Jane Austen among Women

DEBORAH KAPLAN

Jane Austen among Women

THE JOHNS HOPKINS UNIVERSITY PRESS

BALTIMORE & LONDON

For My Mother and Father

© 1992 The Johns Hopkins University Press
All rights reserved
Printed in the United States of America on acid-free paper

Johns Hopkins Paperbacks edition, 1994
03 02 01 00 99 98 97 96 95 94   5 4 3 2 1

The Johns Hopkins University Press
2715 North Charles Street
Baltimore, Maryland 21218-4319
The Johns Hopkins Press Ltd., London

Library of Congress Cataloging-in-Publication Data
Kaplan, Deborah, 1950 –
Jane Austen among women / by Deborah Kaplan.
p.   cm.
Includes bibliographical references (p.   ) and index.
ISBN 0-8018-4360-X   ISBN 0-8018-4970-5 (pbk.)
1. Austen, Jane, 1775-1817.   2. Novelists, English—19th century—
Biography.   3. Woman and literature—England—History—19th
century.   I. Title.
PR4036.K3 1992
823´.7—dc20   91-41186

A catalog record for this book is available from the British Library.

Bliss Domestic, Inward Peace,
These attend, how e'er I roam,
These can throw, though Years encrease,
Rays of Comfort 'round my Home.

Children, best of earthly treasures,
Soothe us with their tender smiles,
Heartfelt, genuine, purest pleasures,
Free from Vice or worldly Wiles.

Who'd exchange such Joys as these,
Simple Whims, & Infant Play,
Artless Efforts form'd to please,
Fond endearments, Spirits gay,

Who'd exchange their infant prattle,
Innocent & fondling kiss,
For the World's incessant rattle,
Languid substitute for bliss?

Blest with these, and tried Affection,
Let us hail the heav'nly throne;
Trusting to Divine protection;
Not our Will but God's be done!

From a birthday tribute to Anne Powlett,
written by her husband, Charles Powlett
June 7, 1814

Contents

[vii]

ACKNOWLEDGMENTS

PART of Chapter 7, in a somewhat different form, was published in *Criticism* 29, no. 2 (1987): 163–78; a portion of Chapter 4, also in a somewhat different form, appeared in *Persuasions*, no. 10 (1988): 65–69. Chapters 2 and 3 revise and expand the argument originally made by "Representing Two Cultures: Jane Austen's Letters," in *The Private Self: Theory and Practice of Women's Autobiographical Writings*, ed. Shari Benstock (Chapel Hill: Univ. of North Carolina Press, 1988), 211–29. I thank the publishers of these works for allowing me to reprint material from them here. For permission to quote from their manuscript collections, I gratefully acknowledge, in England, the Hampshire Record Office, the Centre for Kentish Studies, the National Maritime Museum, the Jane Austen Memorial Trust, and, in New York, the Pierpont Morgan Library. I thank as well the Lord Brabourne, the Lord Harris, Joan Impey, Helen Lefroy, Rear-Admiral P. F. Powlett, and one of the great-great grandsons of Charles Austen. Jean Bowden, Curator of the Jane Austen House, facilitated my research there; the Right Honorable the Earl St Aldwyn allowed me to consult his family archive; George Holbert Tucker helped me to gain access to some Austen family papers; and Deirdre Le Faye answered all my inquiries. Archivists and librarians at the institutions listed above, as well as, in England, the Public Record Office, the British Library, the Royal Commission on Historical Manuscripts and, in the United States, the Library of Congress and Fenwick Library at George Mason University have also given me valuable assistance in locating materials for this study.

Work on this book was supported by an Andrew Mellon Post-Doctoral Fellowship at the Center for the Humanities at Wesleyan University, by a National Endowment for the Humanities Fellowship for College Teachers and Travel to Collections grant, and by a Faculty Study Leave and other timely research grants from George Mason University.

Past and present George Mason English department chairpersons Michael Sundell, Jan Cohn, and Hans Bergmann have fostered my research. In the time that I have worked on this manuscript, I have also been aided by Sharon Cameron's and Helen Lefroy's wise counsel,

Acknowledgments

Dina Copelman's and Jack Breihan's wide-ranging knowledge of British history, and Debora Greger's serendipitous yard-sale discoveries. The Kaplan and Rosenzweig families have helped by putting up with me and this project for many years. I thank them for their care and patience.

Several people read all or most of this book. I have benefited from the encouragement and tried to profit from the insights and erudition of Jean-Christophe Agnew, Elizabeth Blackmar, Devon Hodges, Lorna Irvine, David Kaufmann, and Catherine Parke. Juliet McMaster understood my intentions and gave me invaluable substantive and stylistic advice on two drafts of the manuscript. Four other people, over a number of years, have also scrutinized successive drafts of this book and have sustained me through the process of writing them. Barbara Melosh provided incisive and eloquent comments on the chapters and taught me to relish the peculiar and comic aspects of academic life. For many years Patricia Spacks has helped me to pursue my research interests. She encouraged this project from its inception, and her exhilarating conversation and illuminating criticism of the chapters were crucial resources all along the way. Having exchanged work with Eileen Sypher for more than ten years, I cannot imagine publishing anything that she has not first read—and reread. Her intellectual companionship gave purpose to my efforts and enabled me to finish this book. Roy Rosenzweig, to whom I owe the greatest debt, had faith in and empathy for my work at all stages. He offered astute, challenging criticism of my chapters; inspired me both to imagine and to seek out readers; and heartened me with his wit, common sense, generosity, and optimism.

INTRODUCTION

I N the late 1780s Jane Austen's Hampshire neighbor at Hackwood, the Duchess of Bolton, was organizing a private entertainment, a performance of Nicholas Rowe's 1714 play, *The Tragedy of Jane Shore*. Lady Catherine Paulett, a daughter of the Duchess, was to play the pitiful heroine. For the other female role, the passionate Alicia, the two women turned to their friend Anne Lefroy, living nearby at Ashe. Lefroy, wife of the rector of that parish, wanted neither to act the part nor to disappoint her titled friends. In an effort to appease, she fashioned an answer to the Duchess in heroic couplets:

> All to the Task unused my faultering Tongue
> Would mar the tuneful strains that Rowe has sung
> Can I a Wife, a Mother, tread the stage
> Burn with pale fire and glow with mimic Rage,
> Quit of domestic peace the calm retreat
> As mad Alicia teach my Heart to beat.
> And while my Bosom bleeds for Shore's sad Fate
> Spurn the dejected Mourner from my Gate?
> Too well her woes by Catherine exprest.
> Compassion's sighs would heave my artless Breast.
> Ah spare me then unable to withstand,
> When lovely Catherine asks and you command.[1]

Anne Lefroy wished to decline because she could not reconcile her roles as wife and mother with the part of a woman furious at her lover, Lord Hastings, and wildly jealous of the woman he has come to prefer, Jane Shore. The role of Alicia requires expressions of rage, but Lefroy was "unused" to such outbreaks. Her female identity was felt in the body ("tongue," "heart," "bosom," "breast"), and she would have to "teach" it to feel and to act out anger. She doubted that she would be successful, indeed that she would be able to act at all. Her customary feeling and expressions—"compassion's sighs"—"would heave" her "artless breast," overriding the role's called-for fury.

Although Anne Lefroy thought she would not succeed in the role of Alicia, she apparently thought Lady Catherine would make a fine Jane Shore, expressing the character's "woes" only "too well." What might seem a compliment to Lady Catherine's acting was more likely

[1]

praise of her friend's female identity. In Rowe's play the character of Jane Shore (historically, the former mistress of Edward IV) is chaste, penitent, and generous to the needy. Resisting the sexual advances of Lord Hastings, she is reconciled with her husband just before her death. Lady Catherine presumably would not have to "teach" her "heart to beat" in a different way: her feelings and conduct would find an appropriate outlet in the role of Jane Shore.

Lefroy's poem, then, espouses a female identity, a femininity, that restricts self-expression. This identity, generated by the ideology of domesticity, incorporates compassion, chastity, piety, and self-denial and excludes anger, sexual passion, independent action, and self-concern.[2] The poem does not take a stand against home theatricals or women playing roles in them, although some advocates of the ideology did.[3] It implies, however, that women will rarely find acting roles in which to express the narrow range of feelings and conduct appropriate to them. What they should not be, they should not play at being.

The ideology of domesticity voiced by Anne Lefroy inhibited not only potential actresses but also those women who would express themselves in other art forms. It will be familiar to those who know the work of two "mothers" of American feminist literary criticism, Virginia Woolf and Tillie Olsen, and some of their most important successors writing in the late 1970s and 1980s—Elaine Showalter, Sandra Gilbert, Susan Gubar, and Mary Poovey.[4] Concerned with the self-expression historically possible for women, they have called attention to material and cultural constraints, particularly in the eighteenth and nineteenth centuries, that all too frequently silenced would-be women writers. When women were not poor and illiterate, when they did have rooms of their own and access to books and writing materials, they were still often relegated by their societies' gender ideologies to constricted female identities that inhibited many forms of creative achievement. Feminist criticism has particularly emphasized not only social opposition to women's writing and women's own internalizations of such proscriptions, but also their severe consequent conflicts over both composition and publication. It thus evokes the many women who may have wished to write but who, like Anne Lefroy, had also come to believe in limiting their range of self-expression.

With all the discouragement that British and American women writers encountered, what, then, *enabled* their literary careers? What made it possible for them both to take up writing at all and to transcend imaginatively, in their representations of women in particular, the narrow range of feeling and experience assigned to them? Those very critics who have made us sensitive to Anglo-American cultural biases against women as writers have not been able to place them in a credible, facilitating context. Gilbert and Gubar, for example, have given a large and dramatic role to social influences in their work on women writers, but that role is wholly negative. "Denied the economic, social, and psychological status ordinarily essential to creativity," the woman writer, they suggest, was greatly handicapped.[5] Some critics acknowledge the inspiration of books by other women, and these no doubt did help. But could their influence outweigh for the would-be writer what Gilbert and Gubar see as her "debilitating" social circumstances? The woman who did manage to write, so we can infer, was brilliant, cagey, and *alone*. Through sheer talent, presumably, she rose to fame for her imaginative and wide-ranging productions from the ranks of victimized women.

For Anne Lefroy's neighbor and friend Jane Austen, as well as for many other women writers, conventional biographies have not supplied satisfying explanations either. Although the story of Austen's life has been told and retold for more than a century and a half, narratives of her literary development have not given systematic consideration to those social and psychological supports that made Austen's writing possible and helped to enliven and extend her representational range. Biographies attribute her success to an inner genius severed from all social conditions, or they praise the support of her family, particularly her father and brothers. Such accounts, however, imply that her family was immune to their social world's domestic ideology. A few biographies have singled out a more likely source of encouragement in a patriarchal society—the novelist's sister, Cassandra—but they have tended to focus simply on her willingness to take on most of the housekeeping at Chawton and to guard her sister's privacy while she was at work. Only Austen's most recent biographer, Park Honan, has called attention as well to Cassandra's intellectual support, presenting her as a capable critic of her sister's novels.[6] The impact of Cassandra Austen on the novelist's career, however, cannot be fully understood and appreciated until we situate their tie in the wider social and cultural context of contemporary female friendship. It is the central argument of this biographical and critical study that Austen found crucial support for her writing career not from her sister alone but also from the women's culture that Austen's female friends made.

The novelist belonged to a provincial community that included men as well as women, but she also participated in another distinct set of relationships composed of women exclusively. Because the female affiliations were situated *within* the larger social group, their experiences frequently overlapped. These groups often understood the experiences differently, however. They generated two distinct cultures—symbols, values, perspectives, and practices—which diverged primarily over the nature and role of the female. Austen and her female friends consequently experienced cultural duality. They subscribed to the larger, mixed community's patriarchal conception of the female, organized by the ideology of domesticity. They also produced among themselves an alternative vision of an independent, self-assertive female, implicitly and explicitly critical of the dominant patriarchal version of the female self and her domestic duties.

The larger community, which included Austen's family members, did offer invaluable encouragements to the apprenticing writer, but it did so in her early adolescence, before that community's cultural constraints on womanhood would have made her writing troubling. Austen's female friends, however, created and maintained the enabling context in which Austen developed as an adult writer. Their culture, albeit provisionally, offered not only a refuge but also the resources for female creativity within the larger patriarchal culture. Austen's close female friends formed her audience for work in draft and discussed it with her. Even more fundamentally, the image of female self-assertion that they generated among themselves helped her to turn away from domestic duties to her extended, absorbing writing projects and to develop a sense of herself as a professional writer. The self-confident discourse these women used with one another served also as a key bridge for Austen between the self-effacing expressions advocated by the ideology of domesticity and the authority necessary for narration. And, finally, that discourse and the relationships generating it served as an inspiration for some of her most distinctive, "unfeminine" representations.

I have borrowed the concepts of *cultural duality* and *women's culture*, central to this study, from the work of historians of American women.[7] Feminist historians began in the 1970s to analyze communities of women and the activities, values, and viewpoints specific to them, though "women's culture" did not become widely used in such studies until after the 1980 publication of "Politics and Culture in Women's History: A Symposium" in *Feminist Studies*.[8] "If one speaks of women's activities and goals from a woman-centered point of view," Gerda Lerner wrote in that landmark debate, "one calls that which women do and the way in which they do it, woman's culture." She continued: "Women live their social existence within the general culture and, whenever they are confined by patriarchal restraint or segregation into separateness (which always has subordination as its purpose), they transform this restraint into complementarity (asserting the importance of woman's function, even its 'superiority') and redefine it. Thus, women live a duality—as members of the general culture and as partakers of women's cultures."[9] Lerner also used "women's culture" in conscious contrast to another term, "women's sphere," which names the arena of subordination designated by the ideology of domesticity. It is the experience of subordination in the "women's sphere" that women reperceive and redefine, thereby creating women's culture.[10]

The cross-disciplinary borrowing on which my work depends has been common in feminist scholarship, facilitating or enhancing research in the disciplines to which concepts and methods are imported.[11] In this study such borrowing makes possible the discovery of same-sex social ties and a culture that had a crucial impact on Jane Austen's experience. It also makes available Austen's complex, conflicting allegiances to her two cultures. But excursions across disciplines may also be unsettling for the appropriating discipline. The concepts of women's culture and cultural duality carry with them from the discipline of history some assumptions not entirely at home in literary studies. Because not all literary critics would currently embrace these assumptions, I shall articulate a few of them at the outset. Moreover, because feminist literary criticism is pluralistic in its premises as well as in its methodologies, the identification of these assumptions will help the reader to locate the present work within the spectrum of feminist criticism.

Whereas feminist and nonfeminist postmodern literary critics deconstruct the subject, the concepts of women's culture and cultural duality grant selfhood to women.[12] "Cultural duality" directs attention to the divisions and contradictions in subjectivity, but both concepts nevertheless acknowledge women's self-understandings. Furthermore, whereas some contemporary literary criticism describes ideologies as so powerful or pervasive that they determine subjectivity,[13] the concepts of women's culture and cultural duality attribute to individuals at least some capacity to resist ideologies. These concepts do not deny that ideologies reach into the unconscious, but they focus attention on women's conscious, independent actions in response to patriarchal ideologies.[14]

Empirical evidence lends support for the assumption that individuals are not always in the grip of ideologies. In describing their experience, women in Jane Austen's social group saw resistance or adherence to the ideology of domesticity as a matter of choice. But I also want to acknowledge that that assumption, which is of particular interest to me, has had a fundamental influence on the shape of this study. The question that forms its starting point—what made it possible for Jane Austen to write?—and the material I have marshaled in reply were themselves informed by my concern with women's ability to determine their own experience and, ultimately, to effect personal and social change. I have found the concepts of women's culture and cultural duality in American women's history so compelling precisely because they rest on a belief in agency.

These concepts also assume the importance not just of community but of communality, a supposition not unanimously endorsed by literary critics, feminist or not, for some are still attached to the romantic myth of solitary production. "Women's culture" is attentive to individual actions, but it and, in my study, "gentry's culture" to some degree also emphasize the more salutary effects that group life and culture may have on individuals. This crucial assumption organizes my study.

It is customary to begin biographical studies of an author's life and works with an account of his or her personal history. Instead this book opens with a description of the cultures of Austen's genteel community and the women's affiliations within it, because her social and cultural contexts in effect preceded and were crucial to the production of her professional identity and her fiction. In Part One (Chapters 1–3) I present her community's lived experience of the domestic ideology. I then consider women's dual responses to it. As participants in the larger community, they endorsed it; in their intimate friendships with other women, they expressed distance from and discontent with the identity and duties it constructed.

Part One includes evidence from late eighteenth- and early nineteenth-century conduct books that outline the ideology of domesticity for women. I also explore writings that were not intended for publication. I examine Jane Austen's letters, of course, but situate them in the context of letters, diaries, poems, and memoirs by other members of her community, women as well as men. As Anne Lefroy's poem to the Duchess of Bolton indicates, women who felt that theatrical expressions of rage were improper did not hesitate to express their feelings in more private media. And while, like Anne Lefroy, they conveyed sentiments consistent with conduct-book precepts in their private communications, some also voiced sentiments at odds with them.

Among their private writings, letters are the genre in which women most typically voiced this dissent, that is, the discourse of their women's culture. But letters rarely carried only this discourse. What is most striking about them is their intermingling of affirmations and criticism of the feminine identity and roles constructed by domestic ideology. Such letters are oddly inclusive, incorporating incompatible discourses. Because they represent, more than any other genre, not only the culture of intimate female friends but women's divided loyalties, letters have a prominent place in this study.

Other private writings are also important in this work, forming along with the letters a crucial supplement to conduct books. We still too often forget that conduct books offer prescription, not description. If literary critics hope to ascertain how men and women subjectively experienced ideologies in the past, we will need to join social historians in archives and attics in search of testimony, not just of a Jane Austen but also of her more ordinary contemporaries.

My search turned up a number of documents, some of them in county record offices, others still in private hands, many of them not previously consulted for studies of Jane Austen. I found letters, diaries, memoirs, and poems by neighbors living around Austen's Hampshire homes at Steventon and Chawton and around her brother Edward's Kent estate at Godmersham (to which Jane and Cassandra paid long visits). Proximity, though important, was not my only criterion of selection because it did not, by itself, determine the composition of Jane Austen's social world. This book explores the writings of those who made up what Raymond Williams, describing social experience in Austen's novels, has called the "knowable community." It was "outstandingly face-to-face" but "very precisely selective." "To be face-to-face in this world," Williams has explained, "is already to belong to a class."[15] The private writings treated in the following pages, then, include those by friends and kin living at a distance from Jane Austen as long as she was on visiting or corresponding terms with them. By the same criterion, they exclude those few surviving writings by tradespeople, servants, farm laborers, and other groups in Austen's neighborhood with whom she did not socialize.

A few writings by Austen family members provide particularly comprehensive lists of those with whom Jane Austen would have mixed. This poem composed by Mrs. Austen in 1794, for example, cleverly parades the names of "the company who graced the ball," recently attended by two of her children, Henry and Cassandra:

> First then, the couple from the Vine;
> Next, Squire Hicks and his fair spouse—
> They came from Mr. Bramston's house,
> With Madam, and her maiden Sister;

(Had she been absent, who'd have miss'd her?)
And fair Miss Woodward, that sweet singer,
For Mrs. Bramston liked to bring her;
With Alethea too, and Harriet
They came in Mrs. Hicks' chariot;
Perhaps they did, I am not certain.
Then there were four good folk from Worting:
For with the Clerks there came two more
Some friends of theirs, their name was Hoare.
With Mr., Mrs., Miss Lefroy
Came Henry Rice, that pleasant boy; . . .[16]

Mrs. Austen's poem proceeds tirelessly on to several other persons, including three members of the Terry family and clergyman Charles Powlett.

Austen's own letters provide a good guide to those whom she recognized and who recognized her. They catalogue, for more than a twenty-year span, visitors, dance partners, dinner guests, and companions in walking, riding, shopping, and theater-going. Austen may not have been acquainted with one or two of the individuals whose private writings are analyzed in this study; her letters offer no evidence that she knew the Reverend James Wiggett, for example. But she does mention Wiggett's daughter Caroline, a playmate of one of her nieces, and, while living at Steventon, she saw Wiggett's cousins Thomas and William Chute and Mary Bramston with some regularity. Moreover, one of Wiggett's letters, written in 1818 while he was staying with the Bramstons at Oakley Hall, refers to a morning visit from "the Austens."[17] These Austens would have been family members of the novelist's brother James—probably his wife, Mary, and their younger daughter. If Jane Austen did not know the Wiltshire clergyman, her knowable community and his certainly overlapped.

As Austen's letters indicate, inhabitants of her knowable community, though all elite, varied somewhat in status. Here and there an aristocrat moved through her social world: Lady Dorchester invited Austen to her ball; at another ball Austen narrowly avoided being partnered by the Duchess of Bolton's eldest son, "who danced too ill to be endured"; and at yet another she chatted with Lord Portsmouth, who asked to be remembered to Cassandra, off visiting in Kent.[18] But for the most part the Austens socialized with gentry—owners, like aristocrats, of landed estates but generally with more modest landholdings, smaller annual incomes, and, if titled, with no honor above a baronetcy. The Austens also socialized with those whom historian David Spring calls the pseudogentry—"pseudo" because they owned little (under a hundred acres) or no land, supporting themselves instead from genteel professions.[19] According to Spring, members of the pseudogentry were strivers: "They had a sharp eye for the social escalators, were skilled in getting on them, and (what was more important) no less skilled in staying on them."[20] The fate of Austen's own father, the son of a country surgeon who rose to the more gentlemanly rank of clergyman, exemplifies the fortunes of this group.

Although Spring's distinction between the gentry and the pseudogentry is important, I have chosen to retain the single term *gentry* to identify all members of Austen's knowable community because of the close ties between the landed and the nonlanded groups. The "social escalators" went down as well as up: many professionals and rentiers were not men on the rise but younger sons, who were directed into professions while their older brothers inherited family estates. They were thus inextricably intertwined by kinship and patronage with their generally more prosperous, landowning neighbors. Moreover, they hunted together, attended the same balls and private parties, worshipped at the same Anglican country churches, and with only a few exceptions had the same Tory politics.[21] Although they were sharply aware of their subtle and not-so-subtle differences in wealth and its sources, they acted and perceived themselves as part of the same culture.

For the sake of clarity, I refer to the ties and culture of female friends within this larger group simply by the category of gender ("women") and not of status ("gentry"). It is important to remember, however, that these female intimates, some of whom were kin, were also privileged, at least in the context of the society as a whole. To be sure, there were variations in social prestige and wealth among them. But Spring's distinction between the gentry and the pseudogentry does not make possible the identification of these variations because it is gender blind. Although some single gentlewomen had annuities and some married women had money from marriage settlements (usually pin money during marriage and jointures as widows), few owned more than a hundred acres or, indeed, any land.[22] The daughters, wives, and sisters of the landed gentry were, if we wish to consider women separately from their menfolk, then, just as much pseudogentry as the female kin of professionals.

In attending only to writings of those with whom Austen mingled socially, this book insists on the relatively specific and local social and cultural circumstances influencing Jane Austen's development as a writer. "Early Modern English society," historian Lawrence Stone has observed, "was composed of a number of very distinct status groups and classes. . . . These constituted more or less self-contained cultural units, with their own communication networks, their own systems of value and their own patterns of acceptable behaviour."[23] Broad generalizations about the subjective experiences of women and women writers in the late eighteenth and early nineteenth centuries, however compelling, often overlook these cultural variations and are thus highly vulnerable.

In its focus on the private writings of those who belonged to Austen's knowable communities, this book is also temporally specific. Most of the writings it cites fall within or only just outside of the span of Austen's life: 1775–1817. During that approximately forty-year period, efforts to advocate the ideology of domesticity sometimes—as in the 1790s—intensified, but without altering either the wider community's or the women's culture as a whole. Still, we should not leap to conclude that these cultures are ahistorical. Women's cultures are a response to specific social circumstances. They generally spring up in societies at times, as Gerda Lerner has noted, when women "are confined by patriarchal restraint or segregation into separateness." Patriarchal social arrangements themselves have had a very long history, certainly, but they are not eternal.

We should also not conclude that the two cultures are transparent expressions of a male or female nature (though the word *culture* itself should warn us away from this conclusion). It is tempting to single out the culture of women in particular as the collective process and product of innate female instincts, because alternative, social sources for the women's culture in this period are hard to pinpoint. Late twentieth-century readers who prefer the female identity generated by the women's culture to the ideal of womanhood promoted by the gentry's culture may also be tempted to attribute to the women's culture the primacy of nature. Nevertheless, the values and meanings that circulated among close female friends, like those endorsed by the wider community, were social constructions.

After establishing the contexts for Austen's career in Part One, I turn in Part Two (Chapters 4 and 5) to Jane Austen's specific experiences as a woman writer. The chapters in this section focus on two key issues, directly addressing the problem of who encouraged Austen's writing and the important, related question of why she never married. This second section reconsiders concerns typical of traditional biographies in light of the dual social and cultural contexts explored in Part One. My analysis of elite women's letters, in particular, provides a frame for interpreting in new ways Austen's resources, choices, and achievements.

[10]

Cultural duality, expressed in the letters of Austen and her female kin and neighbors, also throws into relief other biographical interpretations which have so far served to construct the Austen we know. Thus, as it reperceives some of Austen's experiences, Part Two probes prior studies of the novelist's life. I examine the evidence on which their interpretations rest, highlighting moments in the novelist's history about which there is little or no surviving evidence and the efforts that biographers have made to fill such gaps for the sake of narrative coherence. And, mindful of the diverse perspectives Austen and other female members of her community held, I call attention to the particular point of view generally expressed by these biographical accounts.

Austen's most important biographers in the nineteenth and early twentieth centuries were her male kin—her brother, her nephew, and her grandnephew and great-grand nephew. They wrote from within the culture of Austen's genteel community or from within subsequent cultures as much in the service of male interests as the culture of Austen's own genteel community was. Some of Austen's female relatives lent crucial aid in the preparation of these works, particularly to nephew James Edward Austen-Leigh's *Memoir of Jane Austen*. Some twentieth-century biographies have even been penned by women. Nevertheless, as Part Two reveals, most of the interpretations generated by the Austen biography industry have, sometimes inadvertently, expressed and helped to perpetuate patriarchal biases.

Whereas in Part Two I consider the effect of the women's culture and cultural duality on Austen's life and rely on those concepts when analyzing previous biographical accounts of the novelist, I look in Part Three (Chapters 6–8) at Austen's efforts to incorporate expressions of the women's and gentry's cultures in her fiction. She made these efforts over a period of time whose considerable duration scholars do not always take into account. Although Austen is known primarily for the six novels published between 1811 and 1818 (she turned thirty-six in 1811 and died in July 1817), her earliest manuscripts date from 1787, the year in which she turned twelve. By the time she became known in print as "A Lady," the signature for her first published novel, she had already had a long career as a writer of private fictions. Important to any history of Austen's literary development, these fictions are a central focus of Part Three.

In this section of my study I attend to changes over time in Austen's representations of her women's culture. Because Austen was also, always, simultaneously committed to the culture of her wider community, I chart her divided loyalties in textual evidence of cultural duality as well. Both expressions—of the women's culture and of cultural duality—were troubling for Austen, the first because it made for alternative, subversive, representations of women's ties within a genre, the novel, not directed solely to an alternative, subversive, all-female audience, and the second because it brought ambiguity or contradiction to a novel form that Austen was striving increasingly to make coherent, consistent, "seamless."

Austen wrote her childhood and adolescent pieces—her juvenilia—as home entertainments for male and female relatives and a few close female friends. Many of the earliest of these pieces parody formal and thematic conventions of the eighteenth-century courtship novel, taking as one of their targets fictional representations of domestic femininity. But it is impossible to tell whether they are attacking domestic femininity itself or the tendency of the novel medium to distort and compromise it. A few of the later juvenilia revise courtship-novel conventions instead of parodying them. In the effort to create a more realistic fiction, Austen sought familiar versions of womanhood, but because she drew on the resources of both the gentry's and women's cultures these later pieces are ambiguous, too. That they are fragments, with little plot development and no conclusions, only heightens their ambiguity. Although it is impossible to know for certain, Austen may have resorted to indeterminacy as a conscious strategy to avoid having to choose to align in the juvenilia with one *or* the other of her cultures.

From her late adolescence and on, Austen became interested in writing sustained works for publication, not an ambition generally deemed appropriate for women by the gentry's culture. At this crucial juncture, finding support in her close ties with women, Austen made efforts to represent not only these same-sex relationships but also their culture's depictions of a bolder, more independent female identity. These efforts, in what I call Austen's "middle" period, constitute her most daring innovations. She may not have invented any character to rival Rowe's raging Alicia, but her portraits of independent, assertive female characters and their powerful female bonds in *Lady Susan* and *The Watsons* go well beyond the contemporary, conventionally narrow range of proper "feminine" self-expression. Moreover, these representations express an even greater identification with the women's culture by challenging the very plot structure of the comic courtship novel. Such works are organized by the hero's wooing of the heroine and resolved by the couple's marriage, but Austen's portraits of women and their friendships in these works threaten to override the convention of hierarchical and heterosexual union.

From such subversion Austen ultimately drew back, reversing abruptly *Lady Susan*'s point of view and stopping *The Watsons* in midstream. Although she wished to give voice to her women's culture in the novel, she also wished to endorse her wider community's culture and to "write *something*," as she once pleaded with a niece about one of the young woman's confiding letters, "that may do to be read or told."[24] These pieces, then, unlike the juvenilia, textually inscribe her conflicting allegiances.

I also devote attention in Part Three to Austen's shift from private to public writing. Taking *Pride and Prejudice* as an example, I show that she tempered expressions of her women's culture and her dual alliances in works offered to the general public. Although *Pride and Prejudice* does represent the women's culture, particularly in the heroine's talk, it also curtails that representation in crucial ways, so that its social subversiveness is muted. The novel at the same time amplifies and renders appealing the values of the gentry's culture. As a result, its depictions of both the women's culture and the contradictions of cultural duality are much less overt than in *Lady Susan* and *The Watsons*. Although Austen's other novels are not precisely modeled on *Pride and Prejudice*, they, too, evince traces of the women's culture and amplify the gentry's culture. They, too, provide subtler versions of the women's culture and cultural duality than do Austen's middle works.

I analyze only one of Austen's six novels in order to consider, while performing that analysis, questions of methodology. Cultural duality becomes, in the consideration of Austen's fiction, a literary critical approach that shares many of the premises and strategies of American feminist literary criticism. However, it differs in the kind of interpretations it produces, particularly of *Pride and Prejudice* and the other Austen novels published in the second decade of the nineteenth century. Like American feminist criticism, cultural duality as a methodological approach finds and values in these works covert or oblique expressions of Austen's subversive perspectives. But it also attends closely to moments when Austen's novels champion the gentry's culture. And it neither trivializes nor condescends to these renderings.

American feminist criticism tends to isolate gender from other aspects of social identity. Thus any feature of the woman writer's text that is not subversive (and truly expressive of a woman's identity) is usually seen as a superficial façade, whose purpose is only to mask dissent, or as false consciousness. By contrast, the framework of cultural duality encourages us to see gender as inseparably connected to other aspects of identity derived from the general culture. In the case of Jane Austen's community, the wider culture of the gentry, within which the women's culture was situated, emphasized and maintained the elite status of its participants, and its status concerns permeated the interpolated culture of women. Because for Austen gender was inseparable from elite rank, just as the women's culture was inextricably bound to the gentry's culture, we need to take seriously (indeed, see as in her own interests) her hearty endorsements of the gentry's patriarchal values.

The framework of cultural duality gives us a version of Austen's novels that falls short of our late twentieth-century feminist critical expectations. The cross-disciplinary borrowing that makes available to literary criticism the concepts of women's culture and cultural duality requires us to give up the gratifying vision of Austen and her novels as thoroughly rebellious. But this historically grounded feminist literary criticism also has important compensations. By taking specific social circumstances into account, it makes possible the study of women's differing experiences of subordination. The approach also calls attention to the differences between past and present. It shows us the contingency, the wonderful vulnerability to change, of all our social arrangements. If it distances Austen and her works from us, it also submits women's divided loyalties, and the inegalitarian societies that have necessitated them, to time and transformation.

PART ONE

Divided Loyalties

CHAPTER 1

Genteel Domesticity

1

IN 1793 William Chute, Member of Parliament, sportsman, and owner of a large Hampshire estate, the Vyne, surprised his family and friends with the announcement of his engagement to Elizabeth Smith. Few had met her, and for some weeks they had to rely on his cheerful praise of his fiancée—"very accomplished and brought up in a way likely to make a very good domestic wife."[1] Twelve years later, his neighbor at the Steventon parsonage, the Reverend James Austen, wrote in similar terms about his brother Frank's fiancée. A captain in the navy, Frank was waiting impatiently on board the *Leopard* for an opportunity to marry Mary Gibson. "May you have a speedy return," James wrote to him, "& reap the reward which your Principles & Exertions deserve in the enjoyment of Domestic Comforts & the Society of Her who can best make your Home comfortable to you."[2]

In describing ideal wives as "domestic," William Chute and James Austen were revealing the mediation of their personal desires by a popular ideology of married life and of gender. They were also helping to enforce this ideology. The familial relationships and gender identities represented by the ideology of domesticity were not, of course, new.[3] But their objectification and codification in books dated back only to the end of the seventeenth century, and wide dissemination of the ideology did not occur until conduct books, sermons, and educational treatises specifically concerned with women became popular in the second half of the eighteenth century.[4] Indeed, the heyday of print versions of the ideology—1760 to 1820—covered Jane Austen's lifetime. According to this ideology, men and women married for love and esteem. They experienced passion within their conjugal relations, and, when that faded, they sustained an affectionate friendship. They spent much of their time in one another's company and in the company of their children to whom they were lovingly attentive. And the setting for these relationships was always the home, over which women reigned.[5]

This popular ideology included a particular version of the female, created by making social roles and social spaces gender specific—the "separate spheres" that we associate with the mature industrial and capitalist economy of Victorian England. As James Austen's prayer hints, the realm of domesticity was managed by the female, and it had its opposite and complement in a male realm of public "exertions." The men of the middling and upper ranks, like the later, stereotypical middle-class captains of industry, were viewed as public persons whose intercourse with the world was likely to be demanding, even vexing. They could find respite only at home under a woman's care. As conduct-book writer Hester Chapone advised in her *Letter to a New-Married Lady* in 1777, when the husband "returns to his own house, let him there find everything serene and peaceful, and let your cheerful complacency restore his good humour, and quiet every uneasy passion."[6]

The domestic wife's sensibility and responsibilities were constructed in conscious opposition not only to a public world of male work but also to popular conceptions of the aristocratic wife's life-style.[7] When William Chute suggested that his fiancée was "brought up in a way likely to make a very good domestic wife," he was implying that she could have been brought up in another way, to become the wife who was rarely at home, turned her children over to wet-nurses and servants, and devoted herself to an incessant round of social gatherings and public entertainments. Eighteenth-century conduct literature condemned this alternative in almost hysterical tones. "Remember your domestic duties," warned the author of *An Enquiry into the Duties of the Female Sex*, "inform your mind; advance in piety; be not snatched into the wild vortex of amusements."[8]

If gentlemen wanted domestic wives, women sought an appreciation for domestic values in potential husbands. While the young Hampshire clergyman Charles Powlett courted Anne Temple in the early 1790s, her mother worried about his fashionable, extravagant life-style. Although he was of aristocratic descent—a grandson in the illegitimate line of the third Duke of Bolton—and though he spent much of his time at Hackwood, the estate of the sixth Duke of Bolton, he had a very small income of his own. In 1791 he wrote to assure Anne and her mother that the time he spent at Hackwood in the company of aristocrats and even the Prince Regent, who came to Hampshire for the hunting, had not corrupted him: "It would indeed evince a very weak Mind, were I to expect or even wish that, because I sometimes live with Peers in their houses, I should live like Peers in my own."[9]

Powlett justified his aristocratic social life in two ways: it enabled him to study "Men, Manners, & Things," and it would, he hoped, secure him patrons. He insisted, however, that "Happiness is only the Lot of a Man who is married to a Woman that he most ardently loves without any other prospect of Interest than the hopes of a mutual affection."[10] A home in the country with the woman he loved was a domestic ideal with which Powlett never lost faith, although, despite his claims to the contrary, it was not the only influence on his conduct. Because of his elegant life-style, the neighborhood was already anticipating Powlett's bankruptcy two years after he and Anne married. "Charles Powlett gave a dance on Thursday, to the great disturbance of all his neighbours, of course," Jane Austen reported to her sister in 1798, "who . . . live in hopes of his being soon ruined."[11] He did, in fact, have to go into hiding more than once during his lifetime to escape his creditors, although the first crisis did not occur until 1809.[12]

Powlett's experience reminds us that domesticity was, at least in Austen's day, still a high-status ideology. It was part of the culture, the "central system of practices, meanings and values" in literary critic Raymond Williams's words, of elite social groups.[13] Powlett understood the folly of trying to live like an aristocrat on a clergyman's income, but neither he nor his wife would have welcomed (indeed, could have imagined) life together devoid of the habits of conspicuous consumption that signaled elite rank—at least not until Powlett's first financial crisis. In one of her letters written during that period the deeply anxious Anne told her husband apologetically: "I grieve that I have been obliged to buy any wine, but as soon as I am more composed and can eat a little I will try to leave it off."[14]

Because this high-status version of domesticity both expressed and helped to shape the desires and experiences of Jane Austen's social group, it forms the subject of this and the next two chapters. Because the ideology virtually defined the female, I will look particularly at genteel domesticity as experienced by Austen's female friends, kin, and neighbors. We cannot understand how Jane Austen came to be a writer without investigating this aspect of her cultural context. Late eighteenth- and early nineteenth-century conduct books will, of course, be crucial to this investigation. Because their authors were diverse, conduct books vary in, for example, the amount and kind of education they deem suitable for women or the emphasis they place on religious devotions. Nevertheless whether written by men or women, Evangelicals or Anglican clergymen, bluestockings, ex-governesses, physicians, women novelists, or aristocratic ladies fallen on hard times, they provide a consistent view of women's subordinate identity and substantial overlap in their instructions on conduct. Moreover, since most were written for women of the middling and upper ranks, they routinely depict the gentility of this ideology of the heart. Conduct books generally situate their advice in the context of an elevated style of living, including, for example, suggestions on the management of servants and on manifold ways to fill leisure time. They also portray the sometimes uneasy interplay of affective and prudential values that characterized groups devoted to both family feeling and social rank.

Just as a conduct book's actual readers were not identical to its textual depictions of readers, so Austen's social group's genteel version of domesticity was not identical to conduct-book portraits of the ideology. Gentlemen such as Chute, Austen, and Powlett may often have found conduct-book words for their desires, but we must still not allow the books to stand in for their readers. These chapters will therefore juxtapose conduct-book representations and the gentry's practice of domesticity as it was rendered and remembered in their private writings. They will also track some of the interactions of these public and private discourses, enabling us to listen for the echoes and arguments circulating in Austen's social world.

2

Marriage to the right person, claimed *A Mother's Advice to Her Absent Daughters*, "constitutes the highest satisfaction of human life."[15] *Letters to a Young Lady* went even further in declaring that women "unquestionably were created to be the wedded mates of man."[16] But Jane Austen's female friends, neighbors, and kin did not all fulfill a destiny that these and most other conduct books assured them was the summit of female happiness or even a divinely authorized condition. We can see the varying fates of many of these women by looking at the family circles that appear in a retrospective account of some Hampshire households. Caroline Wiggett Workman's "Reminiscences of Life at the Vyne" provides an unusually detailed portrait of the gentry living just northeast of Jane Austen's first home at Steventon.[17] Caroline's mother had died in 1802, leaving her overwhelmed husband, the Reverend James Wiggett of Wiltshire, with seven children. When William and Elizabeth Chute, still childless after ten years of marriage, decided to adopt a child, they thought of Wiggett, a boyhood friend and cousin of William Chute's. He was understandably willing to spare one of his children to affectionate and affluent guardians. Caroline thus came to the Vyne in 1803, and her "Reminiscences" evoke the neighborhood between that estate and Steventon in the first decade of the nineteenth century.

According to Caroline Wiggett Workman, a neighboring estate, Beaurepaire, was uninhabited except once every two or three years by "old Mrs. Brocas." In nearby West Sherborne lived its elderly rector, Dr. Hall, with his sister and wife. Caroline also recalled three families at Worting: Mrs. C. Blackstone and her daughter Margaret; at the upper house, an elderly Mrs. Blackstone and her daughter Harriet and her nephew, who was then the rector; and at the great house, Mr. and Mrs. Clarke with several children. At Manydown lived Mr. Bigg-Wither, a widower, and three of his children: the widow Mrs. Heath-cote, along with her son William; the unmarried Alethea Bigg; and Catherine Bigg, who was to marry in 1808. A Colonel and Mrs. Cunnynghame and their seven children lived at Malshanger. The elderly Mrs. Sclater and two maiden sisters lived at Tangier. Wither and Mary Bramston lived at Oakley Hall along with Wither Bramston's unmarried sister, Augusta Bramston. William Chute's unmarried sister, Elizabeth, also lived nearby in a small house at Oakley. And Steventon was inhabited by the "Austens"—no longer George and Cassandra Austen and their two daughters, Jane and Cassandra, who had moved to Bath in 1801, but their eldest son, James, his wife Mary, and their three children.

Caroline's mental neighborhood map reveals a large number of un-attached women in these households. That number swells further if we consider the lone women who made extended annual visits to some of these families, no doubt for the company and the economic support with which such visits provided them. To the Vyne, for example, came not only Thomas Chute, William's bachelor brother, but Mrs. Scowen, "a dear old lady"; Lady Frances Compton, a relative by marriage of Mrs. Chute's; and Mrs. Norman, "a clever agreeable old lady." Some of these women had never married, although they had probably ex-pected or hoped to do so. Marriage was the only option that enabled women of the lesser gentry to secure their social status economically. Even women with substantial legacies could not achieve adequate so-cial repute without realizing the conjugal destiny marked out for them in conduct books. Without husbands and families of their own, many of these women could only attach themselves as dependents to the domestic circles of their relatives.

Historical demographers' estimates of the percentage of people who never married support Caroline Wiggett Workman's local observations. The celibacy rate for the entire English population fell during the eighteenth century. In the second half of the seventeenth century almost 23 percent of the population between the ages of forty and forty-four had never married. A century later the number had dropped to approximately 9 percent.[18] By contrast, the celibacy rate among the daughters of the aristocracy and gentry hovered between 20 and 25 percent in the last two decades of the eighteenth century.[19] This rate had been even higher earlier in the century—slightly over 25 per cent—but it was still markedly elevated. Such numbers of elite women remained unmarried as a result of the intensification of patrilineage customs in the seventeenth and eighteenth centuries. These customs created a greater demand for brides who were well-financed by their own families. Because more money was concentrated in the hands of fewer eldest sons and because women from nonlanded but wealthy families also entered this marriage market, a woman's "portion" (the capital sum given daughters and younger sons when they married or came of age) had to be substantial to meet expectations that increased over the course of the eighteenth century.[20] Women of more modest means had a hard time finding spouses even among younger sons. Patrilineal customs left younger sons, many of whom could not find professional niches that paid very well, with fewer inherited resources and therefore with a greater need for affluent brides or with less inclination to marry.[21] The celibacy rate among younger sons of the aristocracy and gentry was over 20 percent at the end of the eighteenth century.[22]

Elite communities such as Austen's, in short, could not provide the resources of men and money that would have made marriage universally attainable. Even the most enthusiastic advocates of domesticity generally disapproved of marrying into affection-filled poverty. Among the gentry, the ideology of domesticity, then, was made to accommodate patrilineal customs, which it could rationalize but could not override. Nor did this social group's interpretation of domesticity veer from conduct-book representations, for the books' authors had made the same accommodation.

Although they advanced marriage as women's destiny, conduct-book writers also generally considered it in a practical and materialistic light. Most opposed the purely mercenary marriage. In *Letters on the Improvement of the Mind,* for example, Hester Chapone referred to such unions as "a detestable prostitution."[23] Writers stressed instead the importance of love and respect. Yet they usually suggested that these were insufficient bases for marriage, reminding any overly romantic readers that an income or "competence" was also absolutely necessary. "Permit me," wrote Jane West in *Letters to a Young Lady,* "to assure every young woman who is inclined to underrate the consideration of competence, that she is very unlikely to feel herself happy in a station in life *below* that which she filled in her single state. An income inadequate to our real (not our imaginary) wants, is a calamity of sufficient weight to overthrow the fairest fabric of happiness, and to oppress the most amiable temper."[24] John Gregory's *A Father's Legacy to His Daughters* describes the competence necessary to a newly married couple in these mysteriously ample terms: "If you have as much between you as to satisfy all your demands, it is sufficient."[25]

Many eighteenth-century moralists admitted that not all women would be able to find spouses with the many credentials—moral, emotional, and material—that would make for a genteel domesticity. Thus, in the midst of elaborating on the "destiny" of women, they often acknowledged the many women rendered superfluous by the dynastic ambitions of landed families. In his advice to wives "On the Duties of Matrimonial Life," clergyman Thomas Gisborne told his readers: "There is sometimes seen in families an inmate, commonly a female relation of the master or of the mistress of the house, who, though admitted to live in the parlour, is, in truth, an humble dependent." Gisborne recommended to the "mistress of the house" kindness and respect: "Remember the awkwardness of her situation, and consult her comfort."[26]

Of those members of Austen's community who married, some did so at ages well beyond twenty-three, the mean age of marriage for all British women at the start of the nineteenth century.[27] Some wedded widowers who already had several children. Although such unions were socially acceptable, they were not viewed, at least by women, as highly desirable. Ann Rachel Chute, William Chute's older sister, married a man she did not know well when she was thirty-eight.[28] Catherine Bigg married at the age of thirty-five, Philadelphia Walter when she was nearly fifty. Jane Pym Hales, whose family were neighbors of the Bridges family in Kent, wed when she was thirty. At thirty-six Caroline Wiggett was united to widower Thomas Workman, who had seven "delicate" children.[29] When she was sixty-three, Martha Lloyd became Frank Austen's second wife and stepmother to his numerous children. Fanny Knight (whose father changed the family's name from Austen to Knight in 1812 to comply with his benefactor Thomas Knight's will) married at twenty-seven a man who also had several children. These late marriages testify to the difficulties of finding a spouse who fulfilled the demanding criteria of the gentry's culture. A few of the brides may have held out for and ultimately found husbands who were both affluent and lovable or at least estimable. But some of these marriages attest to a woman's drive simply to marry and to her willingness to compromise on the criteria of affection, compatibility, and even esteem in order to do so.

Caroline Wiggett Workman's mental map reveals that some of the unattached women within family circles were widows rather than people who had never married. Their presence also shows that the ideology of domesticity operated within a context of concern over the maintenance of estates and elite status. By the eighteenth century the life expectancies of both men and women had increased markedly, and women began to live longer than their husbands because they had more resistance to the degenerative diseases that accompany aging.[30] But widows were also remarrying less and less frequently. In the sixteenth century 20 percent of widows remarried, but in the seventeenth and eighteenth centuries only 10 percent did so. By the start of the nineteenth century the rate was down to 3 percent.[31]

Although some women undoubtedly preferred not to remarry in their grief for their dead husbands, others were simply unable to do so. The poorer widows of the gentry, particularly those with children, were not very marketable. Indeed, some—like clergymen's widows whose livings died with their husbands—were more likely to be the object of charitable subscriptions than marriage proposals. When the new curate of the Overton parish died suddenly in 1815 at the house of neighboring clergyman John Harwood of Deane, Harwood collected a large sum from among his friends for the curate's widow and many children. Even with that fund and with places found for some of the older boys at charitable schools, the widow could only manage to settle in a cottage, "a real cottage," Jane Austen's niece Caroline remembered, "not much above a labourer's."[32] Although the same deterrent—poverty—did not operate in the case of the widows of large estate owners, a different pressure did. Women who married a second time transferred any wealth they inherited from their first husband into the families of their second husbands. Although the gentry did not uniformly object, such marriages were always controversial.[33] Sometimes, social disapproval was given a legal form when a widow's jointure (the annual income settled on a woman by her husband for her use if she survived him) was made contingent on her not remarrying.[34]

Finally, widows who were neither very poor nor very rich knew all the problems of scarce resources that unmarried women encountered in the marriage market and often had children to consider as well. When Elizabeth Heathcote's clergyman husband died in 1802, for example, his estate, which she inherited, was valued at £2,000, and she also received some support from her father, Lovelace Bigg-Wither, the squire of Manydown.[35] Over time she and John Harwood, who had been a close friend of her husband's, formed an attachment.[36] They never married, however, because his clergyman's salary was apparently not adequate and because his father had contracted debts that had left his family in serious financial difficulties.[37] In the *Reminiscences of Caroline Austen*, the novelist's niece described their love as

> not of that romantic, youthful nature, which foresees no evil in poverty, and in the change of social position that is sure to follow. The lady had been accustomed to all the comforts of life, and also she had a young son to care for, and for his sake, even if not for her own, she would feel it both unfitting and unseemly to enter into a ruined family; and the gentleman probably having his own full share of proper pride, refrained from offering his "nothing" to her acceptance.[38]

Caroline Wiggett Workman's Hampshire neighborhood map provides a less distinct view of the large number of children that many couples bore than it does of the marital status of women. We know, however, that if marriage lay at the center of the domestic ideology for women, so did childbearing and child-care. Many of those who did marry found themselves with almost more family than they could readily manage or afford. Historian Lawrence Stone has estimated the average number of children born to the upper-class wife at four or fewer for the late eighteenth and early nineteenth centuries,[39] but this average obscures actual childbirth patterns. In most instances, when the couple was fertile, when the wife began her childbearing career while still in her twenties, and when she did not die young of medical complications resulting from childbirth, marriages inevitably resulted in a very large number of offspring. If a wife did die young and a husband remarried, the number of his offspring might be even larger. Historical demographers E. A. Wrigley and R. S. Schofield have calculated the average number of *live-born* children born to women of all ranks in the period 1750–99 at approximately seven, a figure that seems to match more closely the reproductive experiences of Austen's social group.[40] That statistic also reminds us that the number of pregnancies could exceed the reported number of children, although hard evidence of miscarriages and stillbirths is often unavailable. Our look, therefore, at the large numbers of children that husbands and wives produced will undoubtedly underestimate some couples' reproductive histories.[41]

Although only four members of the Chute family are mentioned by Caroline Wiggett Workman—William, Thomas, Elizabeth, and Mary Bramston—they had come from a family in which there had been ten births, with eight children surviving at least to adolescence. Lovelace Bigg-Wither lived with three daughters in the early nineteenth century, but he had had nine children altogether with his second wife (his first wife died in childbirth). The Reverend George Austen and his wife Cassandra had had eight children.[42] The Powletts, whose reproductive experience is unusually well documented, had only four children who survived to adulthood, but Anne gave birth ten times and had at least one miscarriage. Thomas and Elizabeth Terry, also Hampshire neighbors of the Chutes and the Austens, had eleven children. The Reverend John Benn and his wife Elizabeth had at least thirteen. Seven children were born to the Reverend Isaac Peter George Lefroy and his wife Anne. The Debarys had at least six. In Kent Jane Austen's brother Edward and his wife Elizabeth had eleven children. And Elizabeth's parents, Sir Brook and Lady Bridges, had had thirteen offspring. Elizabeth's sister Sophia and her husband, William Deedes, had twenty children. Of Edward and Elizabeth Austen's neighbors, Thomas and Anne Papillon of Acrise had fourteen children, although not all survived to adulthood. Thomas Papillon had come from a family with ten children. Eight children of Anne and Stephen Rumbold Lushington survived; there were others who died in infancy. Sir Edward Knatchbull, the eighth Baronet, had two children by his first wife, eight by his second, and ten by his third. So often did he remarry and so rapidly did he reproduce that Copley, hired in 1800 to paint a family portrait, had to adjust his already crowded composition twice in order to include a new wife and a new child during the two and a half years he worked on the painting.[43] Sir Edward's eldest son, also Edward Knatchbull, and his wife Annabella had six children in seven and a half years of marriage, although one died quite young. Knatchbull subsequently married Fanny Knight and produced nine more.

The large size of these gentry families is not evidence for "natural fertility," the absence of any deliberate efforts to control pregnancy.[44] Austen's relatives and friends knew that a too-rapid series of pregnancies might endanger the health of the mother or, assuming that many of the pregnancies were successful, could drain the economic resources of the family. They acted in ways intended to have at least some impact on their high pregnancy rates. Men were unlikely to have used condoms, although they would have been familiar with them, because this barrier method was linked in people's minds with vice: condoms were still primarily being used by promiscuous cosmopolitans for the prevention of venereal disease. They may have attempted coitus interruptus; Anne Powlett's father, the Reverend William Temple (one of James Boswell's correspondents), had tried it in Cornwall with his wife, probably in the late 1760s and 1770s.[45] But the available letters and memoirs of those who were part of Austen's community make no mention of this method. Jane Austen's widowed brother Frank made sure his second marriage would produce no offspring (he already had eleven children) by selecting a postmenopausal woman,[46] but this frequently recommended strategy also does not appear to have been very common in Austen's community.[47] Rather, the letters and memoirs of Jane Austen's Hampshire and Kent neighbors suggest that they relied for the most part on abstinence.

On the birth of his fourteenth child in 1817, Thomas Papillon received this advice within a letter of congratulations from his wife's uncle, Sir Richard Hardinge: "It is now recommended to you to deprive Yourself of the Power of Further Propagation. You have both done Well and Sufficiently."[48] Although the baronet may have been advising coitus interruptus, more likely, he was suggesting "the simple regimen of separate rooms," which an exasperated Jane Austen recommended in the same year in response to William and Sophia Deedes's seemingly record-breaking fecundity.[49] Some couples may have abstained by stopping altogether, and separate bedrooms would have helped them to maintain their resolve. Others may have abstained periodically, just after the wife had finished menstruating, in the mistaken belief that she was most fertile at that time, or while the wife breastfed. More and more gentlewomen were breastfeeding their children in the late eighteenth and early nineteenth centuries, and, although lactation provided some protection against pregnancy, they received additional protection because many people believed that sexual intercourse during the months when a woman breastfed would be injurious to the mother and child.[50]

Although the gentry were concerned with family planning, still, when we consider the size of their families, we have to acknowledge that they did not make either very successful or very intensive efforts to limit them. Women could, for example, have imposed a longer period of celibacy by breastfeeding for more months than they did;

many had children at intervals of less than two years.[51] It is worth noting, too, that Sir Richard Hardinge and Jane Austen did not recommend abstention until family sizes had reached two-digit figures. The gentry expected large families. Their attitudes and beliefs converged to make rapid reproduction acceptable, if worrisome.

The ideology of domesticity, with its high valuation on children and family life, offered encouragement and rationalizations for reproduction.[52] At the very least, couples who modeled their relationships on the companionate marriage were spending a good deal of time together and were therefore more likely to reproduce frequently. The ideology was reinforced by religious convictions. Theology still exercised much control over sexuality and no doubt promoted the fecundity of a social group many of whose members were clergymen. Nationalistic feeling also played a role. In recommending that the Papillons cease to reproduce, Sir Richard Hardinge argued that his niece and nephew had fulfilled their duty "of keeping up the Population" and could now leave that burden to others.[53] And, finally, because gentlemen, at least, were given to boasting, we can see that the gentry viewed fertility and the birth of children as a banner of their sexuality. In 1792 the Reverend James Wiggett described the birth of his first child to his cousin and boyhood friend William Chute as a "triumph" and couldn't resist adding: "I believe she has rather been in haste to make her entrance into the World, for that day nine Months was our wedding day. We have therefore you see lost no time."[54]

The ideology of domesticity and other cultural attitudes encouraged childbearing, but the generally rapid rates of reproduction, ironically, gave added incentive to some members of the gentry to choose celibacy or at least to postpone marriage when they did not think their incomes sufficient.[55] Genteel domesticity with so many children could be extremely costly, and even late marriages had an impact on reproduction at a time when "to marry," as historian Angus McLaren has remarked, "was to become, or to anticipate becoming, a parent."[56]

Indeed, the strategy of delay was one of the gentry's most effective methods both for building up the necessary income for marriage and for controlling reproduction, and it was not uncommon for friends and kin to urge restraint on eager, love-struck men. When in 1805, for example, twenty-year-old Christopher Edward Lefroy announced his desire to marry, his clergyman father objected not only because the intended bride, a Miss W., was a dissenter but also because of his son's youth. Christopher Edward's older brother, J. H. George, took pains to assure him that, by contrast to their father, he was an advocate of early marriages. He maintained "that a happy marriage is the greatest earthly blessing, & next to religion the most effectual spur to virtue & restraint from Vice, & that early matches founded upon sincere & mutual affection are the most likely to prove happy."[57] And yet his position was not as different from his father's as he wanted, in his sympathy for his brother's plight, to suggest. His enthusiasm for domesticity did not lead him to ignore the economic base required for a genteel household. In a letter that he wrote a few weeks later, he carefully qualified his stance on early marriages: "I have, as You know, always been very much in favour of early marriages *when it is possible they should take place*" [emphasis mine].[58] Although Miss W.'s father had been willing to enter negotiations with the Lefroys for her marriage to Christopher Edward, his father was apparently unwilling or unable to offer financial support for that union. As the young man had not started any kind of professional training yet, his hopes were ultimately frustrated. More to our purpose here, so were Miss W.'s.

Genteel domesticity put marriage and childbearing at the center of women's lives. But it was an ideology that promoted a family life that was intended to affirm but could also erode elite social status. Some women, especially when they had substantial portions of their own, succeeded in finding compatible mates with sufficient incomes, and they established households and large families in material comfort. Others, such as Anne Powlett, married in hope of finding domestic happiness supported by a sufficient competence, but they miscalculated or were misled. Still others saw that it would be impossible to become the central actors in a domestic circle without sacrificing their rank and its standard of living. Thus, while some women found in domesticity a meaningful framework for their married lives, others discovered that it taught them duties and desires that they would have to learn to fulfill less directly, not as wives and mothers but as sisters, daughters, and aunts.

3

The domestic wife and mother represented by conduct books never wants for employment. She cannot participate in the public sphere, in part because her family circle needs her constantly. "The duties that it requires," Jane West told the female reader, "are of such hourly, such momentary recurrence, that the impropriety of our engaging in public concerns becomes evident, from the consequent unavoidable neglect of our immediate affairs."[59] The most important of the domestic woman's duties was to care for her children. Maria Edgeworth and Richard

L. Edgeworth informed their readers in *Practical Education* that "the female sex are, from their situation, their manners, and talents, peculiarly suited to the superintendence of the early years of childhood."[60] And Hannah More suggested that "the great object to which you who are, or may be mothers, are more especially called is the education of your children."[61] One goal of this education, although conduct books and educational treatises do not exactly put it this way, was to perpetuate the family's status by creating the next generation of gentry.

The mother was to form this generation not simply by instilling in her children the different responsibilities of each social rank and gender but also by teaching them in accordance with conduct-book advice: to pray and to espouse particular church doctrines; to detect and eschew vanity and pride; to control their tempers; to take walks or ride on horseback for exercise; to play musical instruments; to read and to develop particular literary tastes; to dress modestly; to perform charitable acts among the villagers; to establish benevolent but not overly familiar relationships with their servants. By raising her children according to conduct-book instructions, she was attempting, in effect, to produce identities not only shaped but *recognizable* by means of the ideology of genteel domesticity.

In the practices of the mothers within Jane Austen's social group, we see such efforts to transmit the cultural identity of the gentry. Though they did not, of course, replicate the exact instructions in any single conduct book, they adopted the role marked out for them by conduct books as the machinery of acculturation—as, in effect, the agent or even the surrogate for conduct books. The letters they wrote testify to their commitment to the task of acculturation even when their children were at a distance. Those letters typically offered instruction on a wide range of the behaviors and values that composed a gentleman's or lady's identity. When Anne Lefroy, for example, described her visit to a dying woman, she was trying to impart religious faith to her son by making him a "spectator," too:

> These are impressive scenes my dearest Edward, they speak to the heart with irresistable authority, to me they are not melancholy, the death bed of a good person is cheered by such glorious hopes, that a ray of light seems to fall upon every surrounding spectator, which opens to them a nearer prospect of the happiness of a future state.[62]

She also gave advice on the development of polite manners: "I am sorry you did not go to the Ball," she wrote him in September 1801, "not only because it would have amused you, but because I think it is always an advantage to mix in good company when you can properly do so."[63] Elizabeth Heathcote, writing to her son in 1818 just after he entered Oxford, similarly mingled advice, now on health ("a little Epsom Salts" for his bilious feeling) and now on the enjoyment of the arts (the proper amount of time to devote to music).[64]

Mothers were not expected to impart all the knowledge or skills that would help create elite identities, but they were responsible for the supervision of any personnel hired to help with the project. The wealthy households that some women directed, for example, employed nursemaids, governesses, and, periodically, portrait painters, hair-dressers, and special masters to teach drawing, dancing, and music—ornaments of conspicuous leisure. Even less prosperous families occasionally hired teachers, although the children often traveled to them for lessons. Because she believed that "there was one grace and accomplishment . . . essential to the condition of a gentlewoman: a good air and carriage, and good dancing," Mrs. Lloyd, wife of a clergyman, sent her daughters, Eliza, Martha, and Mary, to an instructor. For several years (probably in the 1770s and 1780s) they went to him once a week for "a whole day of dancing," as Caroline Austen reported.[65] The widowed Charles Austen, temporarily living in London in 1817 and drawing half pay, filled in as the mother when he sent one of his daughters to a dancing teacher.[66]

Fanny (Austen) Knight's letters to her former governess Dorothy Chapman, dating from 1803, provide us with an unusually detailed record of her mother's efforts to cultivate at the same time that she produced a large and prosperous family. In 1803 Fanny, at ten, was the eldest of seven children. In the next five years her mother would bear four more, while she also planned her children's meals, nursed them through illnesses, chose and helped to make their clothes, supplied them with elegant entertainments, shaped their manners, and presided over their schooling. Elizabeth Austen educated her children when they were very young. Her boys went to boarding school when they were eight, while a governess (and Fanny, too, as she grew older) taught her girls, but even then Elizabeth's influence over at least the girls' schooling did not cease. She determined their hours of school, selected the subjects and skills they learned, and hired their instructors—again and again. Few governesses stayed long, and Fanny's letters recount repeated efforts to find gentlewomen of many and varied accomplishments. Elizabeth fired only one governess, a Miss Maitland, because her French was not good enough, although according to Fanny "she was exactly the thing in other respects & a most delightful young woman."[67]

Women who had no children were still involved in the domestic project of reproducing the gentry. Couples with substantial property but without heirs sometimes adopted male relations who assumed their name. This strategy for family continuity, done for the sake of the husband's family, was often mediated by wives who interested themselves in the children of their kin. Jane Austen's brother Edward became the Knights' surrogate son in just this way. As Mrs. Knight testified to Edward in 1797, "From the time that my partiality for you induced Mr. Knight to treat you as our adopted child I have felt for you the tenderness of a Mother."[68] Childless couples not concerned with nurturing an heir also adopted, often at the wife's prompting. Although it was Elizabeth Chute's husband who turned their attention in 1803 to the children of the Reverend James Wiggett, his widowed cousin, Elizabeth had first expressed the wish to bring a child to live at the Vyne.[69]

Unmarried women were also involved in the reproduction of the gentry's cultural identity, helping female relatives who had children. There was a strangely felicitous fit between those women without marital attachments and those with husbands and large families. The contributions of labor by female members of their own family and status group won women with large families interludes of leisure or helped to ease their households through the domestic crises brought on by their periodic confinements or illnesses. For the unattached woman such contributions provided the pleasures of company and, sometimes, material luxuries not available to them in their own homes. Most important, their lives became more purposeful (in the terms, of course, provided by their culture) when they acted, in effect, as surrogate mothers.

Two of Elizabeth Austen's sisters, Louisa and Harriet Bridges, made frequent and prolonged visits to Godmersham (although for Harriet this pattern terminated after her marriage to the Reverend George Moore in 1806).[70] So did her sisters-in-law, Jane and Cassandra Austen. In both Fanny (Austen) Knight's and Jane Austen's letters we see how completely the unattached woman could insert herself into the large family's affairs, engrossing a child in play, helping to make the husband's shirts, or staying with the children while their parents took trips elsewhere.[71] In June of 1808, Jane Austen visited Godmersham; Elizabeth was five months pregnant. Although she could not "discover, even through Fanny, that her mother is fatigued by her attendance on the children," Austen wrote to her sister, "I have, of course, tendered my services, and when Louisa is gone, who sometimes hears the little girls read, will try to be accepted in her stead."[72]

As Elizabeth's due date approached in September, several women temporarily joined the burgeoning household. "Aunt Cassandra, I am happy to say, is coming to stay here sometime," Fanny wrote to Dorothy Chapman. "It will be a great comfort to me to have her assistance in the lessons during Mamas confinement."[73] Elizabeth's widowed mother, Lady Bridges, also came, as did her unmarried Aunt "Fatty" Fielding.

Two weeks after her eleventh child was born, Elizabeth died. Again, her female kin played a key role in her household. Cassandra, still at Godmersham, helped to manage the house and the extensive preparations for mourning and comforted her brother, Fanny, and the other children.[74] Jane, at home at that time in Southampton, was anxious to be of help and wished very much to have charge of her nephews Edward and George, whom Mary Austen had immediately fetched from school in Winchester and had taken to nearby Steventon. What Jane did for them, when they arrived, was to help them to grieve *and* to manage their grief in a manner befitting their rank. *"They behaved extremely* well in every respect," wrote Jane to Cassandra, "showing quite as much feeling as one wishes to see."[75]

If one of a woman's primary domestic duties, caring for children, was also an attempt to ensure the perpetuation of her family's rank from one generation to another, she participated in another activity that sustained that status in a day-to-day way. That activity—social interactions with friends, neighbors, and kin—constituted an important part of a woman's service to her family. Thus, women were not nearly as isolated as they may seem when we concentrate only on their child-care efforts or if we substitute a conduct book's prescriptive version of domesticity for the actual practices of Austen's community. If domesticity was generally conceptualized in opposition to "society," particularly London or resort-town society, the duality should not blind us to the very sociable lives of the gentry. Their private realm was a good deal more porous, more public than we might imagine.

Few of the women whom Jane Austen knew had much opportunity to succumb to the "wild vortex" of London's public amusements. The cosmopolitan social scene of London generally required an expensive life-style better suited to families with aristocratic fortunes. Those who took houses in London for the season needed an income of at least £5,000 per annum in the last years of the eighteenth century and double that during most of the nineteenth century.[76] The majority of Austen's family, friends, and neighbors lacked the wealth that would underwrite life in London society, and they also—conveniently—lacked the desire for such a life. Announcing in 1791 the marriage of her daughter Elizabeth to Edward Austen, Lady Bridges informed a cousin that the couple's income would at first be small and would thus limit their access to society: "They must be contented to live in the Country," Lady Bridges wrote, "which I think will be no hardship to either party, as they have no high ideas."[77]

Most conduct books, however, did not oppose the social whirl of London only; they urged women to avoid mixing much with neighbors and other acquaintances anywhere. Conduct-book writer John Gregory insisted that women must "necessarily" spend "many solitary hours . . . at home," and he advised them "to have your pleasures as independent of others as possible. By continually gadding abroad in search of amusement, you lose the respect of all your acquaintances, whom you oppress with those visits, which, by a more discreet management, might have been courted."[78] The women of Austen's community ignored such severe prohibitions. As part of the effort to maintain their family's social status, women were the main intermediaries in the frequent and continuous contacts that the gentry typically sustained. It was usually the wife, daughter, or sister who kept in touch with members and branches of her own family at a distance and with other elite families. As the representative of her household, she exchanged visits and letters with male and, more often, female relatives and, generally, with the female members of neighboring families. These contacts ritualistically asserted the status of each woman's family and defined the boundaries of the gentry's community. They were important because a family had status only as long as it was represented within the community—in person and in the more indirect symbolic depictions of oral and written gossip, of *news*. However involved they were in the care of their homes and the management of children, women also devoted much time to creating and sustaining these "appearances" in their letters and visits.

These contacts could occasionally have some additional, more tangible advantages. They mapped potential relationships of patronage, of "friends."[79] T. S. Hancock, married to Jane Austen's Aunt Philadelphia, articulated this latter service only too clearly in his anxiety to achieve financial security. "The General," he wrote to his wife from India, where he had gone to try to make a fortune, "promised his Interest to support me: pray if you can, visit his Lady to Congratulate Her on his Arrival. The Omission might be of bad Consequence to me as He will be a Man of great Power, you perfectly know his vanity and my Necessities."[80] Contacts also created a context of opportunities for marriage, helping to insure that gentlemen and ladies would marry within their social group. More specifically, women who maintained a connection between two families through their meetings and correspondence might be paving the way for a member of one woman's family someday to marry a member of the other's.

This sketch of women's letter-writing and visiting must be qualified in two ways. First, men also wrote letters and paid visits. But the evidence of contemporary correspondence—not just the surviving letters themselves but also the communication patterns they depict—indicates that most men, engaged in professions, politics, or the supervision of their estates, made such contacts less frequently and often used them to transact matters of business.[81] For example, although he had been out of contact with William Chute for at least a year, James Wiggett began a letter to him in 1800 by refusing to apologize because, as he told Chute, "We dont I think pretend to correspond unless upon particular occasions."[82] It was women who were expected to construct "appearances" in their persons and in day-to-day news about members of their families and about neighbors' families.

A letter from Mrs. Knight to her relation Edward Knatchbull around 1808 expressed precisely this notion of her sex as the more devoted and competent communicators of family and community news. Mrs. Knight had a steady correspondence not with Edward but with his wife, Annabella. As Annabella had recently hurt her finger, the correspondence had come to a temporary halt. Edward had stepped into the breach not with a letter but with a package of smelts. Chastised by his wife for not writing, he did, then, apparently follow the gift with a letter. Mrs. Knight's response to both his communications began:

> Indeed, my dear Edward, I am very glad your wife gave you a scold: as I did not know that another sore finger prevented her holding a Pen, I was quite surprised at not hearing from her—her constant attention has spoiled me and made me unreasonable. Yesterday, however, a kind present from *Col.* Knatchbull satisfied me that *you* were alive, whatever might have happened to your wife and children.[83]

Mrs. Knight went on to discuss two of her Knatchbull nephews, the third marriage of Edward's father, the strained relations between father and son, and the health and plans of her neighbors, the Tokes. She concluded with the consciousness of gender and letter-writing with which she began: "You will be glad to resign the correspondence to your wife, if you are to be plagued with such long letters. I expect you will put this into her hand before you have got half through it."[84]

Second, women's letters and visits could satisfy their own desires for sociability and serve no other purpose. But the patterns of association—the sheer volume and constancy of women's contacts—point to the dominance of their families' material and symbolic needs. Fanny Knight, for example, had so many correspondents that she kept diaries almost all her life, partly for the purpose of keeping track of the letters she sent and received. Although her correspondents and the frequency of the exchanges of letters shifted over time, in a three-month period in 1816, for example, the twenty-three-year-old Fanny participated in correspondences with twenty-seven different people. The only males she wrote to—six in all—were her brothers and father. The rest of the letters were addressed to two of her sisters, several aunts, cousins and more distant relatives, the family's governess and nursemaid, and several women from other elite Kent families.[85]

Short visits to several neighboring families were also conducted on a daily basis, routinely filling a substantial portion of the day. The diaries of Caroline Pym Hales, the youngest daughter of the Kent baronet Sir Thomas Pym Hales, give us a sense of the continual comings and goings of women. In the late 1780s, when the extant diaries begin, Caroline was living at Deane House, six miles from Canterbury, with her widowed mother Lady Hales, four older sisters, and a half-brother and sister from her mother's first marriage. A typical entry—this one for December 23, 1788—reports:

> Mama, Marianne, Jane & Elizabeth went very early to Canterbury to make a great many visits. Mrs. Deedes, Mrs. Hales's, both Mrs. Knatchbulls, etc. They came home about 5 Mrs Hougham & Miss Sands came here in the morning.[86]

Once, on a day in March of 1789, she apparently felt that her family had received too many visitors to name: "We went to Church—A 1000 people came in the morning."[87] Almost ten years later, in 1808, Jane Austen went to Canterbury to stay two days with Mrs. Knight. In a letter to her sister, Austen similarly enumerated some of the many calls paid and received in a single day among, roughly, the same circle of gentry:

> Very soon after breakfast on friday Mrs. C.K.—who is just what we have always seen her—went with me to Mrs. Brydges' & Mrs. Moore's, paid some other visits while I remained with the latter, & we finished with Mrs. C. Milles, who luckily was not at home, & whose new House is a very convenient short cut from the Oaks to the W. Friars [Mrs. Knight's house]—We found Mrs. Knight up and better—but early as it was—only 12 o'clock—we had scarcely taken off our Bonnets before company came, Ly. Knatchbull & her Mother; & after them succeeded Mrs. White, Mrs. Hughes & her two Children, Mr. Moore, Harriot & Louisa, & John Bridges.[88]

The rearing of children and the maintenance of networks merged frequently as women trained the next generation of females in the decorum of association. They tried, for example, to instill in young girls both the skills and desire for letter-writing. In her own beautifully formed handwriting, Annabella Knatchbull wrote to her daughter, Mary, in 1814: "I was very much pleased with your Letter I hope you take great pains with your writing Master and never make an I instead of an L."[89] Two years later Mary's aunt gave her a writing box that she had temptingly fitted up "with writing paper, blotting paper, pens, sealing wax & wafers." She sent additional encouragement in the note which accompanied her gift: "I long to receive your letter, for I am told you are much improv'd in writing."[90] The habit of letter-writing was fostered even in little girls who had not yet learned how to write. Fanny Palmer Austen noted approvingly that her five-year-old daughter "composed a very nice little letter to her Papa [Charles Austen]," which her Aunt Cassandra had "commited to paper" and sent for her.[91] Women taught the other form of association, visiting, as well. In play with her young nieces, for example, Jane Austen dramatized the experience. "*She* would often be the entertaining visitor in our make beleive house," a niece remembered long after Austen's death. "She amused us in various ways—*once* I remember in giving a conversation as between myself and my two cousins, supposed to be grown up, the day after a Ball."[92] As this example suggests, mothers, female relations, and governesses imparted to the young the manners of discourse—not just desirable topics of conversation but also appropriate occasions for communication and conventional forms of expression. Austen's letters to Cassandra, for example, sometimes included obviously coached messages from one little girl cousin to another. "I have asked Sophie if she has anything to say to Lizzy in acknowledgement of the little bird," went a letter of Austen's in 1805, "and her message is that, with her love, she is very glad Lizzy sent it. She volunteers, moreover, her love to little Marianne."[93]

In this context the earliest surviving letters of Fanny (Austen) Knight have a special interest for us because they show a child struggling to assume the conventional letter-writing behavior and language of a gentlewoman. Fanny tried particularly hard because she was writing to one of her former teachers and role models of decorum. She was obviously struggling to make letter-writing a daily habit but found the task a bit overwhelming: "I have not had any time to write to you lately," she apologized in one of these early letters, "as I have written 2 or 3 times to Mama and Sackree which takes a great deal of time and I cannot write two letters in one day."[94] She also struggled with her penmanship and the mechanics of writing, often adding postscripts such as: "Excuse monstrous bad writing & horrid mistakes."[95] She had greater success at copying conventional expressions. "I hope you find yourself a great deal better than when you left us," she said in a letter when she was ten years old, "and that you will soon write, to tell me so."[96] At twelve she wrote, "I *long* to see you again & *to talk over old times*, so I do hope you will fix a day for coming, & not defer the pleasure of our meeting any longer."[97]

The letters Fanny wrote much later as an adult have a continuing interest because they illustrate the destiny of little girls trained in the decorum of association. As an adult letter-writer, Fanny continued to apologize for not writing sooner or for writing "blunders."[98] Yet by then she had certainly mastered the skills of writing. She was simply too distracted to be what she felt was an adequate correspondent. For a woman with a large circle of acquaintances and several children, interruptions were a constant feature of experience. Jane Austen observed the insistent push and pull of family life at Godmersham when she stayed there in 1813. In a letter to her sister she noted, "Fanny and I are to go on with Modern Europe together, but hitherto have advanced only 25 Pages, something or other has always happened to delay or curtail the reading hour."[99] Fanny was never able to cultivate the capacity for sustained concentration. At nineteen she marveled at her former governess's patience and perseverance at learning chess. "It would tire me to death in a few minutes," she admitted.[100]

4

Fanny's experience serves to introduce the costs and drawbacks of genteel domesticity for women. Compared, of course, with the lives of laboring women, Austen's female friends, relatives, and kin had privileged, pleasant social circumstances. But though the yoke often sat lightly, the elite woman's domestic role was still psychologically and socially repressive. At worst, the domestic role could even be fatal. The inability to concentrate was a small cost compared to the still very substantial health risks of frequent pregnancies. From the sixteenth through the eighteenth centuries, the hazards of childbirth meant that mothers died at the rate of at least one for every forty baptisms. Wives, according to medical historian B. M. Willmott Dobbie, were more than twice as likely as husbands to die within the first ten years of marriage.[101] Lawrence Stone and Jeanne Fawtier Stone put the figure higher when they consider the first marriages of heirs: "Wives were four times more likely than husbands to die within the first ten years of marriage and twice as likely within the second. . . . Nor do their chances seem to have improved after 1750 when men began to enter the obstetrical profession, to supplement female midwives . . . if anything after 1750 the ratio of wives' deaths to those of husbands during the first ten years of marriage seems to have deteriorated rather than improved."[102]

The gentry justly dreaded the moment of childbirth. As his wife came to term in the spring of 1807, J. H. George Lefroy, Anne Lefroy's oldest son, wrote to a younger brother: "We are, as we have been for some time indeed, in hourly expectation of her being taken ill. I know not how to wish the event to take place, tho' if it please God that she does well I shall feel most thankful when it is over."[103] Jane Austen's mother, who wished in 1798 not to know about her daughter-in-law Mary's labor until it was over, was to learn in the next three decades how warranted her nervous fears were.[104] Of the four of her sons who married and had children—James, Edward, Frank, and Charles—three were to lose wives in childbirth.

Those women who bore large families and survived were often plagued with illness. In 1801, a year before his wife died, the Reverend James Wiggett reported to William Chute about her: "She has lately been too much of an invalid. Her complaint is general weakness, the cause of which it is not difficult to conjecture when one looks at her family."[105] Although no woman would have attempted to delay marriage to an eligible, desirable mate in order to avoid too many pregnancies too soon, Jane Austen did offer the consolation of avoiding pregnancy to her niece Fanny when the young girl began regretting the loss of a suitor whom she had discouraged on other grounds. "By not beginning the business of Mothering quite so early in life," she told her niece in 1817, "you will be young in Constitution, spirits, figure & countenance, while Mrs. Wm Hammond [a friend of Fanny's] is growing old by confinements & nursing."[106]

Women's domestic role could be downright dangerous. It was also not held in much esteem. Men wanted to have pleasant homes and loving and genteel children and to be part of an elite community, but they did not accord much stature to the variety of efforts involved in achieving these outcomes. Conduct books themselves were inconsistent on the value of these efforts. Before the 1790s most writers of these manuals did not view domesticity as a crucial role. In that decade, disturbed by the French Revolution and wars with France, many began to attribute to women a power to influence the characters and conduct of their kin.[107] Moralists envisioned women cultivating domestic virtues within their families as an effective antidote to French revolt, French invasion, and French manners in general. Literary critic Judith Lowder Newton has suggested that the moral influence ascribed to women in late eighteenth- and also nineteenth-century conduct books functioned strategically as well "to sustain unequal power relations between middle-class women and middle-class men." Women were offered influence in place of the power of control or self-determination.[108] But conduct books show that even this trade-off was worrisome, and to moralists of diverse backgrounds. At the same time that they conferred influence on women and their domestic sphere, they imposed limits on it.

Gisborne in *An Enquiry into the Duties of the Female Sex* claimed that women have "real and deeply interesting effects" not just on their families but "on the happiness of society."[109] Later in the book, however, he warned:

> Whatever be the influence which the amiable virtues of a wife may obtain over her husband, let not the consciousness of it ever lead her to seek opportunities of displaying it, nor to cherish a wish to intrude into those departments which belong not to her jurisdiction. . . . let her equally guard against desiring to possess undue weight over her husband's conduct.[110]

In *Letters to a Young Lady*, West gave to women, by an extension of their domestic role, more power to end the conflict with France than belonged to either the government or the military:

> As mothers and mistresses of families, we possess so much influence, that if we were uniformly to exert it in the manner which the times require, we might produce a most happy change in the morals of the people; and in peril of being thought superstitious, I avow my firm belief, that such a change would conduce more to extricate us from our present difficulties, than the wisdom of our counsellors, or the valour of our fleets and armies.[111]

But West's *Letters* too acknowledges elsewhere that men, for most of their lives, are actually immune to women's powers of influence: "The stubborn clay of man is never pliant but in early life; the storms of contention, and the pressure of business, give it an impenetrability which, however suited to the rude buffets that it is designed to endure, prevent its being made malleable by the soft strokes of feminine influence."[112]

Even in the midst of encomiums on women's influence, both books refer to the insignificance of the domestic realm and its activities. Gisborne described domestic activities as "unassuming," made up not of "great" events but of "small but perpetually recurring incidents of good and evil."[113] West simply told her readers that men are engaged in "more important business."[114] Domestic activities were, after all, not public, not part of the domain of history and of fame.

If conduct books mixed their messages on the subject of the domestic woman's import, the members of Austen's community were generally less strategic and less conflicted in their view of the domestic role. They had little to say about influence. For them, the domestic was a necessary but decidedly unremarkable role. Although, for example, Charles Powlett, during his courtship of Anne Temple in 1791, told her that "everything where you are concern'd is interesting to me, I wish to hear of your rides, your Visits, your Employments," he could not deny that he thought these were "trifles." By contrast to their own experiences, those of domesticity had for men no history. Charles Powlett believed that a woman's family life in a "retir'd spot . . . affords few events."[115] The same view appeared, somewhat paradoxically, in the first biography written about Jane Austen in 1818, a year after her death. Her brother Henry Austen assured the public that because Jane Austen was devoted to her family and home life, hers "was not by any means a life of events."[116]

However affectionate, such comments remind us that genteel domesticity, although it stressed affection and mutuality between the sexes, was still the particular medium, in textual representations and social group practices, of patriarchal social relationships. We might have expected otherwise because, as historian Randolph Trumbach has pointed out, patriarchy and domesticity are actually "opposing models of household organization." "Patriarchy," according to Trumbach, "presumed that there was property not only in things but in persons and that ownership lay with the heads of households. It meant that some men were owned by others, and all women and children by their husbands and fathers." By contrast, domesticity was part of a trend toward egalitarian social relationships in the seventeenth and eighteenth centuries. Trumbach has noted, however, that "the clearest victories of egalitarian ideas occurred in the relationships between adult men" and that the relationships of men to women were slow to change.[117]

Genteel domesticity assigned to women a devalued role and only that role. As it was practiced by Austen's community, domesticity effectively inhibited other ways of life. The perpetuation of status through the reproduction and acculturation of children and through the orchestration of family appearances was virtually the only "career" open to women. Certainly, some women sometimes found the activities prescribed for them to their liking. Young, unmarried women, to take one example, may have sustained a particular enthusiasm for the social round as a change from their domestic tasks or as a series of opportunities to make contact with an eligible man or his family. The seventeen-year-old Caroline Pym Hales would complain in her diary when "nobody came all day—horrid—stupid."[118] But other women, especially after they married or as they aged, could not always muster the energy or enthusiasm for almost incessant socializing. On one of the days of Jane Austen's visit to Mrs. Knight in 1808, her hostess had "had a sad headache which kept her in bed. She had had too much company the day before."[119]

Mrs. Knight's "sad headache" points us toward a related problem with domesticity, which we will explore more fully in the next chapter. It limited women's self-expressiveness by offering not only just one way of life but that particular life-style: one which required self-restraint and self-denial. *Control yourself*, conduct books urged women again and again. Writing "On the Government of the Temper," Hester Chapone maintained that "an enraged woman is one of the most disgusting sights in nature"; she insisted that "the most passionate people can command themselves"; and she recommended as their goal "gentleness, meekness, and patience."[120] Gregory thought women should dance but told them "never allow yourselves to be so transported with mirth as to forget the delicacy of your sex."[121] He distrusted indulgences in wit or humor.[122] He also hoped that women's modesty would "naturally" cause them "to be rather silent in company, especially in a large one" and told them to avoid revealing "good sense" or "any learning" lest they seem vain.[123] In short, women were not to gratify themselves in any way. "A life of uselessness and indulgence," Jane West confidently asserted, "can never be a life of happiness."[124] Because women could hope to find happiness only through devotion to their families, those who hoped to marry in particular needed, according to West, "a disposition that can yield to the desires of others, not only without *apparent* reluctance but without *enduring* pain."[125]

These restrictions on life-choice and self-expression have obvious bearing on any consideration of Jane Austen's life and achievements. They not only led women away from novel-writing careers but also prescribed a self-effacing conduct and discourse for them that would seem, certainly at first glance, not to be a medium conducive to imaginative creativity. But before we turn to the problem of Jane Austen's artistic development, we need first to pursue women's own responses to domesticity. How did they envision female identity? What did they do? And what did they say?

CHAPTER 2

Compliant Women

1
———

A NNE HARRIS achieved her feminine "destiny" in India when
she married Stephen Rumbold Lushington. He was to have a
long parliamentary career—Lushington was elected first from Rye in
1807 and then from Canterbury in 1812—but he did not appear to be
a particularly promising catch when he asked for Anne's hand in 1797.
The second son of clergyman James Stephen Lushington, he had gone
to India to make his fortune and in 1795 became private secretary to
Anne's father, an army officer. Major General Harris mistrusted his
sincerity and was convinced that the young man married his daughter
for the money that he hoped she would receive. Lushington's manners
were to continue to provoke suspicion. When she met him more than
fifteen years later, Jane Austen facetiously described him as "quite an
M.P.—very smiling, with an exceeding good address, & readiness of
Language."[1] But for all his ambitious yearnings for fortune and fame
and despite what must have been a rather slick self-presentation, his
letters indicate that he was genuinely in love with his wife. And her
letters reveal that she not only adored but readily subordinated herself
to her husband: domestic ideology shaped her view of her marital
responsibilities.[2]

She was deeply committed to the role it marked out for women, even
when her own bad health prevented her from fulfilling it. In a letter
to her father in 1800, she proudly assured him that she had become "a
careful little Housekeeper."[3] In her attempt to please her father (as
well as her husband) she offered this self-portrait with the diminutive,
evidently to offset any impression of vanity. But a year later she be-

came quite ill, and in 1803 she was near despair, not about the burdens of domesticity but about her inability to carry them. "Time only," she wrote her father, "can sufficiently invigorate it [her constitution] to render me again equal to the performance of those duties which as Wife Mother & Mistress of a family it is my highest ambition to fulfill—for the last two years I have bitterly felt myself a useless being in the creation—I have been obliged to rely on the assistance of others, instead of extending it to those who demand my tenderest cares—and to become the nursling of my family instead of their support."[4]

Anne Lushington's strict adherence to the ideology of domesticity was typical. The private writings of Jane Austen's female friends, kin, and neighbors, which this chapter and the next will explore, express a complex response to the ideology, but compliance constituted one loud and clear part of that response. These women, when speaking of themselves or other women, as we shall see, often sounded like the texts that influenced their vision of private life. We encounter the same allegiance that Anne Lushington showed to the ideology and its imagery of the female in the letters Austen's niece Fanny Knight wrote to her fiancé in September 1820. As Fanny was in good health and had already had substantial experience of the domestic role, she could, unlike Anne Lushington, confidently portray a self that was fulfilling her culture's feminine ideal. Indeed, her letters to her future husband, Sir Edward Knatchbull, were paradigmatic representations of the feminine woman. They had to be. Knatchbull was a cautious man with exacting standards who had already known family happiness with his first wife, Annabella Honywood.

Devastated by Annabella's death in childbirth in 1814 and uncomfortable with his father's excesses in conjugal life—the eighth baronet had married three times and would have by the time of his death a score of children—Knatchbull made no immediate efforts to find another wife. But very gradually he began to think about it. Once a year he reviewed his life in a diary, and in 1816 he wrote, "My great Anxiety regards My Children. I hardly know how to manage them without their Mother's Assistance."[5] In 1817 he finally voiced the question. "My domestic happiness has ceas'd," his diary reads, "I have lately consider'd whether it is well for me or for My Children, that I should continue a Widower—My Mind is unsettled."[6] In 1818 he was still uncertain: "Will it be better for me and My Children, that I should again marry, or that I should remain a Widower?"[7] Although the death of one of his six children later that year must have played a part in his decision, it was his father's death in 1819 that finally determined him to remarry. Inheriting his father's title and very large estate,

Mersham Hatch, and, in effect, his public office, Sir Edward Knatch-bull, ninth baronet and Member of Parliament for Kent, needed a wife. His diary entry for April, 1820, concludes: "Here [at Provender, the estate he had inherited through his mother] I think I should have remain'd a Widower—at Hatch the Case must be otherwise—this for My Children & My Family's Sake—God grant I may do what is best for My dear Children!"[8]

On August 29 of the same year, he proposed to Fanny Knight and she accepted. Although the Knight and Knatchbull families knew one another socially and were even related through Mrs. Knight—she and the eighth baronet were cousins—he did not know Fanny very well, perhaps because she was twelve years his junior. But all outward signs spoke in her favor: she had been competently managing her widowed father's household for more than a decade. Knatchbull was not to be disappointed. Less than two weeks later, the bride-to-be began proffer-ing what must have been reassuring images of her present and their future life in the prolific correspondence that they conducted while Knatchbull was traveling.

She opposed, and showed that she opposed, putting herself forward. Like Anne Lushington she took pains, for example, to avoid even the appearance of boasting about her self-effacing devotion to her family. Concerned about how her father would manage without her, she sug-gested, "Some additional cares I am afraid he must have, for he has been so long in the habit of leaving all family & domestic arrange-ments to me (from being himself constantly occupied with concerns of more importance,). . . . I trust my dearest Love you will not for a moment think I am endeavouring to make myself of too much con-sequence! I detest the idea of such a thing!"[9]

She disliked being the center of attention even when widespread notice was sanctioned by convention. Her engagement caused her so-cial embarrassment, the description of which must have delighted her fiancé. While visiting her married sister, she encountered one day "a whole party of shooters," brought home by her brother-in-law. "We had such a room full of people," she wrote to Knatchbull, "that I could not bear it, & after getting redder & redder every moment I took courage to walk out of the room, & remained upstairs till the gentle-men were gone—I hope they did not think it uncivil, & that *you* will not think me foolish—it is not that I am not happy I may say *proud* of my attachment, but I cannot bear to know other people are thinking of it, & looking at me."[10]

Over and over she asserted her wish to live for her new family. "My earnest endeavours," she told him, will be "to promote the present as

well as future welfare & happiness of yourself and your dear children."
She even seemed anxious to put this self-effacing devotion to the test.
She was becoming acquainted with his oldest child, twelve-year-old
Mary, and was convinced, so she told him, that "I shall have much
more pleasure than trouble in my charge. Had it been otherwise, I
hope you will believe me, when I say, there is no sacrifice I would not
joyfully have made for your sake."[11] Because it was not, apparently,
going to be difficult for her to assume the care of his children, she
seemed to be searching for some other sacrifice. Six days later she
settled on her music. "Unless it would be a pleasure to *you* as well as
myself, it would hardly be worth while to be at the expense of a Harp,
or to give up the time necessary to practise—so tell me *exactly* what
you wish, & I shall have no will but yours."[12]

Although the sacrifice of her music seems merely symbolic and to
have been no genuine loss at all, Fanny did have to face one quite real
trial, and her compliance proves the sincerity of her commitment to
the domestic ideology. Sir Edward, she discovered, wanted to marry
soon, in October, while Fanny wished to spend one more Christmas
with her family at Godmersham. She made her wishes known to her
fiancé but couched their conflict in terms that submerged her will:
should she please her family or her fiancé? She could think of only one
way to resolve the conflict, hoping, no doubt, that her deference and
generosity would win her a winter wedding. *"You* must direct me My
beloved friend," she told him, "& I prove how highly I value your
disinterested judgement by referring to you on such an occasion. You
shall tell me how to act so as to fulfill every duty, & I am sure you will
consider every body as I wish to do myself."[13] They were married in
October.

It is not surprising that Fanny Knight wrote this way to Edward
Knatchbull. Her letters, so perfectly adapted to the tastes and desires
of their recipient, were one of the promising performances that belong
to the periods of courtship and engagement. Nor is it surprising that
Anne Lushington generated similar images of femininity in letters
meant to please or elicit sympathy from her father. But when women
wrote to other women without wishing or expecting their letters to be
read by men, they still espoused the ideal of domestic femininity. In
Practical Education the Edgeworths argued that "girls should be more
inured to restraint than boys, because they are likely to meet with
more restraint in society," and women indicated to their female correspondents that they were looking for such restraint and its companion trait of deference in their sisters, daughters, nieces, and female
acquaintances.[14]

In 1799, for example, Anne Powlett wrote to her friend Padgy Peters of her younger sister Laura: "She is rather improved—her manners are in some degree feminized and she attends more to neatness and propriety in her Dress . . . I begin to hope that she may pass through the World with tolerable decency and decorum."[15] In a letter she wrote to her friend in 1801, Anne reported about her daughter, "My dear little Caroline improves daily, but she has a spirit which will, I fear, require some restraint."[16] In 1809 Jane Austen commented to her sister about their niece Fanny, "While she gives happiness to those about her, she is pretty sure of her own share."[17] And in the same year Fanny wrote disapprovingly about a woman of her acquaintance to her former governess, Dorothy Chapman. Lady Sondes, a widow with six children, had agreed to remarry. "I am rather surprised at her marrying at all, with such a family," Fanny commmented. As "an inveterate enemy to second marriages," Fanny was espousing the subordination of women's individual desires to the dynastic ambitions of the patriarchal family.[18]

Women did not merely recommend a female conduct of self-suppression; they *enacted* it in their letters. Their discourse dramatized domestic femininity when they adopted the perspective of men—expressing their interests, their experience, their opinions—and, in effect, wrote women out of their letters. Sometimes their letters literally used the language of men. For example, when women wrote to other women, as they so often did in order to sustain contacts between families and family branches, their letters often became corporate productions. Such letters, reporting news of their households, often included messages written by a male relation of the woman writer addressed to another male relation in the female recipient's household. Or women spoke for their own and to another woman's male kin, conveying their concerns and desires, as when Jane Austen wrote to her sister in 1798, "You must tell Edward that my father gives 25s. a piece to Seward for his last lot of sheep, and, in return for this news, my father wishes to receive some of Edward's pigs."[19] Even when they did not repeat men's exact words or provide paraphrases of them, women often expressed the interests and opinions of their husbands, fathers, and brothers, identifying themselves as "we." When they did so, they were ignoring socially determined differences and inequities in the experiences of men and women.

In 1790, for example, Mary Bramston was so interested in her brother William Chute's efforts to stand for M.P. of Hants that she neglected one of her own family obligations. "I had intended to have answered your letter by the next post," she wrote to her husband's cousin Henrietta Hicks Beach, "but really my thoughts are so taken up with Elections that I entirely forgot." The letter she had now finally written continues to demonstrate interest in elections, providing among other things an estimation of Chute and Heathcote's likelihood of success. "We had a good majority," she wrote, while "they are driven to their last stake & about that they quarrel."[20] Bramston's "we" suggests that she was writing for her husband and brother to Henrietta Hicks Beach and probably to her husband and father. Her next letter, again about the contest, just a few days later confirms that impression: "Mr B[ramston] being very busy & as Mr Beach & yourselves will I know like particulars I shall give you a whole account."[21]

Similarly, Jane Austen voiced the concerns of men in a letter she wrote to Cassandra at Godmersham in 1801 just after their father had decided to retire to Bath. She described in some detail the fate of her father's bailiff, John Bond:

> Mr. Holder was perfectly willing to take him on exactly the same terms with my father, & John seems exceedingly well satisfied.—The comfort of not changing his home is a very material one to him, and since such are his unnatural feelings his belonging to Mr. Holder is the every thing needful; but otherwise there would have been a situation offering to him which I had thought of with particular satisfaction, viz=under Harry Digweed, who if John had quitted Cheesedown would have been eager to engage him as superintendant at Steventon, would have kept an horse for him to ride about on, would probably have supplied him with a more permanent home, & I think would certainly have been a more desirable Master altogether. John & Corbett are not to have any concern with each other;—there are to be two Farms and two Bailiffs.—We are of opinion that it would be better in only one.[22]

Austen's shift in pronouns from "I" to "we" suggests that she too represents the news of her household and particularly of her father in a letter undoubtedly meant to be shared by Cassandra with her brother Edward.

Mary Bramston's alignment with her male kin illustrates how the assumption of "we" inhibited women's consciousness of their own social situation, supplanting their awareness of socially determined sex differences. The identified writer and reader of her letters—as women—could neither govern nor vote. Imaginative identification stood in lieu of political rights, displacing women's perceptions of their constraints. Jane Austen's "we," as well as the specificity of her account, similarly shows that she and Cassandra were imaginatively involved with farm management, a territory of experience in which they actually had no power and nothing to do. Austen could speak as if she did have some authority in this realm because she had taken on her father's interests as her own.

When women did mention their own interests and experiences, they often diminished them, echoing the patriarchal view of their domestic activities as trivial and unimportant. Although their letters frequently conveyed news of their families, women did not view their child-care or socializing as newsworthy. Consequently, their accounts of such activities are often accompanied by apology or self-deprecation, traits that appear in letters written to their male relatives, in their corporate household letters (which men sometimes helped compose or had occasion to read), and in letters intended only for other women. Anne Powlett, for example, referred to her "own little trifling domestic matters" in a 1805 letter to her husband,[23] but Jane Austen was addressing her sister Cassandra when she called her experiences "important nothings" and "little events."[24] Fanny Austen was communicating only with Dorothy Chapman in 1806, when she thanked her ex-governess for caring "about our little concerns."[25] Occasionally, Fanny resorted to hyperbole in her letters to Dorothy Chapman, warning through playful exaggeration that her narration was unimportant: "I . . . will explain our proceedings past present & future for the good of the Nation in general & for your own private amusement."[26] She sometimes achieved hyperbole by applying the language of novels to her own experience, offering, for example in 1809, "the history of my life & adventures."[27]

Again and again women expressed this view of domestic experience. Eliza de Feuillide told Philadelphia Walter in 1791: "I have no news, at least nothing but *home news*, as Swift says, to send you: the most remarkable occurrence of this nature is that my son & heir who promises to be as great a pickle as any who ever deserved that appellation, has laid aside his feminine garb, & now makes a most manly appearance in a jacket & trowsers."[28] In 1805 Elizabeth Chute similarly insisted to her husband that she had "no news." "You will therefore," she noted, "perhaps think this letter too long, & that long since I might have said farewell."[29] And in 1812 Cassandra Austen began a letter to Philadelphia, now Mrs. George Whitaker, with the familiar apology: "I have not written before because I have had nothing to communicate and perhaps the same reason ought to keep me silent longer, but I will write now lest you should think I have forgot you and trust to your thinking my letter worth reading."[30]

Women *enacted* their self-effacement by silencing or diminishing not only female experiences but also, of course, any desires that ran counter to patriarchal prerogatives. Sometimes they seemed to have no such desires. In the following carefully worded consideration of her sister's travel plans, Jane Austen represented only the needs and wishes of her brothers Henry and James. Speaking for her family in general, she wrote out of the discussion any interests that Cassandra might have had that were separate and different from her brothers':

> Henry would send you in his carriage a stage or two, where you might be met by John, whose protection you would we imagine think sufficient for the rest of your Journey. . . . James has offered to meet you anywhere, but as that would be to give him trouble without any counterpoise of convenience, as he has no intention of going to London at present on his own account, we suppose that you would rather accept the attentions of John.[31]

At other times women did voice their own wishes, but they immediately proceeded to override them, deferring to the authority of men. If the Austen sisters' travel plans were dependent on the movements of their brothers, Mary Bramston's and those of all other wives frequently depended on the preferences and schedules of their husbands. In a letter to Henrietta Hicks Beach in 1793, for example, Mary Bramston expressed the hope that Henrietta had derived "the usual benefits from dipping in the sea" and a longing to go to the seashore herself—"I have often wished for a dip too." But it was not to be, she noted uncomplainingly, for "Mr. B has been so busy."[32]

When women did not have to bow to the superior claims of a particular male relative, they still denied their own desires, inhibited by the restrictive vision of domestic femininity. In a letter to Cassandra in 1799, for example, Austen described her plan to accompany her brother Charles partway in the coach that was to carry him to Deal. "I want to go with him," she said, "that I may explain the country to him properly between Canterbury and Rowling, but the unpleasantness of returning by myself deters me."[33] Conditioned to traveling in the company of a male relative, she had learned to prefer this protection. Anne Powlett called upon Padgy Peters for assistance during one of her pregnances but then immediately expressed her readiness to do without the aid if her friend could not travel to her "under a proper protection."[34]

2
———

Why did these women submit to the behavioral and representational restraints of domestic ideology? Why did they so willingly deny themselves assertion and autonomy? Certainly, we should not underestimate the pull of love and esteem. Women's affective ties to their male kin, elaborated within and encouraged by the ideology of domesticity, gave them an incentive to comply. Women were also disposed to subscribe to an ideology that favored men because they were socially and economically dependent on their male relatives for their status identities.

But women tended to remain loyal to the ideology of domesticity even when they were not directly dependent on their male relations. They consented to their own subordination because domestic femininity was inextricably connected to high social status. Had they refused that femininity, they would have been rejecting their community's ideal not of womanhood but of socially elite womanhood. Sociologist Ann Oakley has shown that the ideology of domesticity was not applied by the upper and middle classes to working-class women until the early 1840s,[35] and perceptions of women servants and laborers articulated by the gentlewomen of Austen's community confirm that in the early nineteenth century they still linked domestic femininity with gentility.

In her "Memoranda," notes made by Jane Austen's niece Anna on her family's history, she described several of the working women in the neighborhood of Steventon. Her recollections reveal the way in which she and her family had viewed them in the early years of the century. Apparently Anna had been able to enjoy and appreciate rather than condemn at least some of their conduct; because they were situated in a different rank, she did not expect them to adhere to the ideology of domesticity. True, Henny Lavender had been "so neat, so clean and industrious," but she was also "so discontented, and dissatisfied." "It was almost a treat," Anna claimed, "to listen to her grumblings, or a vexation, as the case might be." She and her family viewed Bet Littleworth as a "heroine" but not because she was a paragon of femininity. "Though a rather small and delicate looking woman," according to Anna, "she had all her life by choice done the work of a man." And though she had a suitor for several years, she refused to marry, choosing instead to spend "her strength and earnings in the maintenance of the two illegitimate children of a niece." The sexuality of Bet Armstrong, Littleworth's niece, of course, disqualified her from both domestic femininity and the company of ladies: "A very dissipated character was that niece . . . but *she* seldom came amongst us."[36] Women in Austen's social community, then, who refused to adopt its ideal of femininity could experience a symbolic if not literal descent or disappearance into the ranks of this otherness.

High social status mitigated some of the worst aspects of the male domination that British women *in all ranks* faced (working women, of course, felt the impact of that domination most). An incident in the life of Jane Austen's niece Caroline illustrates the mixed impact of genteel domesticity. In 1818 James Austen, the novelist's oldest brother, informed his son James Edward, then at Oxford, of measures he and his wife were planning to take in order to economize. "Your mother," wrote James to his son, "has persuaded me not to enter our carriage this year." They had also decided to remove their thirteen-year-old daughter Caroline from school.[37] But the Austens were evidently unwilling to curb any of their son's expenses. "If I were to give up hunting for the next year or two," James Edward replied to his parents, "there would be no occasion for more than two horses [at home] which with keep and tax & other little concomitant expenses would be, I am sure, a considerable saving." He insists, in anticipation of his parents' objections, that "giving up hunting would be no great sacrifice" and concludes with a final plea: "I am sure it is highly improper that I should be *indulging myself* with my own horse in sports while you cannot afford to give my sister the *necessary* education of a gentlewoman."[38] James Edward's counterproposal only underscores the conventional biases of his culture: men were expected to indulge, women to sacrifice.[39]

The ideology of domesticity was an instrument of sexual oppression for elite women, but it also softened the penalties of that oppression.[40] It did so because its vision of women's subordination was circumscribed and cushioned by gentility. The sacrifice Caroline's parents wished to impose on her was not life-threatening. What she risked without the "education of a gentlewoman" was a reduction of social status. Caroline Austen did not, as she grew older, lose her genteel status, although after her father's death in 1819 she and her mother suffered the economic decline not uncommon to gentlewomen on the death of their clergymen kin. They moved several times, living always in rented homes, until Mary Austen died in 1843.[41] Caroline never married, but she never had to hire out as a governess or take in needlework, either. She remained a welcome visitor to the homes of her nieces and nephews, who admired her "excellent memory," "original and cultivated mind," "sweet, gentle manner," gift for storytelling, and, last but not least, "the unselfishness of her nature."[42] She spent the last twenty years of her life keeping house for two of her nephews. The ideology of domesticity exacted the sacrifice of perpetual "unselfishness" from Caroline Austen, but it kept her safe as well.

That the community was also prepared to enforce compliance with its values became apparent in the rare cases of women who did not perceive the advantages of self-denial and rebelled. The fates of the few women who refused the ideal of femininity constituted compelling "negative incentives" for Jane Austen's female kin and acquaintances. In their reminiscences both Caroline Austen and Caroline Wiggett Workman tell the story of Hester Wheeler, evidently because her unconventional behavior and the responses that it elicited made her especially memorable. When Hester disregarded the self-abnegating conduct of the feminine woman and asserted herself, she met with condemnation and repression from the gentlemen and ladies of Jane Austen's Hampshire neighborhood.

Caroline Wiggett Workman's guardians, the Chutes, had long been associated with Hester's considerably less prosperous family of tradespeople and teachers. Hester's great-aunt had been a governess to Mary Bramston (née Chute) and one of her sisters. Out of loyalty to her, the Chutes helped her niece, Hester's mother, to find a position as a governess, and when Hester's mother died, they arranged to educate Hester. In 1814, the Chutes brought the eleven-year-old girl to the Vyne so that she could be taught with Caroline Wiggett.

Caroline Wiggett Workman suggests rather enigmatically that her "Uncles soon discovered when she was older, that she was not a good companion for me, so Hester was sent to a school at Winchester."[43] Her defects are explained in Caroline Austen's account of what happened next: "Poor Hester, with all her charmingness, was far from perfect. She was self-willed and she could be rebellious, and before the next summer holidays came round, serious differences arose between her and her school mistress, differences which were terminated by Hester's walking away from Kingsgate Street altogether." The girl was returned to her guardians by the family to whom she had fled, and at the Vyne she was, according to Caroline Austen, "considered to be 'en penitence,' but 'penitent,' in English," she adds, "I do not think she *was*."[44] Fearing her influence, all of the adults—Chutes, Bramstons, and Austens—united in their refusal to let Hester associate with other young girls and in their silence about her after they sent her away to relatives in Norfolk. "The subject," Caroline Austen recalls, "was never mentioned, after just the first."[45] Although several years later Caroline heard that Hester was happily married—albeit to a mere linen draper in Scotland—her adolescent "escapade," according to Caroline Austen, had "raised anxious thoughts as to her future life and conduct."[46]

Orphaned and dependent, Hester Wheeler could be banished from sight and even from verbal representations. Lady Frances Honywood, when she challenged the authority of her family's head, was not so easily disposed of. While Hester was stationed at the lower margins of Hampshire's gentry, Lady Honywood was situated in the upper reaches of polite society in Kent. Nevertheless, her experience must also have served as a disturbing lesson to the members of her social circle.

The daughter of a viscount, she had married a baronet in 1781 with an estate worth £7,000 to £10,000 per annum. Much of the estate was entailed, however, and over the years her husband also contracted very large debts. At his death in 1806, consequently, she possessed only what she perceived as a very inadequate jointure of £1,000 per annum. According to Lady Honywood, before her husband died, he had exacted a promise from their son John Courtenay to increase his mother's jointure from £1,000 to £1,500 and to provide her with a house, furniture, and a carriage and horses. Courtenay came of age and inherited the estate in 1808 but made no move to fulfill that promise. After several frustrating interchanges with him, Lady Honywood tried to force him to honor his word. Without a legal claim, she could appeal only to his sense of honor and filial duty. Finally, she attempted to shame him publicly. In debt to her upholsterer for more than £1,500, she threatened her son with her arrest and imprisonment and with the publication of letters she had written about her plight to two of his friends and advisors: Sir Edward Knatchbull (the eighth baronet) and Thomas Brett.

This series of events is recounted in *The Memorial of the Honourable Lady Honywood Written for the Use of Her Referees*, which an enraged Lady Honywood had published in 1812 when all negotiations with her son had collapsed.[47] What is astonishing about the document is that Lady Honywood shows little consciousness of the extreme impropriety, according to contemporary norms, of her aggressive behavior and public expressions of anger. Absorbed in her own defense and what she believes to be her son's scandalous behavior, she cannot understand how she appears to her community. But the views of her contemporaries seep into her account despite her lack of self-awareness. Although she depicts the responses of others to show that they are cruel or greedy (and to modern eyes they may seem so), we perceive a social set united in their view and treatment of her.

Fearing her as a threat to her son's estate and reputation, that social set longed to cut the spendthrift, noisy woman off from the young baronet. Thomas Brett told Mary Anne Cooper just before she married Courtenay in 1808, "Sir John will do very well if he can be kept from his mother."[48] Edward Knatchbull, son of the eighth baronet and at the time married to Annabella, another of Lady Honywood's children, was called upon not so much in his capacity as an in-law as in that of a barrister to help protect the son from his mother. At a private meeting that Lady Honywood described in her *Memorial*, he warned Sir John not to make his mother any promises, "though," he assured him, "you are not bound by any thing you say here." He proposed to Sir John that his mother "give up her jointure, and accept of what you choose to allow her" and sought assurances from Lady Honywood that if her son gave her some financial help, she would not "trouble him again." He also sternly informed her that her imprisonment would not injure her son's reputation, for, he explained, "it would not be known; or if it were known, it would be in such a confined circle, that he could easily explain his reasons for his conduct." And finally, rather ominously, he asked her if she had made a will.[49]

Her female acquaintances cooperated in seeking Lady Honywood's removal from their society. In a letter that Lady Cooper wrote to her daughter, Mary Anne, now the young baronet's wife (which Lady Honywood somehow gained access to and published in the *Memorial*), she urged that "after Lady Honywood's business is arranged, she would be given to understand that her visit must end, and never be repeated." Lady Cooper added, "This last piece of artifice and atrocity to Courtenay must render her character more than ever odious in the sight of all well-judging and respectable people."[50] Although she had her own way of interpreting it, Lady Honywood had met with a sample of this condemnation from Lady Elizabeth, wife of another of Courtenay's Kent friends, George Finch Hatton. As she told Finch Hatton, "The recollection of Lady Elizabeth's behavior to me at the late Lady Darlington's . . . tended to confirm me in the opinion that I had been infamously misrepresented to your family."[51] No one could be more firm in disapproving of the aggressive behavior of women than other women.

At eleven years of age, Hester Wheeler did not restrain herself, perhaps because she did not adequately appreciate the opportunities for social advancement that the Chutes' patronage could offer her. But Lady Honywood lost all restraint and went to war with her son, ironically, in order to protect her status. An addition of five hundred pounds to her jointure, she maintained, "is not more than sufficient to provide me the necessaries of life, and to enable me to live with comfort in my own sphere in society."[52] She chose the wrong tactics, however. Although she sought authority for her claims in her father's aristocratic rank and her husband's intentions, now that her father and husband were dead, her son's wishes were preeminent. Whether Lady Honywood received more money from her son or not, she was ostracized by her social circle because she had refused to defer to him.

In the extant letters of those who were acquainted with the Honywood family, it is difficult to find references to Lady Honywood after 1812. It is impossible to know whether she was effaced from their representations at that time or only when they subsequently and selectively destroyed some of their private writings. Her son Courtenay's wife, Mary Anne Cooper, is mentioned approvingly, and it is tempting to suppose that those who admired her were considering her in light of what they had heard of the Honywood family feud. While staying with her brother Edward in 1813, for example, Jane Austen wrote to Cassandra about her: "I did not sit near enough to be a perfect Judge, but I thought her extremely pretty & her manners have all the recommendations of ease & goodhumour & unaffectedness;—& going about with 4 Horses, & nicely dressed herself—she is altogether a perfect sort of Woman."[53]

Only once, in November 1812, does the dowager's name emerge in a letter, which her daughter Annabella addressed to her husband, Edward Knatchbull. Annabella, very much the compliant woman, wrote to express her wishes for the disposal of her belongings, "should anything happen to me." We can assume from her letter that Annabella had made no will and that her clothes and jewelry would belong to her husband after her death. She could only hope that he would honor her requests.[54] She was especially concerned about a locket that held her brother's hair and a chain, given her many years earlier by her father. "If You do not disapprove it may Lady Honywood have them from me?" she petitioned.[55] Annabella was not interested in displeasing her husband even with a "dying wish" and for the sake of her mother.

3

In their everyday activities and in their representations of those activities, most Hampshire and Kent gentlewomen unhesitatingly accepted their subordination. Still, they had to work at the self-suppression that it required throughout their lives. Writing on late eighteenth- and early nineteenth-century British literature and society, Mary Poovey has argued that under the influence of conduct-book ideology, women's "desires no doubt did begin to seem—even to them—more or less commensurate with their duties."[56] She suggests further that "as women accepted a definition of 'female nature' that was derived from a social role, they found it increasingly difficult to acknowledge or to integrate into their self-perceptions desires that did not support this stereotype." They "may not consciously have acknowledged their own impermissible desires."[57] The private writings of Austen's female friends, neighbors, and kin, however, indicate that even the most self-effacing and deferential of these women were aware of having desires different from their duties and that they made persistent efforts to subdue or convert them.

Of course, they had help. We never have to look very far to see women soliciting or offering advice on conduct. Older women, in particular, fashioned by domestic ideology to be its inculcators, were called upon by younger women to point them toward a properly feminine self-identity. For example, although Elizabeth Chute, according to her husband William, had been "brought up in a way likely to make a very good domestic wife," that training did not end with her marriage in October 1793. The adjustments marriage required—to a new home, to a husband, and to the anticipated responsibility of children— prompted the new bride to turn to her mother, Sarah Smith. She earnestly wanted to live up to her husband's prediction about her but did not always know how.

When Elizabeth admitted four months after her wedding that she still did not feel comfortable with the physical intimacy of marriage, her mother responded, "I join with you in wishing you could get rid of some of your timidity, & be more at ease with Mr Chute I am sure he tries to court you to familiarity." Elizabeth's plight was probably not uncommon. Having learned a demure style of dress and behavior to men, she could not immediately adopt new ways. Elizabeth had also apparently mentioned that she preferred the modest fashion of a black ruff. Her mother was certain that her husband did not like it, for it hid too much of her daughter's "pretty white throat, you know he early gave you proofs of his partiality to it." Her mother advised her, "You should tell him when you wear it you do it on principle, that by some times like a true Coquet keeping it from his view, he may at other times have more pleasure in seeing of it, that Men are changable, to please them we must vary this little advantage nature has given."[58]

Elizabeth Chute and Sarah Smith were considering how much the young woman should seek to indulge her own wishes. Elizabeth's mother, although not endorsing utter self-abnegation for women, insisted on the priority of men's desires over women's. Elizabeth, she believed, might seek to gratify herself as long as doing so did not conflict with her husband's wants. Although Sarah Smith sympathized with her daughter's bashfulness, she offered her a strategy of compromise, which would enable Elizabeth to indulge her preference for modest dress only if it promised her husband increased sensual pleasure.

Sarah Smith taught more lessons in submissiveness when her daughter wrote to her about two proposed trips to London. The visits would have offered the new bride much gratification because they would have reunited her with her family, who were at the time residing in town. In early February 1794, William Chute asked his wife if she would like to accompany him to London, but, as she afterwards reported to her mother, she had decided not to go. Her mother was quick to analyze her reasons and, gently, to condemn her. Perhaps, she suggested, Elizabeth had imagined that the trip would be too expensive or that her husband was only indulging her because he knew she disliked parting with him. Such motives, she continued, masked the real reason Elizabeth had turned down the trip: she did not want to owe her happiness to her husband. But, her mother argued, "why should you refuse pleasure on *his* terms, you would be happy to give *him* pleasure; yet your proud heart will not let him enjoy the same pleasure by thinking it is he that can give it you."[59] Sarah Smith's reaction pointed to a way in which women could frustrate men's desires and power: by denying themselves the pleasures men proposed for them.[60] Elizabeth's mother adamantly opposed self-denial in the service of that goal, but she approved of it when it served to gratify men. It often did.

Later in the same month Elizabeth had another opportunity to accompany her husband to London but declined it when her husband's local political commitments subsequently diverted his attention. Elizabeth explained the circumstances to her mother and awaited her verdict. This time the response was quite different. "I am truly sorry," her mother wrote, "but far from condemning your giving it up, it is now quite a different case Mr C.—— wishes & Convenience has properly decided your choice, & my Eliza's self approbation will prevent her sacrifice being painful, nor will she find the time of Mr C—— Absence so dull; for I suppose he must attend at Winchester the Sheriffe with all due ceremony; before you gave up your own gratification from false delicacy, now you have a pleasure in reflecting *I might go*, but could I do it when I am sure it was more agreable to Mr Chute to defer our Journey till he could remain quietly in town."[61] Sarah Smith was again suggesting that women's preferences were properly limited and circumscribed by men's, although she knew that it was not always easy for new wives to understand their husbands' wishes or to ferret out their own secret, wayward impulses.

Because Sarah Smith's letters display deliberate efforts to mold her daughter's responses, they underscore the patriarchal otherness of the feminine identity women were struggling to assume. As she wrote on various topics, she was imparting to Elizabeth a way of describing her marital relations. Smith voiced unwavering trust in William Chute's treatment and perception of her daughter ("I am sure he tries to court you to familiarity"). She also assumed and articulated her daughter's devotion to her husband ("you would be happy to give *him* pleasure"). Thus, she supplied Elizabeth with a language of conjugal affection that portrayed the priority of men's views and women's loving endorsement of that precedence. For "very good wives"—and sisters and daughters—spoke and complied with words that were in their own interests but did not always express their own particular social and psychological positions.

In addition to the help they received from other women and their conduct-booklike representations, Austen's female relatives and neighbors often looked to their religion to buttress their efforts of feminine self-denial. Turning to religion as a means of curbing desire and dealing with disappointment was a traditional and widespread psychological resource, of course, and we would expect a culture heavily populated with clergymen to take it to heart. Conduct-book writers had already incorporated it as part of their domestic ideology. Hester Chapone's *Letters on the Improvement of the Mind,* for example, urged its readers not to "persist in desiring what his Providence denies you: but be assured it is not good for you. Refuse not any thing he allots you, but embrace it as the best and properest for you."[62]

Men and women turned to this religious advice, particularly as a means of dealing with illness and death. Stationed in the Mediterranean in April 1815, the recently widowed, grief-stricken Charles Austen was further upset by a letter from his sister-in-law, describing the ill health of his "precious little girls Fanny & Harriet." Writing in his journal, he sought to calm himself: "I must bear whatever it pleases God to inflict on me."[63] And in 1816 Edward Knatchbull reinforced his own resignation by telling his diary, "I have just enter'd on the third Year of My Widowhood—sensibly as I feel the Distress under which I suffer, I bow with Submission to the Will of Providence—I hope My Sorrows have never led me to complain."[64]

Marriages too provided opportunities to advocate such resignation. Cassandra Austen, writing in 1811 to congratulate Philadelphia Walter on her marriage to George Whitaker, offered her the following admonition: "Tho' there may be some things you would wish otherwise, for where is the situation on earth exempt from evils? you are too wise and too good to dwell on the wrong side of the Picture. Use will reconcile you to some things which appear evils at first and others you will bear as the necessary attendants of humanity."[65] Mrs. George Austen even made a poem out of similar counsel, which she sent to her grand-daughter Anna in 1814 on the occasion of her marriage to Benjamin Lefroy:

> I wish you happiness and health
> I wish you an increase of Wealth
> (I'd make you richer if I could)
> I wish you every kind of good
> But ills attend us from our birth
> And will while we remain on earth.
> You must not look for perfect bliss
> That's for a better life than this[66]

Women also counseled and consoled themselves in their Anglican faith when they had to suppress their own desires and accept or obey the wishes of their male kin. When not advising others, they revealed in religious language their struggles to achieve self-suppression. Their letters testify to the conservative uses of religion, as it helped women to accept the subordinations of their identity and role. A woman, for example, would voice a desire in a letter and then refer to the necessity of submitting to God—suggesting that she could not entirely reconcile herself to submission to any earthly authority. Jane Austen, critical of the will of her uncle, James Leigh Perrot, silenced herself with: "But I am getting too near complaint. It has been the appointment of God, however secondary causes may have operated."[67] Anne Lushington found it even more difficult in 1799 to accept her husband's decision to leave her at home while he made a journey. She attempted to rein-force her submission with piety. So strong was her desire to accompany her husband, however, that after acknowledging the "lesson" she be-lieved Providence was offering her, she seemed, in noting that it was unnecessary, almost ready to challenge Providence. "To this disap-pointment," she wrote to her father, "it would be foolish not to submit with resignation. . . . Perhaps my dear Father these trials are meant to remind us more forcibly of the causes we have for gratitude in the numerous blessings we enjoy and I hope the lesson will imprint it on my heart tho' that seems scarcely to have required it as I can truly say it overflows with gratitude towards all."[68]

Sometimes women resorted to literary expressions of pious resigna-tion for help in dealing with their desires. In a letter to her sister in

1813 Jane Austen echoed "An Essay on Man": "If *you* do not regret the loss of Oxfordshire and Gloucestershire *I* will not, though I certainly had wished for your going very much. 'Whatever is, is best.' There has been one infallible Pope in the world."[69] Mary Bramston adopted "whatever is is right" as her motto, and she resorted to it when she wanted to assuage her own disappointments, calm her anxieties, and, in general, accept conditions over which she had no control. One was the collapse of her plan to join Henrietta Hicks Beach in Bath in the winter of 1790. Because of the parliamentary election, "we cant meet," she told Henrietta, "at the appointed time for Mr B cant settle any of his affairs till after this meeting." She asked her cousin to delay her arrival as well, and then she also began to prepare for the frustration of her hopes: "I shall be quite disappointed if we do not meet I shall only be able to reconcile it by referring to my consolation on all occasions 'whatever is is right.'"[70]

Whether she used Pope's words or not, Mary worked—frequently—at taming desire with devotion. When her brother William Chute announced his engagement to Elizabeth Smith, we see that effort especially clearly. He presented as a fait accompli his attachment to a woman whom Mary had never met. Because she had long hoped her brother would marry, she rejoiced. But she also worried. As she told Henrietta Hicks Beach: "I am quite restless to see the Lady & indeed very anxious about things tis a serious time & employs all my thoughts." Unable, as she had no doubt wanted, to play a more active role in shaping her brother's future, unable at the moment even to meet the wife her brother had already selected, she sought to quiet herself: "Providence appoints all things better for us than we can ourselves so in all difficulties that ends my reasonings."[71] And presumably her discontent.

Women did not always find it easy to mold their actions or words to conform to their culture's ideal of womanhood. Indeed, although they did rein in their behavior fairly tightly, they did not always speak the language of domestic femininity. Certain limited circumstances freed them from their patriarchal culture's definitions of the female, if only temporarily. These special conditions and the voice they produced are the subjects of the next chapter.

CHAPTER 3

The Women's Culture

1

WHILE traveling in September of 1820, Sir Edward Knatchbull made a brief stop to see Chawton, the Hampshire estate of his fiancée's father, and to meet some of her relatives visiting or living there. In addition to meeting two of Fanny Knight's brothers, in Hampshire to do some shooting, Sir Edward made the acquaintance of some of the inmates of a cottage on the estate: Fanny's Aunt Cassandra; Martha Lloyd, who had been living with the Austens since 1805; and Anne Sharp, a visitor at the cottage.[1] He offered a very favorable impression of Cassandra Austen in a letter he wrote to Fanny while he was still at Chawton Great House, but in a subsequent letter he was distinctly less enthusiastic about the women at the cottage:

> Miss Lloyd I had never before seen—she is not handsome, & we parted as good Friends as we met, without either of us having made a great Impression on the other—Miss Sharp I almost liked very much because I was told she had been your Governess—& I must like any body or any thing that has been instrumental in making you what you are—"Aunt Cassandra" I must love because you do, & because she seems so very deeply interested in your Welfare—[2]

Sir Edward's language—"almost liked," "must like," "must love"—reveals that he had trouble warming to these women. They were older than the thirty-nine-year-old baronet, a great deal poorer, and not, to his eyes, attractive or captivating. But the real reason for his diffidence emerges in the description of his conversation with Cassandra:

We said but little to each other, tho' I felt I could have said more but I dont like to talk about you to anybody—They talk to me, & say Fanny does this, & Fanny does that—and then I reply yes I believe Miss Knight does, and this seems as if they, whom[ever] they may be, are so much more intimate with you than I am.[3]

Sir Edward's shift into present tense reveals his jealousy. Although he claimed that the women's fond and knowing talk made it only seem "as if" they were more familiar with Fanny than he was, the evidence of female intimacy was still imaginatively present to him, dogging him, after he had left Chawton.

The women *were* more intimate with his fiancée. Sir Edward and Fanny had only begun to know one another during his summertime courtship. Although Fanny, happily, found that she could love her fiancé soon after she accepted his late August marriage proposal, the couple's growing affection and familiarity, advanced primarily by means of their copious correspondence in September, could not yet surpass the strength of the tie between aunt and niece.[4] Jane Austen's close relationship with Fanny is better known because some of the novelist's affectionate letters to her niece from 1814 and 1817 have survived, but Cassandra's intimacy with Fanny in fact predated Jane's. In Fanny's youth and adolescence Cassandra had been the more frequent visitor to Godmersham, was (according to Anna Austen Lefroy's "Reminiscences") more welcome there to Fanny's mother, and was the more regular long-term correspondent with her niece.[5]

Edward Knatchbull's jealousy of his fiancée's bonds with the women at Chawton was unusual, the insecurity of a man not yet "in possession" of his bride. Generally, the men of Jane Austen's community encouraged the friendships of their wives with other women, and even Knatchbull conquered his feelings enough to invite Cassandra to visit him and Fanny at his estate, Mersham Hatch.[6] In their promotion of female friendships, gentlemen concurred with the prevailing wisdom of conduct books, which viewed such relationships through the lens of domestic ideology. Because the ideology made the female into a specialist in sensibility, she was supposed to have a particular propensity and need for friendship. As *A Father's Legacy to His Daughters* asserted, "the temper and disposition of the heart in your sex make you enter more readily and warmly into friendships than men."[7]

Conduct books viewed these friendships as a species of domestic relationship, for marriage was itself often perceived as the "highest kind of friendship."[8] Female friendship properly belonged to the private not the public arena, offering women diversion in the quiet of their homes, particularly when their male kinfolk were out in the public realm. In *Strictures on the Modern System of Female Education*, for example, Hannah More positioned "the interests of true friendship" along with "maternal duty, and conjugal comfort" in opposition to the dissipations of fashionable life.[9] Moreover, female friendships at their best did not compete with a woman's familial ties and duties but served to support them, just as they served to support the domestic feminine identity. The desirable friendship was moral and pedagogical: true friends, so conduct books declared, helped one another to live up to domestic ideology's vision of womanhood. "Reproof and advice are the most sacred and the most frequent duties of friendship," claims West's *Letters to a Young Lady*.[10] Lady Pennington's *A Mother's Advice to Her Absent Daughters* concurs: a friend should be "steady in the correction, but mild in the reproof of your faults—like a guardian angel ever watchful to warn you of unforeseen danger, and, by timely admonitions, to prevent the mistakes incident to human frailty and to self-partiality."[11] Hence, conduct books particularly recommended friendships between mothers or mother substitutes and younger women, and it is in the light of this recommendation that we can best understand the relationship of Sarah Smith and Elizabeth Chute and their correspondence just after Elizabeth married in 1793.[12]

In practice, however, female friendships among women were not always like the ideal relationships sketched out in conduct books. Although sometimes they functioned in the service of genteel domesticity, at other times they enabled women to distance themselves from domestic ideology and to view their duties quite differently. At such moments women expressed common values and perceptions decidedly unlike those encompassed by the domestic ideology. These alternative values and perceptions constituted another, distinct culture specific to women.

The ideology of genteel domesticity was part of the gentry's dominant, patriarchal, and heterosexual culture. Its hegemony, however, did not prevent the formation of an "alternative" culture within it.[13] Nor did the dominant culture inhibit women from forming allegiances to two cultures simultaneously and sustaining two separate and somewhat contradictory sets of values and perceptions.[14] Although women endorsed the values of the gentry's culture, including the necessity of their subordination, they also embraced opportunities to reperceive experiences imposed on them and to find worth in what was considered necessary but trivial. These efforts, it is important to note, differentiate their women's culture from "women's sphere." The latter names the position of subordination demarcated and enforced by the gentry's dominant, patriarchal culture. It is the realm of the compliant woman. The former, as historian Gerda Lerner has suggested, "is women's redefinition in their own terms."[15]

In exploring the women's culture of Austen's social group, we need to keep in mind that the relationship between the culture and its makers was interactive. Although women generated their culture in reaction to the prevailing patriarchy, like that dominant culture it acquired a life of its own. Women created their private culture on a day-to-day basis *and* were influenced by it. Banding together, they produced the women's culture and it, in a manner of speaking, produced their friendships.

We should also keep in mind that the women's culture did not express women's "natural" identity any more than did domestic femininity. Women's egalitarian relationships made acceptable their expressions of self-concern, autonomy, and dissent. Like self-effacement, dependence, and compliance, these were socially generated and approved responses. We can only speculate about the "social texts" that influenced the content of the women's culture, but the domestic ideology itself may, parodoxically, have been a central one.

Finally, it is important to remember the flexibility and variability of both female friendship and female identity. Not all women articulated the women's culture in their affiliations. Some friends, who happened not to be emotionally intimate or who were just unusually devout adherents to the ideology of domesticity, sustained associations expressive of nothing but the gentry's culture. None conveyed in their relationships *only* the women's culture. Rather, women participated in friendships that moved back and forth between the poles of differing values, now reinforcing and now protesting the domestic ideology. These friendships prompted women to view and represent themselves and one another sometimes as domestic, submissive women and sometimes as women opposed to this female identity. Although this chapter offers evidence of dissenting voices to add to the last chapter's evidence of compliance, we must remember that, among themselves, women often heard and said both "yes" and "no."

2
___

Up to a point the women's culture recapitulated aspects of female friendship and of relationships in general as they were portrayed by the ideology of genteel domesticity. The bonds of the women's culture followed the lines of association marked out by the ideology. The family was the key unit of relationship in it; not surprisingly, conduct-book writers often advised readers to make female friends if not of their mothers then of their other kin. Thus Dr. Gregory advised his daughters, "If all other circumstances are equal, there are obvious advantages in your making friends of one another. The ties of blood, and your being so much united in one common interest, form an additional bond of union to your friendship.[16]

In actuality, friends in Austen's community, formed by and forming the women's culture, often were sisters, mothers and daughters, aunts and nieces, and cousins. When they were not in fact relatives, kinship often served as a metaphor for their relationships. Many women signaled their affection by asserting family connections with women to whom they were not related or not as related as their forms of address suggested. In 1796, for example, Jane Austen's mother wrote a letter to Mary Lloyd, welcoming her into the family, in which she asked Mary to tell her sister Martha, of whom she was equally fond, that "she too shall be my Daughter."[17] Similarly, just after Mary Bramston's sister married Henrietta Hicks Beach's brother-in-law, she wrote to Henrietta: "My dear Sister I sit down to write you a few lines that I may have the pleasure of calling you by that title.[18] And in 1793 Elizabeth Chute received a letter from her intimate friend Elizabeth Gosling, addressing her as "my dear adopted Sister."[19]

Social status, also crucial in the domestic ideology, influenced the patterns of association among those who participated in the women's culture. Conduct books were unanimous in their insistence that, in general, social inferiors made poor female friends.[20] "Above all things," one conduct-book writer typically cautioned, "avoid intimacy with those of low birth and education."[21] For all female friends, and not just those shaped by and shaping the women's culture, intimacies had little durability when the participants had differences in status. We have almost no evidence of close, long-lasting ties between a gentlewoman and a woman beneath her in rank. The few exceptions that we know of usually occurred between elite women and very loyal, long-serving upper servants, such as the bond between Fanny Knight and Suzannah Sackree, the family's nursemaid, about whom Fanny once remarked, "We all look upon her as a mother."[22] The widest difference in status that such friendships could tolerate was generally that between a governess, often recruited from the lesser gentry, and the wife or daughters in the prosperous family that employed her. Still, these bonds often lost their intimacy over time. Fanny began writing to Dorothy Chapman after the governess left their family's employ. A comparison of her letters with the pocket diaries Fanny kept and with letters written to her by her aunt, Jane Austen, reveal that as the young girl reached adulthood her relationship with Dorothy Chapman became increasingly distant and conventional. As Fanny grew into her family's status identity, the status difference as well as the absence of kinship began to come between girl and governess.

Fanny's relationship with another of her governesses, Mrs. Morris, helps to show why such intimate bonds could not be sustained: differing status tended to inhibit empathy. Mrs. Morris was Fanny's governess for the years 1806–8. During that time, they became quite fond of one another, and Fanny developed friendships with Mrs. Morris's daughters, Julia and Sophia, as well. In 1808 Mrs. Morris was asked to accompany Sir James Gambier's family to America. Since salaries were higher for governesses who attended families going abroad and consequently Mrs. Morris would be better able to provide for her children, she accepted the offer. In relating this news to Dorothy Chapman, Fanny chose to overlook the unpleasantness and the risks of sea travel as well as the emotional stress that the separation caused mother and children. She also ignored the role that her family must have played in Mrs. Morris's decision. It was *their* salary that Mrs. Morris was seeking to better by taking the dramatic step of leaving England and her family.[23]

The ideology of genteel domesticity influenced a woman's selection of her close friends, those with whom she might generate the women's culture; it also helped to shape the affective content of the affiliations. Among adolescent and young adult women, particularly those who had not yet married, intimate friendships were romantic. Women professed their love for one another and exchanged portraits, hair rings, or other tokens of their fondness. They kept an affectionate record in their diaries of occasions when they had enjoyed each other's company, had slept together in the same bed, or had gone to dinners and dances together. The language that they used to describe their relationships, either as adolescents or later in their lives, gives no evidence, however, that they viewed them erotically.[24] Eliza de Feuillide expressed her feelings for her cousin Philadelphia Walter in more heated diction than that used by many women, and her language was hardly passionate. "Be assured my dear cousin," she wrote to Philadelphia in 1782, "you can have no friend more sincerely attached to you than myself & neither time nor absence can affect the regard I have ever felt for you."[25]

More frequently, women aspired in their friendships to a physical and emotional coziness. "I hope nothing will happen to prevent our being very comfortable & happy there," wrote Mary Bramston to Henrietta Hicks Beach about their prospective meeting in Bath."[26] "Aunt Cassandra comes down," wrote Fanny to Dorothy Chapman, "on Monday next, which will be very comfortable, as she had not been staying here by herself for some time."[27] And Anne Powlett, anticipating a visit from her friend Padgy Peters, told her, "we shall I hope pass many tranquil and comfortable days together in this House."[28]

Whether they were seeking romance or comfort, women were drawing on the ideology of domesticity to define the emotional content of their female friendships. For the gentry, it should be recalled, generally sought "comfort" in the domesticity of family life. James Austen, we saw earlier, hoped that his brother Frank would find in his fiancée someone who could "best make your Home comfortable to you." Women looked forward to being comfortable with their friends because they were so often at a distance from one another—there was pleasure simply in physical proximity—and because they could not feel completely at ease when they encountered one another in the social round as representatives of their families. But this particular application of domestic ideology may also indicate that some did not find family life comfortable enough.

With its depiction of frankness as a desirable ingredient of friendship, the ideology of domesticity further influenced the content of women's relationships, including those that generated and were generated by the women's culture. "If you have the good fortune to meet with any one who deserve the name of friends," suggested Dr. Gregory, "unbosom yourself to them with the most unsuspicious confidence."[29] Lady Pennington similarly told her daughters that to true friends, "let your heart be ever unreservedly open;—conceal no secret thought— disguise no latent weakness."[30] And participants in the women's culture did seek and value such openness. They had, as Jane Austen once said about one of Cassandra's visits with Mrs. Knight, "a great deal of unreserved discourse."[31] Mary Bramston was particularly articulate about this aspect of her relationship with Henrietta Hicks Beach: "To you I am always sincere how few are there in this world to whom I can say this, but the comfort of a friend is to speak ones unreserved Sentiments & I really have vanity enough to believe that your regard for me is so sincere that I may venture always to do so."[32] The wish for candor, like the desire to feel comfortable, indirectly reveals the formality so often governing women's relationships when they were fulfilling the duties of visiting and corresponding, prescribed by the ideology of domesticity.

It also points to the constraints women felt when they spoke and wrote as feminine women to their male kin, and conduct books did not take notice of this important contrast. As Charles Powlett admitted sympathetically to his wife-to-be in 1791: "You have every disadvantage on your Side (but Capacity) in a Correspondence with Me." He described one of the most crucial as "the general disadvantage of your Sex, that you cannot express that freedom of Sentiment that we may."[33] Though sympathetic, he was apparently unwilling to alter the socially constructed relations and images of male and female by encouraging Anne Temple to communicate as his equal before or after they married. She occasionally expressed sentiments that disagreed with his, but she never did so without apologizing or framing those feelings deferentially. When she wrote to her husband in 1801, for example, giving him her views on how to manage her troublesome younger brother Octavius, she followed immediately with: "Excuse, my love, my thus seemingly dictating to you. I know in every thing that relates to my Family you wish me to give my opinion."[34]

The affectionate bonds of the women's culture provided a respite from such prohibitions on expression, freeing women to say about themselves what they might ordinarily suppress. Again, it is Mary Bramston who voiced this function: "It is the privilege of Friendship to share our Cares & I know you will forgive me for having filled two sides of my paper with self, but imparting our cares lessens them it relieves the mind from a weight & to you I am not afraid of imparting all my thoughts."[35] Anne Powlett, writing in 1798 as the recipient of such candor from Padgy Peters, concurred: "My dear Friend why should you throw away your pen because you had nothing to write more interesting than of yourself—do you suppose any subject can be more interesting, particularly when your Mind is affected and uneasy: the prerogative of Friendship is to soothe and console, and I shall not be easily induced to renounce a right which you have allowed for these thirteen years."[36]

Frankness necessitated discretion, a point conduct-book writers made repeatedly. Women were instructed to find friends to whom they could talk and whom they could trust. As Hester Chapone remarked, "You do not want to be told, that the strictest fidelity is required in friendship: and, though possibly instances might be brought, in which even the secret of a friend must be sacrificed to the calls of justice and duty, yet these are rare and doubtful cases."[37] Women took the requirement of discretion quite seriously, and those who were not part of the women's culture became aware of it when they came up against the walls of discretion and sensed their exclusion. Late in her life Marianne Knight recalled that her sister Fanny "being so many years older than the rest of us, was a friend and companion of the two aunts, Cassandra and Jane, particularly of the latter, and they had all sorts of secrets together, whilst we were only children.''[38]

Women often forged the bonds of their culture in the disclosure or guarding of secrets. One, which Philadelphia Walter confided to Eliza de Feuillide, prompted the following response: "I am infinitely obliged to You for the mark of friendship You have given me & . . . I feel the value of the confidence You repose in me.—if possible it has made You dearer than ever to your Eliza.''[39] And in the congratulatory letter Mrs. Austen sent to Mary Lloyd in 1796, she expressed her affection for her sister Martha as well, not only by declaring that "she too shall be my Daughter" but also by revealing that she knew one of Martha's secrets—her affection for a Mr. W. She saw no reason to keep the secret of her knowledge *from* Martha, "as we are now all of one family"; she promised to "keep [Martha's] secret as close as if I had been entrusted with it"; and she assured Martha that neither Mary nor her own daughters had taken advantage of the candor of their friendship by being indiscreet. Rather, she had found out the secret, as she explained, "by my own Sprack wit.''[40]

The exclusive discourse of the women's culture appears clearly in letters. Of course, letter-writing was the sole means of communication with persons at a distance, and letter-receiving constituted a major source of information and entertainment; the writing and receiving of letters were very notable activities within the family, hard to keep utterly private. How could women manage to use their confidential discourse in compositions that were often corporate family productions?

There were times when women wrote without the accompanying instructions of their male relatives and with the assurance that their letters would not be seen by anyone but the letter's addressee, but these occasions were rare. Entries in Fanny Knight's diary for 1814 suggest that she and her correspondents had methods for preserving the exclusiveness of their communications. "I wrote a long private to F. Cage, & to Anna," Fanny recorded in January. And on June 13: "Wrote to Anna by a private hand.''[41] Possibly, Fanny had found a way to send and receive letters in secrecy, but she does not elaborate on her techniques of transmission. More often, women spoke both the discourse of their wider culture's domestic ideology and that of their women's culture and often in a single letter, switching their cultural allegiances sometimes line by line. They did so using strategies followed by both writer and reader that enabled them to keep their women's culture to themselves.

The women routinely shared the letters they received, but sometimes they only showed or read parts. "I had but just time to enjoy your letter yesterday," Austen wrote to her sister from Godmersham in 1813, "before Edward & I set off in the Chair for Canty & I allowed him to hear the *chief of it* as we went along" [emphasis mine].[42] In response to a highly personal letter from her niece in 1814 who had been analyzing her feelings for a suitor, Austen told her, "I shall be most glad to hear from you again my dearest Fanny . . . and write *something* that may do to be read or told."[43] Mary Bramston and Henrietta Hicks Beach tried to be extremely clear about what would happen to any sensitive material they elicited from one another. Wishing to know more about her brother's choice of a bride than he was apparently able or willing to tell her, Mary Bramston went around him, asking Henrietta to satisfy her restless curiosity. In soliciting further impressions of Elizabeth Smith, Mary wrote, "It will be only seen by me, so pray be very particular & precise."[44] Any unflattering remarks about his fiancée would, of course, have constituted criticism of William Chute's taste and wishes.

Letter-writers often helped the recipients to determine what to make public and what to censure. "Between you and me," Mary Bramston began, when she was about to tell Henrietta Hicks Beach something not suitable for other members of the latter's household or community to hear.[45] And because they sometimes feared that the sentiments they expressed might not be completely secure, they not infrequently urged their addressees to destroy the letters entirely before they were seen by others. "Pray do not neglect burning this," Eliza de Feuillide wrote on the outside of one to Philadelphia Walter in 1792.[46] Philadelphia did not obey her friend's wishes on that occasion, but many friends did. As a result, correspondence containing the private discourse of women is hard to find or, as in the case of Jane Austen's letters to Cassandra, hard to find whole. Indeed, gaps and silences have become one of the key traits of the discourse of the women's culture as it has come down to us in women's letters.

3

Although candor and discretion were central to conduct-book discussions of female friendships, few eighteenth- or early nineteenth-century moralists gave much thought to the nature or political implications of the private matters that women might share with one another. They recommended selecting friends capable of discretion because they supposed that a woman whose confidences were revealed would be embarrassed or disgraced by the exposure. But that perspective is smugly one-sided: it does not consider the communications from the woman's point of view, does not suppose that such communications might give voice to sentiments and opinions counter to the domestic ideology.

One of the few handbooks to see female friendship in a different light, Hester Chapone's *Letters on the Improvement of the Mind,* imagines the development of an "odious cabal" generating rebellion but only when adolescent girls of the same age formed a friendship. "If they have no lover, or amour to talk of," Chapone maintained, they look for other matters, "betraying the secrets of their families; or conjuring up fancied hardships to complain of against their parents or relations"—and all for the pleasures of confiding in one another. But such rebellious practices, according to Chapone, belong to silly youth and "those early friendships drop off, as the parties advance in years and understanding."[47] In actuality, were all exchanges about hardships "fancied" and all tellers of such tales adolescents? It is in this matter of confidences that the women's culture, as it is represented in the private letters of Austen's female kin, friends, and neighbors, parts company from the "domesticated" versions of female friendship promoted in contemporary conduct-book literature.

What interests did women's frankness in such letters reveal? What was it that they attempted to keep from their male kin and most of their acquaintances? Lovers and suitors, certainly (a topic whose import we will return to below). More fundamentally, they expressed allegiance to one another and their alienation from men. Although kinship and, even more, status set restrictions on participants in the women's culture, in the expressive content of the culture, gender superseded kinship and status as the primary bond of identification. Female friends created emblems of the same-sex bond in assertions of likeness. As Mary Bramston noted affectionately to Henrietta Hicks Beach in 1793, "I often have the pleasure of finding our Opinions coincide."[48] Much similarity was consciously cultivated. "I love to imitate you," Mary told Henrietta in another letter,[49] and she lived up to her words, adopting her friend's plan for a Sunday school and even dressing like her.[50] Other female friends also enjoyed dressing alike. Anna Austen Lefroy remembered that her aunts Jane and Cassandra, for example, had identical bonnets.[51] Because they were affirmations of mutual affection, many women noted look-alike dressing in their memoirs and diaries. When some of Caroline Pym Hales's family went to Ranelagh in 1791, she and her older sister Jane, as she told her diary, "were dressed exactly the same."[52]

Women's assertions of same-sex ties in these declarations and demonstrations of similarity were not in themselves subversive, but they were often joined with women's sense of their distance from men. Eliza de Feuillide once claimed to Philadelphia: "I don't think either you or I very likely to lose either our gaiety or peace of mind for any male *creature breathing*."[53] Voicing the women's culture, friends were sensitive not only to the distance between themselves and men but also to socially determined differences between men's and women's tastes and experiences. In 1798 Jane Austen expressed the gulf she perceived between her father's concerns and her own: "My father and I dined by ourselves. How strange! He and John Bond [her father's bailiff] are now very happy together, for I have just heard the heavy step of the latter along the passage."[54] While conduct books were urging wives in particular to make their husbands' interests their own ("Endeavor to enter into his pursuits, catch his taste, improve by his knowledge," says one, "nor let any thing that is interesting to him appear a matter of indifference to you"), Elizabeth Chute was carefully distinguishing her pleasures from those of her husband and brother-in-law in a letter to her friend Elizabeth Gosling: "We are at present alone, my two gentlemen & myself: they amuse themselves with hunting twice a week: my amusements are very sedentary as they generally are."[55]

When Austen saw and spoke as a subscriber to domestic femininity, when she assumed the pronoun "we," she could be quite interested in and specific about her father's management of his farm. She spoke as a participant in the women's culture when she was insistently vague and ignorant about the exact same arena of experience:

> John Bond begins to find himself grow old, which John Bonds ought not to do, and unequal to much hard work; a man is therefore hired to supply his place as to labour, and John himself is to have the care of the sheep. There are not more people engaged than before, I believe; only men instead of boys. I fancy so at least, but you know my stupidity as to such matters.[56]

In asserting her "stupidity" on this particular subject, Austen was putting back into her discourse a self separate from the concerns of her male relatives. By acknowledging and embracing socially constructed differences between the sexes, women could reclaim in their discourse self-identities lost when they identified with their male kin.

In a letter she wrote to Philadelphia Walter in 1798, Eliza de Feuillide playfully tested the gender of the first-person-plural pronoun. Eliza had recently married militia officer Henry Austen and was with him in Ipswich. She drew attention to her separate and different identity by refusing to identify vicariously with the interests of men. Indeed, she showed that it would be ludicrous to take the "we" literally. The French were believed to be readying for invasion and, according to Eliza, "Government appears convinced of it, for *we* have received orders to add one hundred & fifty men to *our* regiment, and hold *ourselves* in readiness to march at the shortest notice so that I am going to be *drilled* & to bespeak my regimentals without further delay."[57]

In their private discourse, women distanced and distinguished themselves from men and represented those separate selves; they also gave priority to their concerns and activities over those of their menfolk. Their women's culture inverted the value structure of the domestic ideology, often rendering the greater importance of women's private over men's public experiences through point of view. That is not to say that genteel women were generally oblivious to public events. They often wrote to one another about current social and political problems. In 1800 Elizabeth Chute, for example, examined in a letter to her friend Elizabeth Gosling the causes of social unrest:

> All has been quiet about us with regard to the markets; but the poor are dissatisfied & with reason: I much fear that wheat will not be cheap this year: & every other necessary of life enormously dear: the poor man cannot purchase those comforts he ought to have: beer, bacon, cheese. Can one wonder that discontent lurks in their bosoms: I cannot thi[nk] their wages sufficient.[58]

Mary Bramston remarked several times in letters to Henrietta Hicks Beach on the progress of the war with France, frequently worrying about the possibility of a French invasion: "Do not you tremble a little when they are got so far on their road to London, & they will entirely recruit in Holland."[59] Nevertheless, women created the discourse of their private culture at times by pushing riots or war to a peripheral position and placing family life, household cares, and their friendships in the foreground.

Fanny Knight, when addressing Dorothy Chapman in 1819, for example, represented government efforts to suppress working-class radicalism as significant only in that they prevented her brother Henry from rejoining the family circle. Writing a few months after Peterloo, Fanny lamented that Henry "was obliged to join his regiment, which is now at Nottingham so that we have not seen him since March & I am afraid in the present disturbed state of the Country we are not likely to have him with us for some time. We have however the comfort of hearing that he is quite well."[60] Similarly, in a letter to Padgy Peters in 1803, Anne Powlett found war merely instrumental in the quest for marital happiness. "The *Finale* I believe is still at a distance," she said about her brother Frank Temple's hoped-for marriage to Mary Terry. "Bonaparte must be conquered and a few of his ships brought into our Ports. I am sure neither Frank nor Mary is adapted to live upon a little."[61]

Although she was a concerned and sometimes anxious observer of French-English hostilities during the American Revolution, Eliza de Feuillide could also perceive war as an annoying hindrance to the development of female friendship. "Your request for the picture flatters me exceedingly," she wrote from Paris to Philadelphia Walter in 1782, "as it proves the share I have in your affection; I comply with it with pleasure, & will sit for the picture as soon as possible, but I fear I shall not be able to send it you very soon as I must wait for a safe conveyance which in this time of war is not easy to be met with."[62]

The preference for what were generally understood to be women's over men's experiences is conveyed more explicitly by Eliza in a letter to Philadelphia describing a visit to Oxford University. "We visited several of the colleges, the museum etc," she wrote, "& were very elegantly entertained by our gallant relations at St. John's, where I was mightily taken with the garden & longed to be a *Fellow* that I might walk in it every day, besides I was delighted with the black gown & thought the square cap mighty becoming."[63] Her envy of her male cousins' university life (even of their sex, as the pun on "fellow" suggests) is belied by her focus not on learning but on garden walks and student costume. Indeed, her attention to fashion superimposes what was understood by her contemporaries as a feminine concern on a male arena, thus effacing the male.

As Eliza's report of Oxford University life shows, the more talented and self-conscious writers often used irony to invest women's experience with more significance than men's. The most sophisticated and playful letter-writer among the women of her community, Jane Austen achieved some of her wittiest effects with it. She began a letter to Cassandra in 1798, for example, by announcing that their brother Frank was to be promoted soon, and she followed that news with: "There! I may now finish my letter and go and hang myself, for I am sure I can neither write nor do anything which will not appear insipid to you after this."[64] She implies with her self-belittling claims that her sister will, in fact, find her experiences compelling. And she follows Frank's news with detailed accounts of, among other things, her visit to Manydown, the ball she has recently attended, the new gown she plans to make up, her charities, her plans to dine out, and the company invited to Steventon.[65]

Such attentions to the experiences of women reveal that when generating their own distinct culture, women did not view their domesticity or any of their life circumstances in the same way that the larger patriarchal culture did, that is, as uneventful. The same women who could describe their experiences as "little concerns" or "important nothings" also valued the experiences of daily, domestic life. As Jane Austen told Cassandra, "You know how interesting the purchase of a sponge cake is to me."[66] The discourse of the women's culture thus often focused enthusiastically on "particulars," the details of everyday life. "I will first talk of my visit to Canterbury, as Mrs. J.A.'s letter to Anna cannot have given you every particular of it, which you are likely to wish for," Jane Austen wrote to Cassandra in 1808.[67] The details of their home life always figured prominently in Austen's mental life when she was away on visits. "I hope Martha had a pleasant visit again," she wrote home in 1814, "and that you and my mother could eat your beef-pudding. Depend upon my thinking of the Chimney-Sweeper as soon as I wake tomorrow."[68]

Because contributors to the women's culture viewed their domestic experiences as important, they could take pride in them. In relationship with other women, they developed a sense of achievement to which their social subordination, as it was conceived in the ideology of domesticity, did not readily give them access. Conduct literature, for example, treated women's sewing as a necessary household skill which, when put in the service of decoration and fashion, gave vent to women's vanity. In the context of her relationship with Henrietta Hicks Beach, however, Mary Bramston expressed quite a different attitude. In a letter of 1788, she informed her correspondent that "I have worked an Apron in that pattern we had of Mrs Greens." The work, for Mary Bramston, was a demonstration of not only skill but creativity, as she altered the pattern for greater aesthetic effect. The result delighted her—"You cannot think how well it looks"—and she was not embarrassed to say so, particularly since Henrietta was also planning to sew an apron. "I hope you have not begun yours in any other pattern," she added. She took similar pride in drawing, when she could link her productions with those of her friend. In the same letter she told Henrietta, "I am very glad the Drawings that Mr Green shewd you at Cheltenham has afforded you so much amusement I shall expect to see them very well copied & in process of time I think we shall set up a little Exhibition of our own."[69]

Women also took pride in their management of associations between their own and other families. From the vantage point of their women's culture, they could appreciate the value of this domestic responsibility. In 1793 the link that Mary Bramston and Henrietta Hicks Beach were helping to maintain between their families resulted in a proposal of marriage from Henrietta's brother-in-law, William Hicks, to Mary Bramston's sister Ann Rachel Chute. The two women also helped to engineer the proposal. Henrietta first made her brother-in-law's intentions known; he had asked her to find out through Mary Bramston whether his proposal was likely to be accepted. The two women then determined how the proposal should be communicated (through the mail, they decided, no doubt in part because the suitor stuttered). Then they arranged to bring the prospective bridegroom into Hampshire so that he and the bride might at least get to know one another before the wedding. In one of her letters Mary Bramston expressed her sense of the difficulty and importance of their negotiations. "I wonder there are any Weddings," she told her friend, "for there are so many ettiquettes that it requires as much deliberation as settling the affairs of a Nation."[70] And she was pleased with the roles they were playing: "I cant help smiling at the parts we take in such a great affair, not but that I have vanity to think *we* could manage such an affair very well."[71]

When women spoke the discourse of their exclusively same-sex culture, they presented and preferred their own desires as well as their own activities. In a world in which women generally had to suppress or radically qualify and reframe their desires, a focus on them also inverted the value structure of the domestic ideology. For example, they often expressed wishes for particular suitors or husbands, but what merited secrecy was not simply the identity of the suitors— Martha Lloyd's Mr. W., for example—or the fact of desiring, but their close friends' willingness to validate and encourage those wishes.

Although the edited versions of Eliza de Feuillide's letters to Philadelphia Walter, published in *The Austen Papers*, give the impression that Eliza was primarily interested in herself, the holograph letters indicate that she warmly supported both Philadelphia's brief infatuations ("Pray let me have a full & particular account of all your *Flirtations*," she wrote in 1788) and her long-term romances.[72] For at least four years and possibly more, Philadelphia was in love with one "DBB" in the navy. In her letters during the period 1789–92, Eliza was a strong champion of Philadelphia's hopes, even when Philadelphia herself began to doubt. "Why should You, so chearful on all other oc[casions]," she affectionately wrote in 1791, "seem to see this subject in a gloomy light and declare that 'Happ[iness] never will be your lot,' I hope and trust many Years of Felicity ar[e in] store for You, and that I shall ere a considerable period is elapsed hear You are completely settled in the way most agreeable to your wishes."[73] (Eliza could support Philadelphia's hopes only with her own. DBB withdrew his attentions sometime after 1792.)

Women coaxed one another to voice other kinds of desires, of course, as well. When Philadelphia refused to act in the theatricals performed by the Austen family in the late 1780s (the conduct in which many literary critics have seen the prototype for Fanny Price's refusal to act in *Mansfield Park*), Eliza tried to find out if she was actually deferring to her mother's wishes but, if left to herself, would have agreed: "Shall I be candid & tell you the Thought which has struck me on this occasion?—The insuperable objection to my proposal is, some scruples of your Mother's about your acting." Fearing that she had been too disrespectful, she did not attempt to prevent Philadelphia from knowing her sentiments but added this familiar postscript: "I beg as a particular favor that You will not communicate that part of my Letter which contains *my surmise* concerning your Mother's objections to her or any part of Your Family."[74]

The women's culture criticized the ideology of domesticity by reversing its value structure, by putting women and their experiences and desires first. Nevertheless, such criticism did not challenge the gentry's patriarchal culture. Rather, it enabled accommodation. Because the women's culture viewed domesticity as valuable, it helped women to accept and endure their subordination. Moreover, the criticism was implicit. Women, in association, gained a sense of their own importance and pride in their accomplishments, but they did so without directly addressing sexual inequality. So far, then, we must say that the women's culture and the gentry's wider, patriarchal culture were compatible despite the dramatic differences in the values and perceptions they generated.

There were times, however, when the criticism of domestic ideology generated by this women's culture was explicit. Women sometimes did not just invert values; they objected to the specific roles and responsibilities assigned them by the ideology. They protested the central domestic occupation of mothering, for example. Eliza de Feuillide avowed her dislike of it in a letter of 1786, in which she announced to Philadelphia Walter her pregnancy and her plans to leave France: "On my arrival in England I shall *supplicate* your aid for the brat I mean to introduce to you, & which I am sure I shall be much at a loss what to do with, as never was a being less qualified, nor one who had less taste for the cares of a nursery than your humble servant."[75] Elizabeth Chute went so far as to put the well-being of her friend Elizabeth Gosling ahead of childbearing and long before Gosling had produced what would have been considered a large family: "I hope you are not likely to add a sixth bambino to your nursery; five is enough to have the charge of, & Me de Sévigné our old friend, would tell you how necessary rest is to your health."[76]

They also complained about the domestic task of maintaining contacts with other families. Although Mary Bramston could take pleasure in negotiating, with Henrietta Hicks Beach, the marriage between members of their two families, she occasionally tired of the relentless round of social calls. When the Bramstons built Oakley Hall in the early 1790s, they moved in before the house was quite ready for the reception of visitors. Mary was grateful for the temporary respite, admitting in a letter to Henrietta, "All the people here are not equal to setting one morning in the sun & hearing my charming black birds."[77] Fanny Palmer Austen, docked in Halifax with her husband, Charles, wrote irritably in 1810 to her sister Esther Esten of "receiving & returning a number of stupid visits with Lady W." (The wife who, like Fanny, lived on shipboard with her naval husband might still have a busy round of social calls to make whenever the ship came into port.)[78] And even Jane Austen, though maintaining her wit in this letter to her sister, could weary of sustaining contacts through writing:

> I have written to Mrs. Birch among my other writings, and so I hope to have some account of all the people in that part of the world before long. I have written to Mrs. E. Leigh too, and Mrs. Heathcote has been ill-natured enough to send me a letter of enquiry; so that altogether I am tolerably tired of letter-writing, and, unless I have anything new to tell you of my mother or Mary, I shall not write again for many days; perhaps a little repose may restore my regard for a pen.[79]

Women's complaints about specific domestic tasks could lead them to articulate a more generalized resentment against subordination. In 1800 Elizabeth Chute, for example, shifted her anger from the necessity of sustaining the role of homemaker all the time to the great "difference between husbands & wives." Confiding in Elizabeth Gosling about her husband, she burst out: "He seems to think it strange that I should absent myself from him for four & twenty hours when he is at home, tho' it appears in the natural order of things that he should quit me for business or pleasure, such is the difference between husbands & wives. The latter are sort of tame animals, whom the men always expect to find at home ready to receive them: the former are lords of the creation free to go where they please."[80]

When women contemplated the treatment and behavior of other women, they also sometimes voiced bitterness over subordination itself. Jane Cresset Pelham realized, through her own forgetful slip in a letter, that the inequitable treatment of women began at birth. In the winter of 1793 she was staying at Acrise, the estate of her son-in-law, Thomas Papillon, while her daughter Anne gave birth to her first child. Right after the child was born, she wrote to Thomas Papillon's sister, Elizabeth, and then sent another letter soon afterwards to apologize for her "former hasty scrawl" because she had neglected to mention the sex of the newborn. "I make no doubt but you was convinced of the Childs Sex," she added, "for when you hear Mrs such a one is brought to bed, & as well as can be expected *its always a girl*, otherwise they say Mrs—— has got *a fine boy*." Although she had herself fallen into conventions of birth-announcing that proudly brought the male infant into view and hid the female, the devaluation of the female irritated her. "It is a very small child but thrives & always has looked healthy," she told Elizabeth, "I hope to god it will do well & be worth more than any boy in the World."[81] Growing up did not improve the situation of girls. Jane Austen, visiting at Godmersham in 1813, was similarly annoyed at her twenty-year-old niece Fanny's inferior position in the family, and she too championed women. "We did not go to the Ball," she wrote to Cassandra. "It was left to her to decide, & at last she determined against it. She knew that it would be a sacrifice on the part of her Father and Brothers if they went—& I hope it will prove that *she* has not sacrificed much."[82]

Writing to one another in anger or envy, women usually identified their own subordination as a lack of control over experience. Elizabeth Chute lamented to Elizabeth Gosling in 1800 that she couldn't spend her time as she wished: "I always find tho', it is difficult to read much in society, so many interruptions arise: but your mornings are long, & you have no gentlemen to disturb you."[83] In 1804 Anne Powlett complained to Padgy Peters about her husband's manner of supplementing his income—he took in students. She disliked "the noise and the total interruption to all domestic comfort which six Boys occasion in a Family. Money so earned ought to be well employed," she maintained. "The vacations are the only time I see anything of C.P."[84] Many women saw money as the key to this control. Jane Austen understood that as long as she had to depend on her brothers to pay her travel expenses, she would have to consent to their plans. She criticized one of Edward Austen's itineraries in a letter to her sister in 1808 and yearned for an alternative: "He wishes to reach Guilford on friday night—that we may have a couple of hours to spare for Alton.—I shall be sorry to pass the door at Seale without calling, but it must be so—& I shall be nearer to Bookham than I c^d wish, in going from Dorking to Guilford—but till I have a travelling purse of my own, I must submit to such things."[85] A few women who had adequate economic resources believed that staying single was the key to self-determination. Although she married twice, Eliza de Feuillide expressed a strong inclination to remain unfettered, first as a young and eligible woman and then after her French husband was guillotined. "My impulse in favour of liberty & disfavour of a lord & master," she noted in a letter to Philadelphia written during her widowhood, "is . . . irresistible."[86]

To be sure, although all creators of the women's culture routinely put women first, reversing the values of the gentry's patriarchal culture, few directly and frequently attacked the structure of social relations. Still, it is hard to find a correspondence between close women friends that does not contain some expression of opposition to women's subordination. Even such a zealous adherent to the domestic ideology as Fanny (Knight) Knatchbull, writing to a woman with whom, after the first decade of the nineteenth century, she was no longer particularly intimate, once voiced disenchantment about marriage and motherhood. In her forties, with several children, Fanny wrote to Dorothy Chapman: "I am glad to hear your sisters are all well & was not aware that they were all Widows—I believe *you* are the wisest & best off of us all My dear Miss Chapman."[87]

What was the source of this discontent, generated by the women's culture? The discourse of that culture does not tell us. Women could have cultivated longings for autonomy and equality through the general influence of Enlightenment ideas, for example, or through the more specific mediations of Restoration comedies or the writings of late seventeenth- and eighteenth-century British feminists. But they did not say as much, and they could have met autonomy and equality, oddly enough, in the ideology of domesticity itself. Women could appreciate their own interests and desires by turning the ideology on its head; they may have developed views of autonomy and equality through another such inversion.

Prescriptions for sexual identity and appropriate conduct are necessary or desirable because other ways of being and acting are possible. Whether transmitted by word of mouth or in conduct books, advice on self-restraint and deference often not only implied but even embedded these alternatives. Information on how to be an ideal, feminine woman was often accompanied by negative examples of women taking liberties or seeking their own rather than their male kin's happiness. The author of *Letters to a Young Lady*, for example, hopes that "women will not join in a conspiracy to annihilate the small degree of knightly courtesy which yet exists, by themselves assuming the deport-

ment of amazonian boldness, or affecting amazonian independence."
She also insists that the "business of the wife is to controul her own
inclinations, instead of projecting how she may gratify them."[88] While
women were learning the identity and conduct recommended for them
by the ideology of domesticity, they may also, within the encouraging
context of their intimate, egalitarian relationships, have been absorbing the very different values forwarded after a "not" or "instead of."

Whatever its social source, women's overt criticism and the values
of autonomy and equality that they expressed with it had no effect on
the gentry's patriarchal culture or community. Like implicit criticism
of the domestic ideology, this explicit criticism also functioned to
accommodate women to their subordination and maintain it. The
women's culture served this role because, although contributors to it
expressed strong dissatisfaction with gender-based social inequities,
although they expressed longings for liberty and authority, they communicated these sentiments *only to one another.* Their culture thus
functioned as a safety valve for the release of discontent.

In 1801 Anne Powlett had to tell Padgy Peters the painful news that
her infant son had died. In the same letter she informed her friend,
"You will be surprised to hear that I am again three Months on; but
I dare not complain that it is too quick."[89] She dared not complain—
to anyone but her friend, Padgy. Similarly, Fanny Palmer Austen vent-
ed severe disappointement in a letter to her sister Harriet in 1814 but
noted that she intended to make a very different, cheerful communication to her husband, Charles. Tired of paying a visit to her spouse's
superior and patron, Sir Thomas Williams, and Lady Williams,
Fanny had been hoping to return with Charles to his ship the next day;
he preferred to prolong their visit: "Tho' I receive every kindness &
attention from them both, I cannot help feeling a great desire *to be at
home,* however, uncomfortable that home may be—but I must submit
& pretend to like it. I believe Capt. Austen rather wishes to stay than
otherwise."[90] And in 1813 Jane Austen wrote, in the following complaint to Cassandra, precisely what she as a subordinate and dependent female relation felt that she could not say to her brother Edward:
"Here am I in Kent, with one Brother in the same County & another
Brother's Wife, & see nothing of them—which seems unnatural—It
will not last so for ever I trust.—I shd like to have Mrs. F.A. & her
Children here for a week—but not a syllable of that nature is ever
breathed."[91] Apparently, Austen did not think even polite inquiry appropriate. She elected the passive tactic of waiting.

When Elizabeth Chute was learning from her mother in the winter
of 1793–94 how to please her new husband, her sister Augusta was

looking on at Elizabeth's conduct restlessly. Longing to see her, Augusta was growing impatient with the many feminine proprieties determining Elizabeth's repeated decisions in February of 1794 to put off her visit to her family in London. Thus, while Elizabeth's mother was teaching her the subtleties of her domestic, feminine identity, her sister began urging her in March not to embrace that identity so completely. Augusta accused her sister of being too recessive and silent when William Chute raised the prospect of a visit to London yet again:

> if Mr Chute applies to you to name the time of your departure you need not from Compliments make it a distant one; you have very properly stayed for his business, pleasure & convenience; but now, surely it is not necessary to appear an inanimate machine that has no wish; Mr Chute's frank open temper would not like so much insipidity; every thing has its extreme; come Eliza, assert the Privileges of a Woman & speak boldly, or else I renounce you for one of the Sex.

She threatened to speak to William Chute herself, and yet for all her aggressive posturing, she restricted her own boldness to her sister: "I am half tempted to write M^r. C— a letter; but I think he would not like such a Correspondent, so I forbear; my letter would not be the essence of honey."[92]

Mary Bramston was similarly expressive to another woman while also assuming an *outward* passivity at a potential turning point in her brother Tom's life. Their uncle in Norfolk held a living for Tom, who, though planning to enter the Church, was still in the fencibles, an organization of men recruited to watch the coastline during the wars with France. As their uncle had become very ill, Mary was anxious for her brother to take the living as soon as possible. She expressed her opinion very firmly in a letter to Henrietta Hicks Beach: "These horrid french with their threatened invasion always keeps him undetermined about quitting the fencibles but as he was always designed for the Church I really do not see why he could not on such an occasion resign." She then admitted ignorance on a relevant clerical point but made an aggressive attempt to compensate: "As you have two Clergyman with you I wish you would without mentioning the Circumstances ask how long a person must be ordained before they can hold any living." She did not, however, plan to use any information she gained, for she did not believe that her opinion would count with her male kin. "This is merely for my own satisfaction," she informed her friend, "for my brothers will act as they please."[93]

Because women "ghettoized" the moments when they refused silence and submission, their private culture paradoxically served a conservative purpose, enabling them to subscribe to the ideology of domesticity and sustain domestic practices. However, there is no reason to suppose that the women's culture in itself prevented women from breaking with the domestic ideology and the gentry's culture. As I have suggested, gender identity for Austen's social group was inextricably combined with status identity. To reject one could mean losing the other, and elite status was a good deal to lose in late eighteenth- and early nineteenth-century England. Austen's female friends, relatives, and neighbors would have remained loyal to the values of the gentry's culture with or without a women's culture because they needed and wanted to do so.

What if these women had had no distinct culture of their own? When we consider their culture in this light, we can, justly, switch metaphors: if it was a safety valve, it was also a training ground. We must be cautious, to be sure, about the claims we make about that training ground. Because the friendships that generated and were generated by the women's culture were restricted by rank, the culture did not promote a universal awareness of gender and of solidarity among women. It thus remained uninfluenced, for example, by the democratic radicalism to which Mary Wollstonecraft gave voice in the 1790s—a radicalism which, according to historian Barbara Taylor, linked "the emancipation of women to the social and political liberation of 'the people' as a whole."[94] Nor did the culture promote the social and political rights of women just of the upper and middle ranks. It did not engender a more limited reformist bourgeois feminism. Augusta Smith wanted her sister Elizabeth Chute "to assert the Privileges of a Woman," but a rhetoric of "privileges," which sounds similar to a doctrine of "rights," was not typically expressed in the women's culture. Nevertheless, the women's culture kept discontent and dissent alive, nurturing the seeds of a feminist consciousness among women who were not obvious candidates to be revolutionaries or reformers.

Implicit and explicit sentiments of the women's culture, it is important to remember, mixed with expressions of feminine compliance. Women were apt to receive letters within the space of a few weeks, as Elizabeth Chute did, advising them both to defer and to be self-assertive in dealing with their husbands or they were apt to write, as Eliza de Feuillide did, praising female self-denial while at the same time encouraging female self-gratification. The letter Eliza sent in 1797 to her cousin Philadelphia, who was at home nursing her father, noted admiringly, "how cheerfully you give up all you are so well calculated to enjoy—I know that your happy Temper together with the consciousness of fulfilling the most sacred of all Duties support you under every sacrifice and enable you to submit to confinement, & Seclusion.'' But the letter also alluded to Philadelphia's personal interests and needs. Eliza queried Philadelphia about her old suitor, DBB, with whom she had lately been in touch again, and tried to encourage her in flirtation: "How are all yr other Kentish Beaux?"[95] This fluidity in women's attitudes even within a single letter signals an early, inchoate stage of feminist consciousness. For that reason and because the form of private letters was marked by contradictions as well as fluidity in women's views, these writings are of particular interest.

Their culture had a rudimentary influence on the consciousness of gentlewomen. It also contributed richly to individual women's lives. It provided them with the sympathy and support of fulfilling emotional ties, of a kind not always available to them in heterosexual relationships. The women's culture gave them self-esteem and a sense of the significance of their daily activities. And it offered them an expressive outlet for anger, anxiety, and assertiveness. These important psychological benefits also influenced some women's choices and actions. We shall see that influence in turning now from the collective values and meanings of the gentry's and women's cultures to Jane Austen's particular experiences of them.

She was, of course, not a typical woman, but neither was she cut off from her environment. She couldn't have lived or written the way she did without the gentry's or women's cultures. The next two chapters, then, consider the roles played by Austen's dual cultures in her literary achievement, and they show that Austen's experience of the women's culture was particularly important when, as an adult woman, she encountered the pressures of the ideology of domesticity. With the help of her women's culture she was able to marshal sufficient confidence and autonomy not merely to write but to become a publishing novelist—to become Jane Austen.

PART TWO

Portraits of
the Woman Writer

CHAPTER 4

Circles of Support

1

JANE AUSTEN became a novelist, so many biographers have told us, because she was a genius. That explanation first appeared in postromantic nineteenth-century narratives of the writer's life, but it has received the most play in twentieth-century biographies as diverse as those by Jane Aiken Hodge, David Cecil, and John Halperin.[1] In their renderings, genius is part of Austen's "double life." She is both artistic genius *and* ordinary woman, two strikingly discrete identities. Indeed, in Cecil's *Portrait of Jane Austen*, which offers the most elaborated account of the so-called double life, artist and woman inhabit entirely different realms. Only Austen's life as a woman is subject to empirical investigation; the artist is, by contrast, "a detached invisible figure, observant to gather the fuel that might one day kindle her imaginative spark to flame."

The Austen of Cecil's *Portrait* does not require an encouraging social context in order to realize her talent. Indeed, his vision of the double life suggests that Austen found novel-writing possible only by removing herself from social experience. Although Cecil refers to her as an artist and a woman, he implies that she had to be an artist *or* a woman. The "detached, invisible figure" of genius must have no gender because he identifies women only with their procreative potential. Austen, we are told, "differed from most women. The creative impulse which in them fulfilled itself as a wife and mother in her fulfilled itself as an artist."[2]

This explanation is simplistic, not because it attributes to Austen innate talent—surely she had that—but because it renounces any influence whatever of social life on that talent. Because it is so simplistic, however, Cecil's perception of a double life for Austen makes especially apparent the problem that confronts all who attempt to explain how Austen came to be a writer: her sexual identity. Given her community's adherence to the ideology of domesticity, given that Austen *was* expected to fulfill herself "as a wife and mother," where did she meet with encouragement for writing? The double-life explanation acknowledges (and endorses) the feminine identity that the ideology constructs but gets around it by exempting the presumably rare genius from that identity. Still, there are other, less extreme explanations that do acknowledge social influences on Austen's achievement; how do they treat the issue of her gender?

The most widely recognized influence has been Jane Austen's family. Biographers have credited her relatives with supporting and inspiring her to write. Even biographers who have proffered the view of a double life have, despite the incompatibility, advanced this explanation as well. "Family influence" does not, as does Cecil's "double life," overtly reject the impact of domestic femininity on the extraordinary woman artist, but it is still problematic. Evincing its own patriarchal perspective, the explanation is simply oblivious to the role played by Austen's gender. Because it doesn't consider what it meant to be female in Jane Austen's community, the "family influence" explanation cannot, then, adequately account for Austen's achievement, either.

Drawing on the framework of Austen's dual cultures—gentry and women's—this chapter points to the limitations of the "family influence" explanation for different stages in Austen's literary development. In the process, it also reperceives the customary biographical representation of the novelist's family. To be sure, it is easier to review than to revise the conventional story of Austen's literary development. Biographers have been handicapped by the small number of surviving primary documents. The internal evidence of Austen's letters indicates that she had several correspondents and that she wrote frequently to Cassandra in particular, when they were apart. But only just over 150 of her letters have survived, all of them written between 1796 and the year of her death, 1817.[3] Her sister destroyed many of the novelist's letters after she died, as did her brother Henry and probably others of her relatives. Contemporary testimonies are also sparse. Most, by nieces and nephews, describe her only in the last decades of her life. But the framework of gentry and women's cultures enables us to see some of this evidence differently and, in some instances, to couple or contextualize some of the usual materials with additional and previously ignored sources—the writings of Austen's neighbors and kin, for example.

By situating Austen's family in the context of their community's cultural affiliations and expressions, this chapter shows that biographers usually portray it as an insular and unchanging unit. What they have labeled "family" might be seen more precisely as a shifting circle of supporters over the course of Austen's life. She was born not just into a family but into a community whose culture fostered wide reading and playful writing—rich exercises in literacy that we should not overlook. As Austen matured and encountered the inhibiting pressures of the community's domestic ideology, however, she found still another supportive culture generated by a small group of female kin and friends within her wider community. In this female circle Austen was able to develop her creative voice and a professional writer's identity.

At different moments in her life Austen benefited from encouragements offered by the gentry's and women's cultures. But if it is simplistic to suggest that only an abstract quality of genius made Austen the novelist she became, it is equally simplistic to maintain that her dual cultures alone made her a writer. We might say, rather, that part of Austen's undeniably great talent consisted in recognizing the cultural resources of her social world and in learning how to make use of them.

2

Jane Austen's first extant literary compositions date from 1787, the year in which she was eleven years old, but she may have started writing fiction even earlier. Her spectacularly precocious beginning, recorded in her witty juvenilia, testifies not only to her talent but also to those social circumstances that enabled its expression. Two of her earliest biographers, themselves kin to the novelist, have praised her family and especially some Austen men for motivating her to write. Her brother Henry Austen, whose 1818 "Biographical Notice of the Author" provided the public with the first history of Jane Austen, singled out the impact of their father, the Reverend George Austen: "Being not only a profound scholar, but possessing a most exquisite taste in every species of literature, it is not wonderful that his daughter Jane should, at a very early age, have become sensible to the charms of style, and enthusiastic in the cultivation of her own language."[4] Austen's nephew James Edward Austen-Leigh, whose *Memoir of Jane Austen* appeared in 1870, called attention to the father-figure role of Jane Austen's brother (Austen-Leigh's own father) James: "He was more than ten years older than Jane, and had, I believe, a large share in directing her reading and forming her taste."[5]

Following these precedents, subsequent biographers and critics have acknowledged the influence of her father and oldest brother but have credited, too, the literary atmosphere generated by the whole family. They have been portrayed as lovers of wit, who play-acted and read novels. They are said to have thought and talked critically about contemporary literary tastes and conventions and to have formed an enthusiastic audience for any clever, homemade entertainments.[6] Moreover, many family members, not just the young Jane, are shown to have enjoyed composing. Her mother and sister wrote poems and riddles, and some of her brothers were, as literary critic B. C. Southam has put it, "minor versifiers and essayists."[7] James was particularly and consistently prolific; his numerous surviving poems (including prologues and epilogues for plays performed at Steventon) span a period of almost forty years, from the early 1780s to his death in 1819.[8] As a young man, he also produced a periodical, *The Loiterer*, to which he and Henry Austen contributed more than half the essays. Surrounded by these affectionate and highly receptive scribblers, Jane Austen was apparently prompted to write also.

The Austens *were* unusually literary and did provide a stimulating setting for Jane Austen's girlhood writing. Biographers generally have not acknowledged, however, that the Austens were part of a broader context of encouragement: their genteel community. James Edward Austen-Leigh, for example, does briefly concede the "good taste and cultivated minds" of some Austen neighbors, but family pride and a strong belief in progress led this influential Victorian biographer to look back on late eighteenth- and early nineteenth-century Hampshire and see a shining cluster of talented Austens surrounded by the dull and uneducated. In the world in which his aunt was born, Austen-Leigh tells his readers, "ignorance and coarseness of language . . . were still lingering even upon higher levels of society than might have been expected to retain such mists." To prove his point, he relates the story of "a neighbouring squire, a man of many acres," who "referred the following difficulty to Mr. Austen's decision: 'You know all about these sort of things. Do tell us. Is Paris in France, or France in Paris? for my wife has been disputing with me about it.'"[9] Austen's family members, as biographer David Cecil has suggested, may have been "cleverer" than their neighbors.[10] But the surviving nonvocational writings of even just that segment of Austen's community living in the immediate vicinity of the Steventon parsonage, where Austen grew up, suggest that her Hampshire neighbors were in fact highly—we might almost say hyper—literate, intellectually curious, and playful.[11]

Their letters and diaries offer brief but intriguing references to their wide and varied reading. Mary Bramston of Oakley Hall, for example, had strikingly broad tastes, recommending in her letters to a close friend histories and gothic novels, the works of William Wilberforce and of Lord Byron. Elizabeth Chute of the Vyne had a particular fondness for French literature, and, although she had not read it (as of the summer of 1800), she was interested in what people were saying about radical William Godwin's novel *Caleb Williams*. "In morals, in religion & politics, everyone allows it to be very faulty," she wrote to a friend.[12] As one of Jane Austen's own playful letters informs us, her friends at Manydown, Elizabeth Heathcote and Alethea Bigg, liked "enormous great stupid thick quarto volumes."[13]

The letters and diaries written by members of Austen's Hampshire neighbors, of course, testify not only to their reading but to their writing habits. As we have seen in previous chapters, they were prolific correspondents and diarists. Women more often than men wrote letters of family and personal news and probably kept more of the diaries that functioned partly as social calendars. Men often composed detailed accounts of travel and hunting adventures, though, and both sexes penned family histories, making notes for future generations, and kept logs of daily and monthly expenditures.

Austen's neighbors were capable of a pious, sometimes more formal prose as well. Although not a few gentlemen in the community, having entered the Church, routinely drafted sermons, nonprofessionals devoted their pens to religious concerns too. Lady Frances Heathcote, wife of the third baronet of Hursley and mother-in-law of Austen's friend Elizabeth Heathcote, wrote at least one long sermon in verse, probably for her own private instruction;[14] others wrote prayers.

They also frequently produced and delighted in lighthearted, fanciful compositions. In a world without Hallmark greeting cards they responded to one another's birthdays, weddings, anniversaries, and childbearing with their own homemade, cheerful doggerel. J. H. George Lefroy, oldest son of Jane Austen's friend Anne Lefroy, sent poems to one of his younger brothers in honor of the boy's birthday, incorporating in one of them a fairly realistic assessment of his poetic talents:

> Again, Dear Boy, Novembers blast
> Bids me my tribute pay
> And joyous I resume my task
> And greet thy natal day.
>
> What tho' in me no vivid rays
> Hath Genius bade to glow
> Despise not thou these simple lays
> Affection bids them flow.[15]

Austen's neighbors broke into verse even when not marking the key events of personal life. Wither Bramston of Oakley Hall wrote ten stanzas for his aunt in 1782, describing his efforts to buy her some oranges:

> . . . Stop'd at Cooks, tasted some, but alas! cou'd get none,
> Till I reached Botolph Lane in the City,
> Where I picked up a Chest, that seem'd of the Best,
> If they do not succeed, 'tis a Pity. . . .[16]

Stephen Terry of Dummer wrote poetry about his hunting escapades. And even the commonplace scene of boys playing outdoors could put Anne Lefroy into a rhyming mood. The neighbors also produced numerous charades very like the one *Emma*'s Mr. Elton contributes to Harriet Smith's lavishly ornamented album.

A playful spirit found its way into more extended endeavors. Jane Austen was not the only member of her community to try parody. Elizabeth Heathcote's eleven-year-old son, for example, created "The Mirror," a mock newspaper filled with parodies of international and local events. It reported the loss of Bonaparte's nose, for instance, and the marriage of Miss Blachford (one of Heathcote's cousins) "to John Prion aged 70—the Beauty of her spouse (it is generally believed) is the reason of the Lady's choice being Captivated by him one day as he was cutting wood & sporting off a new pair of hedging gloves & an old wig."[17]

The neighbors also liked and sometimes wrote songs. As county elections neared, many new lyrics set to familiar tunes were produced, describing and lampooning the candidates and their competitions. If Austen's neighbors did not write them (many were published anonymously or under pseudonyms) they certainly relished them. In 1790, for example, "Nurse Jervoise's Lullaby to Lord Jacky" appeared, mocking Lord John Russell, one of Heathcote and Chute's opponents in the Hampshire contest for Parliament. "Jacky shall ride round the County," charged one of its stanzas, "And pop in at every door'a, / Take care it dont miss its way, / It ne'er was in Hampshire before'a."

Mary Bramston so enjoyed the verses that she made a copy for her invalid mother-in-law, residing in Bath, who had her daughter Augusta copy them over and send them to her niece.[18] Wars also inspired song. Perhaps because she believed that there was "nothing more useful in exciting & keeping up the spirit of a nation than popular songs," Anne Lefroy supplied new patriotic words to a Robert Burns poem sung to the tune of "Hey Tittie Tattie."[19] She adapted it to suit a corps of Newport Volunteers, formed in the Isle of Wight to defend the inhabitants in case of an invasion by the French. Finally, gentlemen wrote songs in celebration of sports and fellowship. Charles Powlett's uncle, the Rector of Itchen Abbas, achieved a local reputation as "the Laureate of the Hunt" with rousing verses sung at the Hampshire Hunt dinners.[20]

None of this work, of course, approaches the brilliance of Jane Austen's early writings, "Love and Freindship" in particular, but these widespread, albeit unremarkable, literary undertakings form the broad context for Austen's juvenilia. They also provide the context for many of the other compositions Austen produced over the course of her life—her numerous poems and charades and her household prayers. All these works, as well as those by other Austen family members, expressed and contributed to the wider community's patterns of reading and writing, were part of its culture.

Although some of the writings of members of the Austen family and their community (some personal diaries, for instance) were kept utterly private and some, such as songs, were often offered to the public, many of these works, especially letters and poems, were neither very private nor very public. They were instead the products of domesticity and kinship, written by one family member for others. If these family writings were like today's greeting cards, they were also gifts, offered for the pleasure and sometimes the entertainment of loved ones. The dedications attached to the majority of Jane Austen's childhood parodies make their domestic and familial identity especially clear and closely associate them with the other genteel home productions of her community, such as poems marking birthdays and anniversaries.

Indeed, it is *because* many of these works were expressions of family feeling that they were sometimes preserved. Some of the extant letters of Austen's friends and neighbors have notations on the outside, added by the letter recipient several years after they were received. These notations constitute, in effect, an emotional index, listing the family member who wrote the particular letter, sometimes its date, and its especially meaningful topics. After their author had died, letters and other domestic writings were also handed on by their original recipient, given to surviving family members as mementos of the deceased. Cassandra Austen's treatment of her sister's letters was typical behavior within her community. She withheld a relatively small number of Jane Austen's letters from the fireplace, probably not because she thought their charm and wit ought to be saved for posterity but because she wanted to give her relatives tokens, not unlike a lock of hair, of the dead. She treated the juvenilia as tokens too, giving sections to three members of the family.

3

Biographers and critics, in stressing the role of Austen's kin, have ignored the general impact of their community's culture while insisting that the influence of the novelist's family, after getting her started as a writer, continued unchanging. Throughout her life her family is said to have stimulated and supported her talent.[21] "Her novels remained to the last a kind of family entertainment," according to Mary Lascelles.[22] Mary Poovey concurs with Lascelles's representation of Austen's relatives: "Jane Austen wrote her first stories for the amusement of her family. . . . Austen's first longer works . . . were also apparently family entertainments, and, even after she became a published author, she continued to solicit and value the response of her family as she composed and revised her novels."[23] But just as the family's influence was permeated by the culture of Austen's community in her childhood, so that influence was reshaped by the community's values in Austen's adulthood. "Family" became a smaller circle in Austen's adult life, but that group, though private and exclusive, was still not disconnected from the community and patriarchal culture surrounding it.

The literary interests and pursuits of Jane Austen's family *and* community explain how, as a young girl, she came to be interested in literature and to try imaginative writing, but they cannot account for Austen's mature writing. In the second half of the 1790s Austen was becoming a serious, committed writer. We can follow the transformation by considering her productions. The majority of her juvenilia, like the works of her family and neighbors, are very brief; some mere fragments or, as she called one selection of them, "Scraps." Most of the longer pieces are unfinished. *Lady Susan*, the first composition written after the juvenilia in 1793–94, while not incomplete, is brought to a quick finish with a short, tacked-on conclusion. But beginning in 1795, Austen wrote and completed three extended manuscripts:

"First Impressions," "Elinor and Marianne," and "Susan," and those efforts changed the nature of Austen's creative life, differentiating it both from her work on her earlier fictions and from the leisure-time composing of other members of the gentry. The manuscripts required sustained concentration. They took time.

We have only to remember the dictums of the widespread ideology of domesticity to appreciate the potential subversiveness of that writing. The ideal woman was to engage in activities that served her family, contributing either to the pleasures of her husband or to the education of her children. Certainly, a young girl or even an adult woman who whiled away an occasional solitary afternoon by composing a poem or by writing brief parodies could not be accused of putting herself first in an "unfeminine" way. But to write three books in four years? Although biographers and critics have routinely portrayed the charming family context for Austen's girlhood precociousness, they have not provided a persuasive rendering of that context for the novelist's difficult transition from play to professionalism, a transition that began in the second half of the 1790s and extended into the second decade of the nineteenth century. They have not been able to do so because they have ignored the increasing cultural pressures on females in Jane Austen's community who were becoming adult women.

Was the Austen family somehow indifferent to their culture's domestic ideology? The little surviving evidence of their responses to Austen's novel-writing suggests that they may have been, but only to a degree. Certainly, her father's effort to find a publisher for "First Impressions" in 1797 indicates that he knew and approved of his daughter's work. Nor was he naive or inattentive to the implications of his action: in his letter to publisher Thomas Cadell he compared his daughter's manuscript to Frances Burney's *Evelina*.[24] Her brother Henry often negotiated with her publishers after their father's death, and he proudly blurted out the secret of her authorship to his acquaintances. But some of the novelist's other male kin expressed ambivalence, if not over the novels then over their sister's being known as the author of them. Frank was in favor of maintaining secrecy. James's discomforts with his sister's work are expressed in "Venta," a poem that he composed after she died. It acknowledges an Austen family "prejudice" against "fair female fame," referring to family members who "Maintain that literary taste / In womans mind is much misplaced, / Inflames their vanity & pride, / And draws from useful works aside." And it defends her against this prejudice: although she was a novelist, she was "ready still to share / The labours of domestic care."[25] This defense, however, does not refute the "prejudice." Instead, the elegy's praise sounds like an apology for Jane Austen's literary career.

The novelist's own behavior provides richer evidence, suggesting that she understood that her devotion to writing could create at least tension in some of her family relationships and that she wished to avoid such tension. She attempted to keep her novel-writing and eventually her publishing a secret from her reading public as well as her neighbors. Although she didn't hide the fact of her writing from her male family members, she did keep her time-consuming and self-absorbing labors out of their view.

Some biographers have found these efforts peculiar. The "obsessive secrecy about her writing," claims David Cecil in *A Portrait of Jane Austen*, "is the nearest thing to an eccentricity in her otherwise well-balanced character."[26] According to John Halperin's *Life of Jane Austen*, "her passion for secrecy came close to being a mania."[27] Yet Austen was part of a community in which the guarding of secrets was a common practice, particularly among women who needed to hide desires, interests, and activities not sanctioned by the domestic ideology. And women writers of her day, in general, often resorted to anonymity or pseudonyms when publishing.

Literary critics have studied the strategies for self-effacement practiced by eighteenth- and nineteenth-century British women writers from a variety of cultural milieux.[28] But the letters of Jane Austen's neighbors offer us a very local example. In November 1802, Austen's friend Anne Lefroy announced to her son Christopher Edward that she had recently published an "Explanation of the little horn mentioned in the 7th chapter of the prophet Daniel" anonymously in the *Gentleman's Magazine*. But she quickly added, "You will, of course, not mention who put it in."[29] No such secrecy surrounded the publications of her brother, Egerton Brydges, however. She sent her son his new novel, *Le Forester*, in the same month, "which," she assured him, "you are at perfect liberty to mention as your Uncle's writing."[30]

For the second half of the 1790s it is difficult to determine precisely who knew Austen was writing and when they knew it. The testimony of Austen's niece Anna Austen Lefroy gives some indication of the secret's boundaries, but there are two versions of her story. One comes directly from Anna in her "Reminiscences of Aunt Jane," though she wasn't remembering in this case; she was reporting what her older relatives had told her about her early years. Austen's "earliest Novels," Anna noted, "certainly P. & P were read aloud in the Parsonage at Dean." When the very young Anna began talking about the characters, "it was resolved for prudence sake to read no more of the story aloud in my hearing."[31] Since the manuscripts were read in James and Mary Austen's home, presumably her female and male kin were "in" while servants, neighbors, and children were "out."

The second version appears in *Jane Austen: Her Life and Letters*, a 1913 biography published by W. and R. A. Austen-Leigh, the novelist's grandnephew and great-grandnephew, respectively.[32] Sometime after Anna's mother died, according to this account, the little girl was staying at Steventon, where she was admitted to her aunts' "chocolate-carpeted dressing-room, which was now becoming a place of eager authorship. Anna was a very intelligent, quick-witted child, and, hearing the original draft of *Pride and Prejudice* read aloud by its youthful writer to her sister, she caught up the names of the characters and repeated them so much downstairs that she had to be checked; for the composition of the story was still a secret kept from the knowledge of the elders."[33] This rendering indicates that Cassandra was privy to Jane Austen's work while she was writing and that other family members were being told about or shown the fiction after she was finished. We can infer that some of the Austen family's members were becoming liminal figures, standing between her intimates and members of the community outside the home. They knew less of Austen's work than Austen's confidante, Cassandra, but presumably more than the neighbors.

Austen's letters suggest that by the end of the 1790s she had a small inner circle of enthusiastic female supporters. Only two references to readers of her manuscripts appear in her letters from the period, but we can conclude from them that her writing was a source of entertainment to which those to whom she was closest returned frequently. In 1799 Austen's mocking responses to Cassandra and Martha Lloyd's requests to read one of her manuscripts suggest that both had already done so several times. "I do not wonder," she tells her sister in what must be a sarcastic tone, "at your wanting to read 'First Impressions' again, so seldom as you have gone through it, and that so long ago."[34] Martha's petition she pretends to mistrust: "I would not let Martha read 'First Impressions' again upon any account, and am very glad that I did not leave it in your power. She is very cunning, but I saw through her design; she means to publish it from memory, and one more perusal must enable her to do it."[35]

Although Austen joked about Cassandra and Martha's requests, she was also expressing self-confidence in her response to Martha. Such expressions were not consistent with domestic femininity, though they were typically encouraged by the women's culture. The audience for some of Austen's responses to her own work, however playful, was shifting in the late 1790s. Austen's writing and her consciousness of that effort were becoming part of the distinct culture of her female friendships. To be sure, most of these ties, particularly in future years, were to be to female kin, but "family" nonetheless was beginning to have a meaning different from that evident during Austen's youth and early adolescence.

4

The shift toward a circle of female supporters is much more apparent during Austen's most productive period, beginning in 1809. Between 1800 and 1808 Austen, as far as we know, wrote a portion of a work subsequently titled "The Watsons" and made substantial revisions to "Susan." She may also have done revisions on her other full-length manuscripts, as well. Moreover, she made a second unsuccessful effort to publish. When in 1797 her father offered "First Impressions" on her behalf to Cadell, the publisher had refused to consider it. But in 1803 Henry Austen (through his business associate, Mr. Seymour) submitted "Susan" for her to publisher Richard Crosby, who purchased it but did not bring it out.

That is where matters stood when in 1809 Jane Austen aggressively renewed her attempts to publish and began to revise old works and to write new ones in rapid succession. She wrote to Crosby under the assumed name of "Mrs. Ashton Dennis" or "M.A.D.," as she actually signed the letter. She offered to send him another copy of the manuscript, supposing the original lost, and threatened to seek another publisher. "Should no notice be taken of this address," she insisted, "I shall feel myself at liberty to secure the publication of my work, by applying elsewhere."[36] Crosby's response was not ideal. He was willing only to sell the manuscript to Austen for the ten pounds he had paid for it. Disheartened or, perhaps, unable to spare the money, Austen let the matter drop until 1816, when she finally did buy "Susan" back. Nevertheless, at the same time, she embarked on another, more successful attempt. She turned to "Elinor and Marianne," which she had first written in 1795 or 1796. Austen had already revised it once in 1797, renaming it at that time *Sense and Sensibility*. Now she rewrote it again and, with her brother Henry as the intermediary, sold it to the firm of Thomas Egerton. She became, finally, a published writer when it appeared in 1811. That publication was followed in 1813 by *Pride and Prejudice*, a revision of another early manuscript, "First

Impressions"; in 1814 by *Mansfield Park*; and in 1816 by *Emma*. Austen finished *Persuasion* in 1816 but died in 1817, a year before it and her revision of "Susan," retitled *Northanger Abbey*, appeared.[37]

Those biographers who have specifically commented on the context enabling this wave of creativity and publishing success have made of it an opportunity to reinvoke Austen's earliest family context. Following the example of W. and R. A. Austen-Leigh, they have generally attributed the literary work of this period to the intervention of one of her elder brothers. In the fall of 1808, in the wake of his wife's shockingly sudden death, Edward Austen offered his mother a house on one of his estates. Mrs. Austen, her daughters, and Martha Lloyd chose to settle in a cottage at Chawton. According to W. and R. A. Austen-Leigh's *Jane Austen: Her Life and Letters*, the removal to a country cottage, so remote from the bustle of Bath and Southampton (where Austen had lived since 1801), made possible Austen's series of publications: "She was no doubt aided by the quiet of her home and its friendly surroundings. In this tranquil spot, where the past and present even now join peaceful hands, she found happy leisure, repose of mind, and absence of distraction, such as any sustained creative effort demands."[38] Austen, in this version, owed the work that she did beginning in 1809 to the literal and metaphoric shelter that Edward provided.

The explanation of Edward's patronage in 1808 makes claims for a patriarchal family influence on the career of the novelist, but it has only symbolic weight in W. and R. A. Austen-Leigh's *Life and Letters*. It stands for a family circle that had altered radically since the late 1780s and early 1790s. In 1809 Austen's father had been dead for four years. Her brothers were preoccupied with careers and families of their own—all except George, who had not, in any case, whether because of illness or disability, lived among the family since he was a child.[39] Although Frank and his new wife, Mary, lived with the Austen women in Southampton from the fall of 1806 to 1808, Mary was the more long-term housemate, for Frank was at sea from April 1807 to June 1808. Martha Lloyd had also set up housekeeping with Mrs. Austen and her daughters beginning in 1805. The four people who moved to Chawton Cottage in the spring of 1809, then, constituted a considerably altered, all-female version of the Austen "family." Austen's housemates had a more sustained and immediate effect on her writing than her brother's gift of the cottage.

In these later years Austen continued to try to restrict knowledge of her writing. She signed the first edition of *Sense and Sensibility* "By a Lady" and her subsequent novels "By the Author of," listing some of her earlier works. Family and close friends knew; neighbors and acquaintances she tried to keep in the dark. The Middletons, who leased Chawton Manor from 1808 to 1813, were unaware of the writing going on in the cottage across the road.[40] And one of her letters from January, 1813, shows Austen and her mother trying to keep the authorship of the just-published *Pride and Prejudice* a secret from their houseguest, Miss Benn—even as they read the novel aloud to her.[41] Jane or Cassandra also habitually enjoined family members to be discreet. The September 28, 1811, entry in the diary of their niece Fanny reads, "Another letter from Aunt Cassandra to beg we would not mention that Aunt Jane Austen wrote 'Sense & Sensibility.'"[42] As late as 1817, the year she died, the novelist wrote to Fanny, "I have a something ready for Publication, which may perhaps appear about a twelve-month hence." She followed this announcement with a warning to her niece *not* to pass the news on to her Kent acquaintances: "This is for yourself alone. Neither Mr. Salusbury nor Mr. Wildman are to know of it."[43]

The female *and* male members of her immediate family knew of her work, of course, but because over time her family had not only changed but grown, adding a new generation, Austen's reliance on the support of women is even more visible in this period. Her niece Fanny became part of the inner circle of confidantes, as did Fanny's sister Lizzy. James's daughter, Anna, also probably had intimate knowledge of her aunt's writing when they became quite close in the last four or five years of the novelist's life.[44] The younger nieces and nephews were locked out of the secret, presumably until they were old enough to control their tongues.

Only Anna could report anything of her aunt's years at Steventon, but others of Austen's nieces and nephews were able to remember something of her years at Chawton. Their testimonies inadvertently help to reveal her choice of confidantes. What is striking about their descriptions of their aunt as a writer is how little some of them had to remember. They knew retrospectively that she was beginning a career as a novelist, but they saw very few signs of that career when they called up their memories.

Austen did no fiction writing while fulfilling her domestic duties, even when that meant no more than entertaining young relatives. We know that she did, however, write letters within gatherings, at least of family members, because part or all of her letters voiced their concerns and interests. As Caroline Austen half recalls and half guesses, "My Aunt must have spent much time in writing—her desk lived in the drawing room. I often saw her writing letters on it, and I beleive she wrote much of her Novels in the same way—sitting with her family, when they were quite alone; but I never saw any manuscript of *that* sort, in progress."[45] James Edward Austen-Leigh, who had read Austen's first two novels before he learned that they were written by his aunt, can only assume in his *Memoir* that Austen wrote in the company of just the women closest to her at Chawton: her sister, mother, and Martha Lloyd. But he *knows* that she put the duties enumerated by the domestic ideology before her writing and never revealed any hesitancy to do so. Or, rather, she never revealed any reluctance to him and other kin who were outside her circle of confidantes:

> In that well occupied female party there must have been many precious hours of silence during which the pen was busy at the little mahogany writing-desk, while Fanny Price, or Emma Woodhouse, or Anne Elliot was growing into beauty and interest. I have no doubt that I, and my sisters and cousins, in our visits to Chawton, frequently disturbed this mystic process, without having any idea of the mischief that we were doing; certainly we never should have guessed it by any signs of impatience or irritability in the writer.[46]

One of Austen's nieces, however, was able to recall Austen's writing with more certainty and specificity because older sisters of hers were allowed to hear works in progress. Marianne Knight advanced the "behind shut doors" imagery about her family's estate at Godmersham, which, along with the stories of the squeaky door and the blotting paper at Chawton, biographers have often evoked in order to describe Austen's working conditions. According to Marianne's reminiscence, when Austen stayed with the Knights in Kent, she shared her manuscripts with Fanny, Marianne's eldest sister, and probably with Lizzy, the next eldest sister, but only with them. As Marianne tells it, "I remember that when Aunt Jane came to us at Godmersham she used to bring the MS. of whatever novel she was writing with her, and would shut herself up with my elder sisters in one of the bedrooms to read them aloud. I and the younger ones used to hear peals of laughter through the door, and thought it very hard that we should be shut out from what was so delightful."[47]

In such restricted gatherings Austen received affirmation of her work as a writer. In accordance with feminine dutifulness and deference, she generally hid her work and kept silent about it. Even to show the pages of a manuscript, then, and to read from them was a striking, liberating change. Moreover, by sharing work in progress, she was not only acknowledging the fact of her products but the labor of creating them, and she was welcoming her female audience's participation in that labor. They laughed, but they also offered suggestions and criticisms. One of the youngest of her nieces, Louisa Knight, though no doubt excluded from Austen's private readings, later remembered—perhaps one of her older sisters, Fanny or Lizzy, told her—that Cassandra Austen tried to persuade her sister to change the ending of *Mansfield Park* by allowing Mr. Crawford to marry Fanny Price.[48] And one of Austen's letters to Fanny Knight suggests that they had debated the traits desirable for heroines.[49]

Because Austen's brothers did know that she was writing and publishing, we can compare the ways in which she represented her work to them and to contributors to her women's culture. A few of the remarks Austen made about her writing to female kin and friends and to her brothers were the same. She talked freely to them all about the financial arrangements she had with her publishers (Henry, of course, made many of them for her) and about her desire to make money from her books. She informed her brother Frank in 1813, for example, "You will be glad to hear that every Copy of S. & S. is sold & that it has brought me £140 besides the Copyright, if that shd ever be of any value.—I have now therefore written myself into £250—which only makes me long for more."[50] In response to an inquiry of her niece Fanny's in 1814, she expressed a similar sentiment, "It is not settled yet whether I *do* hazard a 2d Edition [of *Mansfield Park*]. We are to see Egerton today, when it will probably be determined.—People are more ready to borrow & praise, than to buy—which I cannot wonder at;—but tho' I like praise as well as anybody, I like what Edward calls *Pewter* too."[51]

But Austen volunteered less information to the male members of her family than she offered to her small female circle about works in progress, about what and when she was writing. Her allusion to a scene in *Mansfield Park* in a January 1813 letter that she wrote her sister indicates that Cassandra was very familiar with that still unfinished manuscript. By contrast, Austen mentioned it to Frank in July of 1813, when she had already completed the manuscript, telling him simply that a novel was "in hand."[52] And Henry embarked on his first reading of the completed novel in March, 1814, without any prior information on its plot or characters.[53] In a letter to Fanny Knight, written in 1817, we find more evidence that, despite his help with the business of publishing, Henry was—perhaps because he was not discreet enough to suit his sister—generally one of the last to learn of Austen's manuscripts. "Do not be surprised at finding Uncle Henry acquainted with my having another ready for publication," Austen wrote. "I could not say No when he asked me, but he knows nothing more of it."[54]

We can see an even more dramatic difference between what Austen said to contributors to her women's culture and what she said to her brothers and other members of her wider community in the way she represented herself as a writer and assessed her novels. Her biography-writing male relatives, beginning with Henry Austen, have insisted that she had little confidence in her work and was meekness itself in discussions of her writing.[55] More recently, literary critics Susan Gubar and Sandra Gilbert have radically altered this vision of the novelist by arguing that Austen consciously crafted modest, even self-abasing images of herself and her work: "With her self-deprecatory remarks about her inability to join 'strong manly, spirited sketches, full of Variety and Glow' with her 'little bit (two Inches wide) of Ivory,' Jane Austen perpetuated the belief among her friends that her art was just an accomplishment 'by a lady,' if anything 'rather too light and bright and sparkling.'"[56]

Austen's letters suggest that Gilbert and Gubar, though closer to the truth than biographers such as Henry Austen, are still only partially correct. Austen did indeed consciously construct self-deprecating images. She contributed them, however, only to the culture of the gentry. It was to her nephew James Edward that Austen represented her work as "the little bit (two Inches wide) of Ivory on which I work with so fine a Brush, as produces little effect after much labour."[57] To the Prince Regent's Librarian, J. S. Clarke, she offered a similarly self-deprecating pose: "I think I may boast myself to be, with all possible vanity, the most unlearned and uninformed female who ever dared to be an authoress."[58] Austen advanced such humble, albeit witty, self-representations with the intent, no doubt, of countering her society's general distrust of the femininity and gentility of women with public reputations as writers. She was always conscious of how she might appear to others if she were known as a writer. After the publication of *Pride and Prejudice*, a Miss Burdett expressed the desire to meet Austen. "I am rather frightened by hearing that she wishes to be introduced to *me*," Austen wrote her sister in dread of becoming a very unladylike public spectacle. "If I *am* a wild Beast, I cannot help it."[59]

In the discourse of her women's culture, Austen did not similarly depict herself as barely competent. Since her close friends generally promoted female assertiveness and pride in accomplishments, Austen could be sure of appreciative support when she announced to them the success of a dinner, a charitable act, some fine handiwork—or a piece of fiction. Thus, in her private discourse with female friends, Austen was able to develop a self-assured, even professionalized persona as a writer, a self-image that surely helped her to write. She was sometimes critical of or, to be more exact, sometimes a critic of her own writing but hardly in a self-demeaning way. When she told Cassandra that *Pride and Prejudice* was "too light, and bright, and sparkling," she was wondering if "the playfulness and epigrammatism of the general style" would be fully appreciated without "something unconnected with the story; an essay on writing, a critique on Walter Scott, or the history of Buonaparté, or anything that would form a contrast."[60]

She was also proud of her work. She spoke triumphantly to Cassandra, for example, about Elizabeth Bennet and the novel in which she figures, declaring her own superiority over those who either would not like or would not understand *Pride and Prejudice*: "I must confess that I think her as delightful a creature as ever appeared in print, and how I shall be able to tolerate those who do not like *her* at least I do not know. There are a few typical errors; and a 'said he,' or a 'said she,' would sometimes make the dialogue more immediately clear; but," Austen continued, adapting a passage from Scott's *Marmion*, no less, "'I do not write for such dull elves / As have not a great deal of ingenuity themselves.'"[61]

Only to women did she reveal the power she felt as an author. She may have pretended to a trivial "feminine" art before her nephew, but she was quite in earnest when she told her niece Anna about one of her manuscripts: "I *do* think you had better omit Lady Helena's postscript;—to those who are acquainted with P. & P. it will seem an Imitation."[62] Mine is the originating and original work, she was, in effect, declaring. She also admitted to Cassandra her enjoyment of her second publisher's deferential treatment. After complaining to John Murray, "a rogue of course," about the delays in the publication of *Emma*, she was "soothed & complimented" and happily enumerated Murray's gestures of respect: "He has lent us *Miss Williams* & *Scott*, & says that any book of his will always be at *my* service. . . . We are not to have the trouble of returning the sheets to Mr. Murray any longer, the Printer's boys bring & carry."[63]

Only with women friends did she bask in the compliments she received, knowing that they would share her pleasure. We know the names of some of those who admired her work, because she told them to Cassandra and Fanny. In a letter of 1813 she reported to her sister about *Pride and Prejudice*: "Lady Robert [Kerr] is delighted with P. and P., and really *was* so, as I understand, before she knew who wrote it. . . . And Mr. [Warren] Hastings! I am quite delighted with what such a man writes about it. Henry sent him the books after his return from Daylesford, but you will hear the letter too."[64] As she explained to Cassandra after describing in considerable detail Henry's enthusiastic response to *Mansfield Park*: "I tell you all the good I can, as I know how much you will enjoy it."[65] After mentioning the possibility of putting out a second edition of *Mansfield Park*, she similarly noted to Fanny: "I am very greedy & want to make the most of it;—but as you are much above caring about money, I shall not plague you with any particulars.—The pleasures of Vanity are more within your comprehension, & you will enter into mine, at receiving the *praise* which every now & then comes to me, through some channel or other."[66]

The Austen life-writing tradition has not utterly ignored the women to whom Austen was particularly close while she produced her six novels. Park Honan's recent *Jane Austen: Her Life* is the only work, however, to call attention repeatedly and appreciatively to Austen's close female friends, when she was living at Chawton and earlier.[67] It also singles out Cassandra's support, emotional *and* intellectual.[68] Indeed, describing life at the cottage, Honan suggests that Jane Austen was "actively helped by" the "critical opinions" of Martha Lloyd as well as Cassandra.[69] But *Jane Austen: Her Life* does not situate these female bonds in the more general context of a women's culture. Thus it cannot do more than hint, and then only in descriptions of Jane and Cassandra's interactions, that such ties permitted greater freedom in behavior and discourse than did the community's overall culture.[70] Other biographies give considerably less credit to Austen's female ties, even at Chawton. Because these studies have generally overlooked the difficulties for women who wished to write in a community committed to the domestic ideology, they have missed the significance of female ties for Austen's career. They have carefully mapped the Chawton Cottage inmates' daily activities—the gardening, the household chores, the reading, sewing, and walking. They have even asserted the compatibility of Austen's writing and relationships with women. But they have understood compatibility to mean simply that Austen was able to work because her female relations and friends didn't disturb her.

James Edward Austen-Leigh first put forward this vision when he described "that well occupied female party" at Chawton in which "there must have been many precious hours of silence" during which Austen composed.[71] While emphasizing Edward Austen's gift of Chawton Cottage, W. and R. A. Austen-Leigh also noted "the quiet of her home" and the "absence of distraction."[72] Elizabeth Jenkins, in her *Jane Austen*, has elaborated on references to the quiet home, imagining a society very like a nunnery: "The many long spells of quiet when the others had walked out, her mother was in the garden and she had the room to herself; or when the domestic party was assembled, sewing and reading, with nothing but the soft stir of utterly familiar sounds and no tones but the low, infrequent ones of beloved, familiar voices—these were the conditions in which she created *Mansfield Park, Emma,* and *Persuasion.*"[73]

Biographers have made the women so quiet and static that when chroniclers discuss Austen's writing, her companions sometimes seem to disappear. Life-writers, in fact, often invoke visions of Austen as a solitary genius or even of her double life at this point in their narratives. For James Edward Austen-Leigh, the quiet of Austen's female household enabled the "mystic process" of creation.[74] To David Cecil, whose vision of the female society at Chawton is a good deal less reverent than Elizabeth Jenkins's, Austen's life there "apparently so stagnant, served rather to provide the needed time and incentive for her genius to operate."[75] Because none of them supposes that Austen had a community at Chawton worthy of or necessary to her talents, many life-writers have insisted, as John Halperin does, on Austen's "loneliness" as a writer.[76] Even Jane Aiken Hodge, whose biography, *Only a Novel: The Double Life of Jane Austen,* shows a good deal more interest in Austen's relationships with women, has maintained that "the artist is inevitably alone" when describing Austen during this period.[77]

It was not her housemates' quiet or apparent capacity for invisibility that enabled Austen to write her novels. Before and after she moved to Chawton, her all-female "family" served as the crucial bridge between modest, self-effacing femininity and the self-assertion and self-expression of authoring. They formed a social circle among whom she could produce fiction and to whom she could talk—easily, confidently—about that work. We may never know the specific catalyst for the novels on which Austen embarked in 1809, but this much is clear: Had she only devoted herself to the interests of male and female neighbors and kin, had she always spoken a discourse filled up with their voices and concerns, she could not have become a novelist. Thus her alternative culture enabled her to do something for which the gentry's culture alone did not prepare her and to diverge considerably from the domestic ideal of womanhood without coming into conflict with it.

CHAPTER 5

Assuming Spinsterhood

1

ON December 3, 1802, Jane Austen rejected a proposal of marriage from Harris Bigg-Wither. Rather, she said yes on December 2, reportedly spent a sleepless night, and retracted her consent irrevocably the following morning. The final decision is striking not only because marriage was very important to gentlewomen like Austen but also because this marriage offer was especially desirable. The suitor was the brother of two of Austen's closest women friends and the eldest surviving son of a much respected, wealthy landowner, Lovelace Bigg-Wither. The proposal offered far more, materially, than the portionless Jane Austen had a right to expect. Then, too, she was almost twenty-seven years old. Although many gentlewomen, Harris's own sister Catherine among them, married when they were in their late twenties or older, these were late marriages by the norms of the day.

All of Jane Austen's biographers have had to come to terms with this key life event. With very few exceptions, they have treated her decision only as a measure of her and her suitor's fitness for romance. Like Jane Austen's own contemporaries, they have viewed the single woman's status as unattractive, even shameful, and have felt compelled to defend her against their own pejorative assumptions about loveless, passionless spinsters. Preoccupied with this defense, most Austen biographers have not considered that her writing may have been a factor in her decision.[1] By 1802 Austen had already written three novels and tried to have one published. Even with the support of a few critical and appreciative female readers, a married Jane Austen probably could not have continued to write novels or ventured to publish them.

This chapter, then, carries forward my earlier discussion of the enabling conditions of Austen's career by focusing on her crucial decision not to marry. It looks first at the way we have previously been asked by biographers to view Austen's rejection of Bigg-Wither's offer. It next proposes an alternative interpretation of Austen's response, showing how the decision may have been influenced by her literary ambitions. This chapter also draws on the framework of dual cultures because with that framework we can better appreciate the options a novel-writing Austen confronted in 1802 and the meaning of each option *for her.*

All accounts of Jane Austen's decision in 1802 are hypothetical. On the basis of currently available evidence, no one can produce an authoritative interpretation of Austen's response to Bigg-Wither's marriage proposal. Partly in the interests of coherent story-telling, however, biographers have tended to create unhesitating, gap-free narratives. Because Austen apparently struggled with her decision for several hours, life-writers sometimes formulate their explanations of that decision as "the thoughts that must have passed through her mind during that sleepless December night."[2] In fact, we have no direct access to those thoughts. Austen's extant letters come to a halt in the late spring of 1801 and do not resume until the fall of 1804. Although a few Austen descendants have left reports of the event, as we shall see, their explanations of Austen's reasons for refusing Bigg-Wither are far from conclusive.

Like all other interpretations, then, my own representation of Austen's decision in 1802 has the status of a hypothesis, but I hope to show that it is truer, at least to what we know of Austen's values and resources at that time. Moreover, when we turn to the life Austen created following on her decision not to marry, as we do in the last two sections of this chapter, we move to firmer ground. Because biographers have generally assumed that there would be little to say about an aging unmarried woman's life, many have been unwilling to take a close look at it. But the framework of dual cultures also enables us to gather substantial evidence indicating that a seemingly drab spinsterhood obscured a way of life obviously conducive to writing and not accidental in its arrangement.

In portraying Austen's experience after 1802, I do not mean to imply that we can or should use the later life retroactively as evidence to support a particular account of her 1802 decision not to marry Bigg-Wither. We cannot rule out the possibility, even if it seems unlikely, that Austen discovered her vocation only after she had relinquished all opportunities to marry. Rather, I provide an analysis of Austen's single life after 1802 in order to show that, although Austen's women's culture and her desire to write *may* have influenced her decision not to marry, her choice of singlehood and the women's culture that made that choice viable did make a difference to her subsequent literary career. And certainly, by the time Austen began publishing novels, she knew it.

2
—

James Edward Austen-Leigh's *A Memoir of Jane Austen* was the first work to allude to the novelist's rejection of Harris Bigg-Wither, and it set the terms for almost all subsequent discussions of the event. Austen-Leigh referred to the incident in order to assure readers that, although Austen never married, she was lovable: "She did not indeed pass through life without being the object of warm affection. In her youth she had declined the addresses of a gentleman who had the recommendations of good character, and connections, and position in life, of everything, in fact, except the subtle power of touching her heart."[3] Although Austen-Leigh evidently felt a need to introduce the subject of romance, he did not invent this view of the Bigg-Wither incident. He had apparently applied to some of his relatives for information on his aunt's long-ago marital prospects, and they had offered him the romantic rendering of the Bigg-Wither affair.[4] A glance at the origins of their representations should inspire caution.

Not surprisingly, knowledge of Jane Austen's response to Bigg-Wither's proposal circulated originally only among female Austens. Jane Austen apparently confided in her sister-in-law Mary Austen just after the incident occurred. Mary subsequently passed on the story to her stepdaughter, Anna Austen Lefroy, and to her daughter, Caroline Austen, and Anna discussed it with one of her own daughters, Fanny Lefroy. Both Caroline and Anna's daughter, Fanny, recorded what they heard and what they or perhaps Mary and Anna had conjectured. In addition, Cassandra Austen seems to have shown some letters referring to the incident (which she later destroyed) to her brother Frank's daughter, Catherine Hubback.[5] What those letters actually said or how much Jane Austen told her sister-in-law, we will never know. Nor can we assess whether any material was lost or added in transmissions of the incident from one female relative to another. It is also quite possible that the women who recorded Jane Austen's secrets or told them to James Edward Austen-Leigh when he was writing his *Memoir* withheld or changed information to fit their private stories for immediate or eventual passage into the general culture.

Nevertheless, Austen-Leigh confidently portrayed Austen's refusal of Bigg-Wither as an issue of love, and subsequent life-writers have generally followed suit. With the same worries about spinsterhood but with more psychological sophistication, most twentieth-century biographers, however, have slightly altered the angle from which they viewed Austen-Leigh's concern. Austen may have been lovable, but was *she* able to love? Their interpretations of Austen's refusal are in effect defenses against the charge of heartlessness. Austen, they maintain, rejected Bigg-Wither because she *wanted* to love. She was, according to Elizabeth Jenkins, merely fastidious, "difficult to please, but not incapable of being pleased."[6]

The suitor had to have been unappealing. Although until quite recently biographers have not tried to find out just how unappealing he was, they have made what they could out of small bits of readily available evidence. They have pointed to his age—he was younger than Austen—and to a few references in Austen's letters mentioning ill health. Elizabeth Jenkins, for example, has described him as "invalidish."[7] Digging deeper, though selectively, John Halperin learned from an early twentieth-century history of the suitor's family that he was "a recluse who stammered and had a mean temper."[8] But Park Honan has recently provided the fullest and most unpleasant picture of Harris Bigg-Wither.

Honan has relied on that same family history and, for the first time in the twentieth century, the accounts of Fanny Lefroy and Caroline Austen. None of those sources is unmixed. The author of *Materials for a History of the Wither Family* described the suitor as "diligent in magisterial work, kind to the poor, and beloved by his family. Owing to his stammering, he was a man of few words, and rather avoided society. He was, however, very hospitable in his own house, but quick-tempered."[9] Caroline Austen, writing in 1870, referred to him as "very plain in person—awkward, & even uncouth in manner—nothing but his size to recommend him—he was a fine big man." But then she added, "I believe the wife he did get was very fond of him, & that they were a happy couple—He had sense in plenty & went through life very respectably, as a country gentlemen."[10] But Honan's representation is unambiguous: "He was silent, rude, awkward, difficult with his loving father, badly inhibited by a cruel stutter. . . . he was an amiable, silent giant of 21. . . . He was, at the moment, acceptable to almost no one."[11]

So peculiar does he appear in personality and appearance here that it is surprising to discover that both Anne Lefroy and her son, J. H.

George Lefroy, mention him in letters they wrote in the first years of the nineteenth century as if he were an ordinary member of their society rather than a cross between Goofy and Frankenstein's monstrous progeny. He appears in their letters dining at the Ashe rectory, going out shooting with J. H. George Lefroy and another companion, John Harwood, and grieving deeply over the death of his brother-in-law, the Reverend William Heathcote, to whom he was particularly attached. In 1804 Anne Lefroy met and liked Anne Howe Frith, the woman with whom Harris found consolation after Jane Austen refused him, and in November, when they had just married and were staying in the neighborhood, she hoped to "see a good deal of them."[12] The Lefroys' comments on Bigg-Wither serve as an apt reminder that efforts to prove Jane Austen's capacity to love have required sometimes extreme assertions of her suitor's unlovableness. And none of the very different assessments, of course, tells us how Jane Austen perceived the suitor or his offer.

Most biographers have made yet another case for Austen's ability to love with an incident that occurred a few years prior to Bigg-Wither's proposal. The story of this incident was also originally confined to female members of the Austen family. Cassandra recounted it to a few nieces, one of whom told her daughter, and they, again, shared it with James Edward Austen-Leigh when he was preparing his *Memoir*. The versions that Austen's female relatives recorded for Austen-Leigh contain several contradictory details, but one general outline does emerge.[13] In 1798 (or 1799, or 1801) the Austen sisters and their parents visited a seaside resort—probably in Devonshire—where Jane was attracted to a gentleman, possibly a clergyman. When they parted, he expressed a strong desire to see her again. He may even have asked to visit at Steventon. He died soon afterward, however, before he had a chance to propose marriage. *Or* (and this has been a less popular version with biographers) he was not interested in Austen, nor did he die after he parted with her. In this version of the story, with wonderfully ironic justice, Cassandra meets him many years after her sister's death and finds him "stout, red-faced and middle-aged."[14] Austen's emotional response to what was either loss or rejection remains one of the more elusive parts of the story. One relative's testimony—"This attachment must have been very deep"[15]—is contradicted by another's: "Aunt Jane never *had* any attachment that overclouded her happiness, for long. *This* had not gone far enough to leave misery behind."[16] Nevertheless, many of Austen's biographers have confidently asserted that Austen's strong affection for this suitor made it impossible for her to accept Harris Bigg-Wither's proposal. According to David Cecil, for example, Austen discovered when Bigg-Wither made his offer, "the truth she was to state so poignantly in her last novel *Persuasion*: namely that women have a sad ability to go on loving when hope is gone."[17] Austen wouldn't marry without love, and she wouldn't marry Harris Bigg-Wither because she was *still* in love.

If Cecil draws on a nineteenth-century image of womanhood (created by Austen herself), John Halperin, author of another, recent full-scale biography, has shaped his portrait according to a popular late twentieth-century stereotype of women: his Jane Austen could be a frequenter of singles bars. Apparently haunted, like so many other biographers, by pejorative, patriarchal attitudes toward the unmarried woman, he shows not just that Austen knew love but that she was "a veteran of potentially romantic encounters."[18] In his essay, "Jane Austen's Lovers," Harris Bigg-Wither and the mysterious seaside suitor are merely two of the troop of men, twelve in all, who either rejected a pining Austen or pursued an uninterested one. If the logic of his claims—can one be a veteran of potentialities?—or the banal and formulaic quality of the romances, as Halperin renders them, does not undermine the confidence of his readers, the identities of the suitors themselves should.

We are told, for example, that in 1801 Austen, then living in Bath, was hoping to receive a proposal of marriage from a Mr. Evelyn: "The novelist seemed to have her fingers crossed. The day after writing this [a letter to Cassandra] she was taken out by Mr. Evelyn for a ride in his phaeton; but the gentleman, simply making good on a promise, offered no other declaration. That was that."[19] But there are a few things about Mr. Evelyn that Halperin overlooked, although the twenty-five-year-old Austen would not have ignored them: the gentleman happened to be a sixty-seven-year-old married man. Austen, Halperin also tells us, was "quite taken" with Stephen Rumbold Lushington, whom she met while at Godmersham in 1813. But "he did not," according to the biographer, "reciprocate Jane's partiality for him"[20]—perhaps, as Austen, again, would have known, because he too was married and had been so since 1797.

Halperin ignores the apparently trivial detail of marital status in his hunt for suitors. Moreover, many of the eligible men whom he rounds up for Austen can be cast as romantic figures only when he misreads Austen's responses to them, skipping over some of her remarks and ignoring the teasing quality of others. In 1815, for example, while staying with her brother Henry in London, Austen made the acquaintance of Charles Haden, the surgeon taking care of her brother, and, according to Halperin, was "knocked over by the advent of this sexy new playmate."[21] Austen did praise him to her sister as "our Precious" and as "something between a Man & an Angel," but the exaggerated sentimentality of her diction suggests that Austen was *playing* at adoration.[22] Furthermore, the novelist and Haden did not "manage to dine alone together several evenings running," as Halperin claims,[23] because her niece Fanny was also staying at Henry Austen's home. In actuality, Austen suspected that Haden might be attracted to Fanny, though he was never taken seriously as a suitor by any member of Henry Austen's household. In one of her letters to her sister, Austen noted with amusement: "Henry calls himself stronger every day & Mr. H. keeps on approving his Pulse which seems generally better than ever—but still they will not let him be well. . . . Perhaps when Fanny is gone he will be allowed to recover faster."[24]

It is easy to recognize the late twentieth-century view shaping Halperin's interpretation. Some of us may believe that men and women should be romantically "experienced," but did the late eighteenth- and early nineteenth-century gentry wish women to be "veterans" of romance? Even preoccupations with Austen's romantic life less quantitative than Halperin's are somewhat anachronistic. Although the gentry's ideology of domesticity advocated marriages based on love and esteem, it did not neglect prudential motives. Ideally, gentlemen and ladies were to marry for love and economic support—a "competence"—but many, such as a Mrs. Alexander, Anne Powlett's friend, married for the economic support alone. As Powlett explained the union in 1799: "Mr. A. seems a very good kind of Man, but I should not have selected him for the elegant and lively Mary Anne Browne— But *money* . . . has incalculable charms—and I trust she will find it make up for every other deficiency."[25] Caroline Austen's general assessment of Jane Austen's social world is consistent with Anne Powlett's description of Mrs. Alexander's case; writing about Bigg-Wither's proposal in 1870, she recalled that "a great many would have taken him *without* love."[26]

To understand Austen's refusal of Harris Bigg-Wither, then, we need to keep an eye on her particular context. The question is not whether she could love, or whether she did love, but why she wouldn't marry, as so many of her contemporaries did, without love. If we put love aside, we can begin to consider the choice Austen faced in 1802: on one side, a probably nonromantic but definitely materially advantageous union; on the other side—what? There must have been another positive option, though her decision in 1802 has been frequently seen as a negative choice only, as a decision "not to." Why couldn't the other choice have included writing as well as genteel poverty?

The same biographers who repeatedly refer to Austen as a genius do not bring her talent and interests into view when portraying her decision-making.[27] They tend to sever and isolate her genius from her historical life as a woman. On this occasion, Austen is customarily portrayed as a feeling, principled, and ordinary woman. But this tendency to compartmentalize has made it difficult to imagine the obvious. By 1802 Austen had already written three novels and had tried to publish one. In 1803, less than a year after she had turned Bigg-Wither down, she had Henry Austen send another of her works to the publishing firm of Crosby. She wanted to write. Wouldn't she have thought about her writing and about her chances of being able to continue it when considering Bigg-Wither's marriage proposal? Wouldn't she have thought about the offer as a genius/artist as well as a woman? This representation of Austen's options is hypothetical, but it is at least consistent with her sociohistorical context.

Writing and marriage were not necessarily mutually exclusive. To be sure, the number of women writers who never married climbed substantially after 1780,[28] and those who did wed, literary critic Janet Todd has surmised, had a higher incidence of failed marriages than the population as a whole.[29] Nevertheless, many late eighteenth- and early nineteenth-century women writers married and stayed married. My claim is more circumscribed and specific: a woman in Austen's community was unlikely to be able to sustain an ongoing commitment to writing within marriage.

In a culture committed to genteel domesticity, wives had much more social repute than unmarried women. Sarah Smith summed up the attitude of her culture when she assured her daughter Elizabeth Chute, a few months after she wed: "You are now of much more consequence in life."[30] But marriage also potentially intensified a woman's experience of subordination by increasing her domestic ties and duties. A husband's authoritative desires and children—possibly large numbers of them—demanded self-abnegation. Elizabeth Chute, who did not have any children until she and her husband adopted Caroline Wiggett in 1803, still found it hard to control her own time and activities. Her husband and brother-in-law, as she lamented, were only too apt to interrupt and disturb her.[31] Imagine, then, the experience of Anne Howe Frith, after she married Harris Bigg-Wither in 1804. She entered a new, extensive set of relationships with her husband's kin and neighbors and bore ten children in the next eighteen years. In contrast, singleness would have enabled Austen to write by offering her a freedom from *some* of the constraints of domestic femininity without challenging her community's gender ideology. Indeed, Austen's selection of a single life would have been the only strategy for serious writing available to a woman with a strong allegiance to the gentry's culture.[32]

In making up her mind, Austen was likely to have considered her women's culture, which did not, of course, encourage participants to resist marriage. As we have seen, it was not positioned in opposition to the gentry's culture but rather served the dominant culture. It supported the wider culture's ideological insistence on marriage as the proper destiny of women. Moreover, it enabled women to endure the potentially stressful, feminine passivity required of them during courtships. Although women could only hope to be selected as marriage partners, they could at least voice their desires and disappointments to those who would encourage or comfort them. In the private and candid communications that played such a central role in the women's culture, women thus gained actual or imagined control over their experiences.

Jane Austen's letters to Cassandra in the late 1790s provide some of her confidential assessments of the local marriage market and her position in it. She routinely described to her sister the balls she attended with a focus on the appeal and availability of men and on her own popularity. "Our ball was very thin," she wrote Cassandra in 1798, "but by no means unpleasant. There were thirty-one people, and only eleven ladies out of the number, and but five single women in the room."[33] In a letter of 1799 she observed: "I do not think I was very much in request. People were rather apt not to ask me till they could not help it; one's consequence, you know, varies so much at times without any particular reason. There was one gentleman, an officer of the Cheshire, a very good-looking young man, who, I was told, wanted very much to be introduced to me; but as he did not want it quite enough to take much trouble in effecting it, we never could bring it about."[34]

Austen's letters show us not only one woman confiding in another about courtship and marriage but a chain of such communications among women. We know from the letter that Mrs. Austen wrote Mary Lloyd in 1796, welcoming her into the family, that Martha Lloyd's interest in a Mr. W. was the subject of secretive discussions among Jane, Cassandra, Martha, and Mary.[35] Martha's hopes were eventually frustrated, and it took her some time to get the better of her disappointment. In October, 1798 Austen and Cassandra were still discussing Martha's response to the collapse of her prospects: "I hear that Martha is in better looks and spirits than she has enjoyed for a long time," Austen wrote to her sister, "and I flatter myself she will now be able to jest openly about Mr. W."[36]

Austen's women's culture generally promoted women's marriages and coexisted compatibly with marital ties. Just after Elizabeth Chute married, her close friend Elizabeth Gosling wrote to say as much: "I know it is a common opinion that marriage dissolves youthfull friendships, but tho' it may often be the case, it surely is not a necessary consequence of marriage, and I hope we shall prove it for I feel that whatever may be my own situation in life, I shall take a most lively interest in your's."[37] They and many other female friends did prove that they could sustain while married not only the friendships envisioned by the domestic ideology but also the bonds of a women's culture. For many women, marriage even gave rise to or intensified such bonds with other women, namely, their husband's female relations. Mary Bramston and Henrietta Hicks Beach, for example, were originally brought together through Wither Bramston, Mary's husband and Henrietta's cousin. Marriage also had the capacity to bring women of the same family even closer. Had Cassandra or Jane Austen married, one might have been able to offer the other, unmarried sister a home later in life.

And yet, if a woman had other reasons not to marry, the women's culture could serve as an inducement for remaining single. It provided her with compensations for the absence of marriage and other heterosexual relationships, often when—and where—least expected. Women sustained their close relationships within the context of their community and often literally within the context of its social occasions. A prediction Austen made in a letter to her sister in 1798, for example, conveys the multiple functions of balls—as occasions for mingling with neighbors, putting herself in the way of meeting eligible men, *and* having comfortable, personal chats with women friends. "I expect a very stupid Ball," she claimed, "there will be nobody worth dancing with, & nobody worth talking to but Catherine; for I believe Mrs. Lefroy will not be there."[38] In the absence of eligible men at balls, the pleasures of female friendship were even made to stand in lieu of courtship: "There was a scarcity of Men in general, & a still greater scarcity of any that were good for much," Austen confided to her sister in 1800. "I danced nine dances out of ten, five with Stephen Terry, T. Chute & James Digweed & four with Catherine."[39] These descriptions reveal that women always could find at least some of the social and emotional (if not economic) benefits of marriage in their friendships, *even* in the ballroom.

And Austen was quite aware of these benefits. In her description of a visit she made in 1799, she expresses a consciousness that female relationships within the context of her patriarchal community's socializing could temper the marginality she was already beginning to experience as a single woman in a world of genteel domesticity. She and Martha Lloyd were staying at James and Mary Austen's home at Deane. The couple's infant son was still very much the focus of their household: he had just been christened and Mary, according to her sister-in-law, was only beginning to be "more reasonable about her child's beauty."[40] The two unmarried women's status as bystanders to the important domestic event of childbirth was underscored, Austen's rendering suggests, by their spatial position in the small parsonage. Though relegated to the small space of the nursery, however, they managed to turn crowding into the snugness so often generated among members of the women's culture:

> Martha kindly made room for me in her bed, which was the shut-up one in the new nursery. Nurse and the child slept upon the floor, and there we all were in some confusion and great comfort. The bed did exceedingly well for us, both to lie awake in and talk till two o'clock, and to sleep in the rest of the night. I love Martha better than ever, and I mean to go and see her, if I can, when she gets home.[41]

In 1802 Austen would have known that she would not have to live a single life of genteel poverty in isolation. She had already come to see that her women's culture was an important social and emotional resource in the event that she did not marry.[42] This resource must have been additionally attractive because she was already drawing from it the small audience for her developing novels. As we have seen, Austen turned to members of her women's culture for acknowledgment of her creative labors, for encouragement and criticism, for opportunities to express pride in her work and a professional writer's identity. She also found in it a rich social life that may have made writing possible by offsetting the social degradations of singleness.

3

In 1802, it is plausible to conjecture, Jane Austen knew that turning Harris Bigg-Wither down was a conclusive gesture, made in order to avoid the heaviest burdens of domestic femininity and to preserve some time and liberty to write. Moreover, within another five years she was chafing at the everyday obligations imposed even on unmarried women. Still, her divergence from the path marked out by the ideology of domesticity was far from total. Her letters show that in the years after 1802 she continued to endorse marriage for women and tried to help her unmarried friends to "circulate"—if only by getting out of their way. In 1805 while she was visiting Harriet Bridges, one of Elizabeth Austen's sisters, Harriet received a ticket for a "grand ball" at Deal. As Austen wrote to her sister, Harriet was at first "disinclined" to go, "but at length, after many debates, she was persuaded by me and herself together to accept the ticket."[43] Austen also continued to be an earnest advocate of women's deferential role. On her niece Fanny's sixteenth birthday in January 1809, for example, she informed her sister, then at Godmersham: "We thought of and talked of her yesterday with sincere affection, and wished her a long enjoyment of all the happiness to which she seems born.—While she gives happiness to those about her, she is pretty sure of her own share."[44]

Alongside these conventional avowals, her letters increasingly express an undercurrent of complaints about social obligations. By 1807 and 1808 that undercurrent becomes quite distinct. Although Austen also wished "to give happiness to those about her," she was finding entertaining troublesome and sometimes tedious. "When you receive this," she wrote to her sister in these years, "our guests will be all gone or going; and I shall be left to the comfortable disposal of my time, to ease of mind from the torments of rice puddings and apple dumplings, and probably to regret that I did not take more pains to please them all."[45] And in 1808 she compared the effort of giving an evening party to the work and suffering of childbirth. "About an hour & half after your toils on Wednesday ended, ours began," she told Cassandra, who was staying at Godmersham, "at seven o'clock, Mrs. Harrison, her two daughters & two Visitors, with Mr. Debary & his eldest sister walked in; & our Labour was not a great deal shorter than poor Elizabeth's, for it was past eleven before we were delivered."[46]

These complaints can be heard in her letters with growing frequency. In the winter of 1813 Austen repeatedly mentioned, for example, the unpleasantness of playing hostess. In February she wrote to Cassandra, "Before I set out [to Alton] we were visited by Mrs Edwards, & while I was gone Miss Beckford & Maria, & Miss Woolls & Harriet B. called, all of whom my Mother was glad to see, & I very glad to escape."[47] And to Martha she confided less than two weeks later, "We are going to be all alive from this forenoon to tomorrow afternoon;—it will be over when you receive this, & you may think of me as one not sorry that it is so. George, Henry & William [her nephews] will soon be here & are to stay the night—and tomorrow the 2 Deedes' & Henry Bridges will be added to our party;—we shall then have an early dinner & dispatch them all to Winchester."[48] In November of 1815, in London staying with Henry, she similarly longed to be free of guests. She wrote home to Cassandra, "We have been very little plagued with visitors this last week, I remember only Miss Herries the Aunt, but I am in terror for to-day, a fine bright Sunday."[49]

Austen's novel writing primarily accounts for her yearnings to engage in fewer visits and dinners and all other ceremonious efforts to please others. She expressed the wish to Cassandra and Martha to avoid guests or to dispatch them quickly in the winter of 1813, just after she had received *Pride and Prejudice* from the printer and while she was busy writing *Mansfield Park*. And when she wrote to her sister from London in November, 1815, she was in the midst of correcting the proofs of *Emma*. She herself suggested in 1816 that the social role marked out for women by the gentry's culture inhibited her writing:

> I enjoyed Edward's [their nephew's] company very much . . . & yet I was not sorry when friday came. It had been a busy week, & I wanted a few days quiet, & exemption from the Thought & contrivances which any sort of company gives.—I often wonder how *you* can find time for what you do, in addition to the care of the House;—and how good Mrs. West c^d have written such Books & collected so many hard words, with all her family cares, is still more a matter of astonishment! Composition seems to me Impossible, with a head full of Joints of Mutton & doses of rhubarb.[50]

Austen wished for fewer social obligations because she wanted the time for writing and because she was gradually losing interest in such socializing. Her desire to be free of some of the burdens of domesticity, probably a later, ongoing expression of the *cause* of her 1802 decision not to marry, was also an *effect* of that decision. By choosing to remain single, Austen had made herself peripheral to her community's social occasions, a position not lost on her. In a letter to her sister in 1813 she whimsically described her role at an evening party: "By the bye, as I must leave off being young, I find many Douceurs in being a sort of Chaperon for I am put on the Sofa near the Fire & can drink as much wine as I like."[51]

While the gentry put aging single women such as Austen on the sidelines, Austen's marginality increasingly made her feel both remote from and exhausted by various public performances of civility. Playing hostess was not the only effort that she was glad to avoid. Although she worried in 1813 that Fanny might be missing an opportunity to meet eligible men, when her twenty-year-old niece decided against attending a ball, Austen was relieved that she did not have to go: "*I* was very glad to be spared the trouble of dressing & going & being weary before it was half over."[52] Austen called attention to the emotional strain of making polite conversation in a letter to Fanny in

1814: "Though I like Miss H.M. as much as one can at my time of Life after a day's acquaintance, it is uphill work to be talking to those whom one knows so little."[53]

Her discontented remarks about social obligations help us to understand an observation that Austen's niece Caroline made about her and Cassandra. "I beleive my two Aunts were not accounted very good dressers," she recalled, "and were thought to have taken to the garb of middle age unnecessarily soon."[54] Austen was apparently exploiting contemporary stereotypes about spinsters to her advantage. Assuming the dress of rejected, resigned, and inconspicuous women, Jane Austen and her sister Cassandra were presenting themselves as their community was most apt to see (or ignore) its unmarried women. In this manner, although Austen would never have rejected the gentry's culture and its responsibilities, she was able to recede from some of the domestic woman's social duties.

By assuming the guise of spinsterhood, Austen may also have been able to reserve more private time to spend with her most intimate female friends. As the years passed, Austen became increasingly oriented toward the culture that had made possible her decision not to marry as well as her adult writing. Whether she wrote in the company of her female friends or not—and when she was with some of them she did not—Austen could be more self-assertive as well as more comfortable in the greater informality and equality of these relationships. Austen was, of course, critical of and indeed did not care for some of the women she knew well. Although, for example, she had been very close to Mary Lloyd in the late 1780s and the first half of the 1790s, Austen found her bossy, pretentious, and restless after her marriage to Austen's eldest brother, James, in 1797. Conversely, not all women in her circle liked Austen or her writing ability. Anna Austen Lefroy recalled that Elizabeth Austen, Edward's wife, was not fond of the novelist: "She very much preferred the elder sister—a little talent went a great way with the G Bs [probably a shorthand for Elizabeth Austen's kin, the Bridges family, whose Kent estate was Goodnestone]."[55]

Although Austen did not have affectionate or consistently affectionate feelings for all the women she knew well, she did have several emotionally fulfilling ties. Austen's niece Anna Austen Lefroy particularly remembered the intimacy between Jane and Cassandra: "They were so much to each other those Sisters! they seemed to live a life to themselves, & that nobody but themselves knew."[56] The sisters' bond with Martha—"the friend & sister under every circumstance," as Jane told Cassandra in 1808—was drawn even tighter when they and their mother set up housekeeping with her in 1805.[57] And in the years after

1802, Catherine and Alethea Bigg remained good friends to the sisters despite Austen's rejection of their brother Harris's proposal. So dear and familiar were the Bigg sisters that other women could remind Austen of them. In 1805 Austen visited Elizabeth Austen's sisters, Marianne and Harriet Bridges, and reported to her sister the resemblance between Marianne Bridges and Catherine Bigg: "So striking is the voice and manner of speaking that I seem to be really hearing Catherine, and once or twice have been on the point of calling Harriot 'Alethea.' "[58]

Over time some of Austen's bonds with women changed, as in the case of her friendship with Mary (Lloyd) Austen. Some ended; her cousin Jane Cooper, for example, to whom she had been affectionately attached from girlhood, died in a carriage accident in 1798. Anne Lefroy died when she fell from a horse in 1804. But Austen also developed new ties after 1802: to Anne Sharp, whom she first met in 1805 when Sharp was the governess at Godmersham; to Harriet Bridges, at least for a period of time around 1805; and to Catherine Knight. Although she had known the older woman for many years, probably since her childhood, she and Cassandra seem to have become particularly close to Mrs. Knight around 1807. The novelist also found warm friends in her oldest nieces, Anna and Fanny, as the two girls neared adulthood.

Austen's letters portray the sisters' ongoing efforts to be with these friends during or between the many social events in which it was their duty to participate. Although they gave priority to their social obligations, they preferred and, when possible, quietly arranged the more self-gratifying interactions of female intimacies. In May of 1811, for example, Austen was looking for a time during the summer to invite Anne Sharp for a visit. "I have a magnificent project," she announced to her sister:

> The Cookes have put off their visit to us; they are not well enough to leave home at present, & we have no chance of seeing them till I do not know when—probably never, in this house. This circumstance has made me think the present time would be favourable for Miss Sharp's coming to us; it seems a more disengaged period with us, than we are likely to have later in the summer.[59]

Austen also sought to spend time with Martha, Catherine, and Alethea without the inevitable intrusions of other people and the duties and decorum their appearances introduced. "I hope," Austen wrote to her sister in 1808 from Godmersham, "by this early return I am sure of seeing Catherine & Alethea;—& I propose that either with or without them you & I & Martha shall have a snug fortnight while my Mother is at Steventon."[60] And in 1809 she laments to Cassandra, who was now at Godmersham, "We shall not have a Month of Martha after your return—and that Month will be a very interrupted and broken one; but we shall enjoy ourselves the more, when we *can* get a quiet half hour together."[61] Even in January of 1817, when Austen was already suffering from bad health, she wrote encouragingly to Alethea: "We have no chance we know of seeing you between Streatham and Winchester: you go the other road and are engaged to two or three houses; if there should be any change, however, you know how welcome you would be."[62]

A similar wish to enjoy the company of Mrs. Knight appears in a letter Austen wrote to her sister describing a visit she paid the widow in 1808. Mrs. Knight had a great many visitors while Austen was staying with her, and Austen herself had several visits to pay while in Canterbury. It is, she told Cassandra, "a matter of wonder to me, that Mrs. K. & I should ever have been ten minutes alone, or have had any leisure for comfortable Talk.—Yet we had time to say a little of Everything."[63] Austen also enjoyed finding or creating occasions when she and Fanny—"almost another Sister," as Austen told Cassandra in a letter of 1808—could be together undisturbed.[64] In December 1815 while aunt and niece were staying at Henry Austen's, Austen reported to her sister: "Fanny & I were very snug by ourselves, as soon as we were satisfied about our Invalid's [Henry's] being safe at Hanwell.—By Manoeuvring & good luck we foiled all the Malings attempts upon us. Happily I caught a little cold on wednesday, the morns we were in Town, which we made very useful."[65]

Anna Austen Lefroy has provided one of the few testimonies of what some of those "snug" moments, free of the duties of civility, must have been like. Between 1812 and 1817 Anna saw a good deal of her two aunts. As she tells it:

> It was my amusement during one summer visit [at Chawton Cottage] to procure novels from a circulating Library at Alton, & after running them over to relate the stories of them to Aunt Jane, it was *her* amusement also, as she sat over some needle work, work of charity I must observe in which I fear that I took no other part—& greatly we both enjoyed it & so did Aunt C. assuredly & in her quiet way with one piece of nonsense leading to another she wd. exclaim How *can* you both be so foolish! & entreat us not to make her laugh so much.[66]

Austen's behavior in these tête-à-têtes offers a fitting emblem of the way she handled her dual cultural allegiances. Even during these high-spirited sessions—and her sister's reprimands suggest that they frequently threatened to overturn feminine decorum—Austen did not entirely put aside her domestic duties. She had found an unobtrusive way to do some sober and ladylike work for others, while having a good, loud laugh for herself.

4

In the letters she wrote after 1802, Austen appears content with her decision to remain single. In 1808 she came as close to expressing that contentment outright as she ever did in her extant letters. She had recently attended a ball at which memories of her youth and the sight of several unattached, unescorted women triggered the following reflection: "The room was tolerably full," she wrote her sister, "& there were perhaps thirty couple of Dancers;—the melancholy part was, to see so many dozen young Women standing by without partners, & each of them with two ugly naked shoulders!—It was the same room in which we danced 15 years ago!—I thought it all over—& in spite of the shame of being so much older, felt with thankfulness that I was quite as happy now as then."[67] If Austen almost never directly expressed her feelings about her own situation, at least in her surviving letters, she often commented on the lives of other women she knew, and many of her observations offer indirect or refracted assessments of her own circumstances. They help to explain but also to qualify her satisfaction with her own single life, by showing a keen interest in female autonomy and control.

She was always apt to cast a sharp eye on the spouses of her female friends, showing a particular interest in how domineering they were. In 1806 Elizabeth Austen's sister Harriet Bridges, for example, married the Reverend George Moore, whose "manners to her," Austen noted when she first met him in 1808, "want Tenderness." Prone to anger, "he was," Austen continued, "a little violent at last about the impossibility of her going to Eastwell."[68] In 1813 when Austen returned to Kent, she had another opportunity to observe Harriet's husband and again she was most interested in his treatment of his wife. This time her appraisal is a bit more favorable. When the coachman was late bringing Mr. Moore his carriage, he became "very angry, which," Austen wrote her sister, "I was rather glad of. I wanted to see him angry; and, though he spoke to his servant in a very loud voice and with a good deal of heat, I was happy to perceive that he did not scold Harriot at all."[69] Austen was similarly interested in the treatment shown her niece Anna by her husband Benjamin Lefroy after their marriage in 1814. She wrote to Fanny about Anna soon after the marriage: "I received a very kind note from her yesterday, to ask me to come again & stay a night with them; I cannot do it, but I was pleased to find that she had the *power* of doing so right a thing."[70]

Austen's interest in the behavior of husbands toward their wives shows her sensitivity to patriarchal power. Husbands might be consistently kind instead of ill-tempered and dictatorial, but they had the *right* to be either. Just as she believed that other women should marry, so Austen always endorsed her community's cultural belief that women should submit to the will of their husbands. Although she herself said very little to participants in the gentry's culture about her novels, she had a different opinion about what her niece Anna should say to her fiancé about *her* writing: "You have been perfectly right in telling Ben of your work, & I am very glad to hear how much he likes it."[71] Perhaps because she believed that wives should defer to their husbands' authority, she chose not to place herself in a position to defer. What if Ben had disapproved of Anna's work? What if he had resented the assertiveness of her efforts to write? Whether he liked her writing or not, Austen believed that marriage, of necessity, would subdue women's imaginations. Although she generally encouraged her niece Fanny in her desire to marry, she did just once in 1817 lament: "Oh! what a loss it will be when you are married. You are too agreable in your single state, too agreable as a Neice. I shall hate you when your delicious play of Mind is all settled down into conjugal & maternal affections."[72]

Austen was acutely conscious of another manifestation of patriarchal power: the numerous children that many married women bore. Although many of her well-known comments about pregnancies do not specifically attribute responsibility for large families to husbands—"Good Mrs. Deedes! . . . I w^d recommend to her & Mr. D. the simple regimen of separate rooms"—a remark she made about Anna in 1817 indicates that she did indeed believe that men were responsible and women made prisoners of their reproductive capacities.[73] "Anna," she wrote to Fanny, "has not a chance of escape; her husband called here the other day, & said she was *pretty* well but not *equal* to so long a walk; she *must come in* her *Donkey Carriage.*—Poor Animal, she will be worn out before she is thirty.—I am very sorry for her."[74]

Not entirely pleased with her single state, Austen expressed discontent in her letters but about her lack of money rather than of a husband. After her father died in 1805, Austen, her mother, and sister had £460 per annum among them: Cassandra and Mrs. Austen together possessed £210 per annum, and this sum was increased by annual contributions from James, Edward, Frank, and Henry Austen. That was not very much at a time when many of Austen's contemporaries were suggesting that a comfortable, respectable competence for a woman *living alone* was between £400 and £500.[75] A surviving page from an account book Jane Austen kept in 1807 gives some indication of the meagerness of her own personal (not household) budget for that year—about £50—and of her expenditures. She had in reserve approximately £6/4 at the end of the year, after paying sums that included: £3/17 for "Letters and Parcels," £3/10 for "Charity," £6/4 for "Presents," £2/13 to "Hire Piano Forté," and a mere £13/19 for "Cloathes & Pocket."[76] "Single Women," as Austen had good reason to tell Fanny in 1817, "have a dreadful propensity for being poor—which is one very strong argument in favour of Matrimony."[77]

Austen often wished that she could enjoy close friendships with other unattached women within the context of an affluent life-style. But that was not to be, at least, in her homes with her mother, sister, and Martha Lloyd. Still, when she weighed the gratifications of conspicuous consumption made possible by connections to affluent men against the bonds of her women's culture, she chose the latter. In 1808 she wrote to Cassandra from her brother Edward's estate in Kent:

> In another week I shall be at home—& then, my having been at Godmersham will seem like a Dream, as my visit at Brompton seems already. The Orange Wine will want our Care soon.—But in the meantime for Elegance & Ease & Luxury—; the Hattons & Milles' dine here today—& I shall eat Ice & drink French wine, & be above vulgar Economy. Luckily the pleasures of Friendship, of unreserved Conversation, of similarity of Taste & Opinions, will make good amends for Orange Wine.—[78]

In her letters after 1802 Austen less frequently admired the lives of affluent, happily married women than she did those of the few widows or single women with fortunes. Alethea and Catherine Bigg and their widowed sister Elizabeth Heathcote approached Austen's ideal during the many years that they lived with their widowed father at his comfortable estate, Manydown (Elizabeth returned to it after her husband died in 1802; Catherine left when she married the Reverend Herbert Hill in 1808). Austen especially admired their capacity to support friendship in material splendor. Writing to her sister in 1813 just before Cassandra was to leave on a visit to Alethea and Elizabeth, Austen foresaw the pleasures of friendship in prosperous surroundings: "In a few hours you will be transported to Manydown & then for Candour & Comfort & Coffee & Cribbage."[79] In a letter she wrote a week later to Martha, Austen noted that the weather had been bad for Cassandra's visit: "Cassandra has been rather out of luck at Manydown—but that is a House, in which one is tolerably independent of weather."[80]

When Lovelace Bigg-Wither died in 1813, not long after Cassandra's visit to his daughters, Harris inherited Manydown. The sisters, unmarried and widowed, moved as a matter of course to more humble accommodations, renting a house in Winchester. The death of their male kin often, though not always, had a detrimental impact on the social situations of women. By comparison, Austen's friend Mrs. Knight was made independently wealthy by her husband's will. She appreciated her unusually fortunate social position; the information that we have about her suggests that she responded to her late husband's kindness with generosity to others. Her obituary in the *Gentleman's Magazine* particularly notes her "benevolence to the sick, the poor, and the friendless."[81] She was equally generous to family members and friends. In addition to giving Edward Austen in 1797 the estates that were supposed to devolve to him only upon her death, traces of evidence reveal that she enjoyed giving large gifts—to Fanny, an expensive watch,[82] to Jane and Cassandra, money to pay their transportation to see her in Canterbury—so much money, in fact, that Austen was able, as she informed Cassandra in 1808, to "reserve half for my Pelisse."[83] That particular visit was "very agreable," she wrote afterwards. Again, Austen depicted the pleasure of friendship played out in an affluent context. "There was everything to make it so; Kindness, conversation, & variety, without care or cost."[84] Another glimpse she provides of the visit to Mrs. Knight subtly conveys the superiority of the affluent widow's circumstances to those of the wife. Harriet Moore joined Austen and Mrs. Knight for dinner and her husband arrived later. "We sat quietly working & talking till 10, when," according to Austen, "he ordered his wife away, & we adjourned to the Dressing room to eat our Tart & Jelly."[85]

Austen, as she grew older, had more control over some aspects of her life than Harriet, though less than Mrs. Knight. If there was no one to order her home, there were also not sufficient means to supply all the tarts and jellies she might have enjoyed sharing with her friends. She longed for more money in one of the few forms available to her—inheritance (possible, though unlikely). Writing to her sister from Godmersham in June of 1808, she noted wistfully: "Eliza^th has a very sweet scheme of our accompanying Edward into Kent next Christmas. A Legacy might make it very feasible;—a Legacy is our sovereign good."[86] And in another letter to her sister less than two weeks later she burst out: "I do not know where we are to get our Legacy—but we will keep a sharp look-out.—Lady B.[ridges] was all in prosperous Black the other day."[87] In the last year of her life, her uncle James Leigh Perrot died. Austen had been hoping that he would leave something to her mother and to those of her children who most needed money. At that time many of them did, since the banks in which Henry Austen was a partner failed in 1816 and several family members lost money in that collapse. Instead, Leight Perrot's will ignored his sister, and, although it did not forget her children, it did not provide them with any immediate financial assistance. Leigh Perrot left £24,000 to James Austen and his heirs, subject to Mrs. Leigh Perrot's life interest, and £1,000 each to those of Mrs. Austen's children who survived his wife. Austen, already quite ill, became sicker after hearing the terms of the will. As she wrote to her brother Charles: "I am ashamed to say that the shock of my Uncle's Will brought on a relapse. . . . I am the only one of the Legatees who has been so silly, but a weak Body must excuse weak Nerves."[88]

Austen never received a legacy, and perhaps we should be grateful. Literary critic Susan Lanser has shrewdly observed that Austen's single status gave her novel writing "an economic imperative that marriage would have erased."[89] A handsome legacy would similarly have lessened the financial concerns that in part gave impetus to Austen's writing. The sum Austen earned from her novels was, to be sure, modest, but it would have made a significant contribution to her very small income. From the publication of her first four books, she received just under £700, 600 of which she invested in the Navy Five Percents, as a means of building up an annuity. Had she lived, she would have earned more: in 1821 *Northanger Abbey* and *Persuasion* had made Cassandra, as her legatee, just over £515. And it is likely that Austen would have continued to write and publish novels. She began a seventh, "Sanditon," in January 1817 but stopped writing three months later when illness made the effort impossible.

Although nothing like the generous legacy for which she yearned, Austen's earnings were beginning to offer her at least occasional opportunities for independent action. As early as 1813 she had already, as she told her brother Frank, "written myself into £250,"[90] and one of her early purchases with this money was a present for Cassandra. Austen wrote to her from London in 1813, offering the gift with a tact and a barely controlled joy at the prospect of being able to share not just affection but prosperity with her sister:

Instead of saving my superfluous wealth for you to spend, I am going to treat myself with spending it myself. I hope, at least, that I shall find some poplin at Layton and Shear's that will tempt me to buy it. If I do, it shall be sent to Chawton, as half will be for you; for I depend upon your being so kind as to accept it, being the main point. It will be a great pleasure to me. Don't say a word. I only wish you could choose too. I shall send twenty yards.[91]

Austen's experience demonstrates that her women's culture, although it altered none of the institutional structures of her patriarchal community, could be liberating for individuals. The gentry's culture was an encouragingly literate context that stimulated Austen's writing when she was a young girl. Although she remained loyal to the values of that culture throughout her life, she derived the support she needed as an adult writer from the women's culture. In addition to offering her opportunities to write and to test her writing, to speak confidently and happily of her achievements, and to develop a professional identity, it also enabled her to adopt the only acceptable social role in which writing talent would be relatively free to flourish. She could reject marriage in 1802 because her women's culture provided her with the emotional intimacy that only wedlock was thought to offer. And it could do these things precisely because it remained private.

Austen's cultural contexts made her writing possible, and they also influenced what she wrote. Because her women's culture played an especially important enabling role, we might justly expect to see that cultural affiliation, in particular, inscribed in her fiction. Chapters 6, 7, and 8 will be centrally concerned with whether and where it figures.

PART THREE

Representing Two Cultures

CHAPTER 6

The Juvenilia:
Convenient Ambiguities

1

BETWEEN 1787 and 1793, Jane Austen composed several short pieces of fiction that later came to be known as her juvenilia.[1] The dedications she attached to all but one of these works identify her readers as male and female kin and a few female friends. She addressed once, twice, or even three times her sister, five of her brothers (excluding only George), her mother, father, infant nieces Anna and Fanny, cousins Eliza de Feuillide and Jane Cooper, and friends Mary and Martha Lloyd.

Over time Austen transcribed those pieces she wished to preserve in three small notebooks; the large scrawl of her childhood eventually gives way in these manuscripts to the small, neat hand she wrote as an adult.[2] These copies, in turn, circulated among family members—particularly, as time passed, among nieces and nephews, a few of whom wrote their own additions into the notebooks.[3] The path of transmission of the volumes in itself underscores the largely familial context; at least one originally came to Austen as a gift from her father, and after the novelist's death, her sister gave the first volume to their brother Charles, the second to their brother Frank, and the third to their nephew James Edward.

Evidence of Austen attempting to entertain her relatives and of her family enjoying and treasuring her work might lead us to assume that the juvenilia voice the patriarchal values of the Austen family's culture, but critics have disagreed about the values these works express.

On the one hand, A. Walton Litz and B. C. Southam, while not commenting specifically on gender, have asserted the social conservatism of Austen's juvenilia. Litz finds in these works the expression of a "Johnsonian system of morality"; Southam situates them in an eighteenth-century tradition of moral criticism that defended "civilized values and personal rectitude" against fictional representations of self-indulgence and emotional excess.[4] On the other hand, Sandra Gilbert and Susan Gubar have suggested that in the juvenilia Austen "repeatedly demonstrates her alienation from the aggressively patriarchal tradition that constitutes her Augustan inheritance."[5] Although none of these critics offers a sustained discussion of the response of Austen's audience, Litz and Southam assume that Austen's family readily understood and shared the "system of morality" that they believe her works conveyed.[6] Gilbert and Gubar, by contrast, imply that Austen would have slipped by her audience "her alienation from the aggressively patriarchal tradition," for they locate that subversive attitude in the juvenilia under "cover" or, in effect, behind "camouflage-screens."[7]

Was she laughing *with* her family or secretly *at* them—or at least at the males in her audience? Neither of these views adequately describes the juvenilia. Austen inherited literary conventions for the presentation of the ideology of domesticity, and the juvenilia manifest her considerable interest in them. Austen's family, if their enthusiastic responses may be taken as a measure, understood her treatment of the domestic ideology in ways consistent with their particular values (just as modern critics have done). But the pieces themselves provide unusually little guidance. It is not just that the values they express are hard to pin down; the juvenilia rely on strategies that create indeterminacy. Although documentary evidence is slight for Austen's adolescence, although we can only hypothesize about her motives, it is possible that she was in this period already experiencing allegiances to two cultures. Her literary response to divided loyalties may have been equivocation, albeit different versions of it in different works; Austen's juvenilia vary considerably.

Beginning in parody, these compositions move gradually and intermittently toward nonparodic writing, toward the serious comedy of Austen's published novels. The earliest, parodic pieces, considered first in this chapter, offer unmistakable evidence of her surprisingly early dedication not just to writing in general but to writing in a particular genre. Of these works (approximately twenty-eight),[8] only three or four are play excerpts or poems; one is a history. The rest are fictions and, for the most part, a particular kind of fiction popular in Austen's day: the courtship novel. The parodies mock not only individual conventions of this novel form but also the juxtaposition of these conventions within a fiction. They ridicule the eighteenth-century courtship novel as a diverse and frequently incoherent mix of conventions, by stitching together—with jarring effects—numerous stylistic and thematic clichés.

Works such as "Jack & Alice," "Frederic & Elfrida," "Henry and Eliza," and "Love and Freindship" include among their many technical and thematic conventions those which convey domestic femininity: virtuous heroines and their didactic female friendships. Through surprising and humorous juxtapositions, these pieces suggest that the eighteenth-century courtship novel's diverse conventions render representations of domestic ideology ludicrous. But what cultural perspective is behind this charge? Was Austen attacking only what the courtship novel made of domestic femininity? Or was she taking domestic femininity itself as her target? Austen's use of parody creates ambiguity; the eighteenth-century courtship novel is shown to subvert its own representations of domestic ideology, but we cannot tell whether Austen herself was subverting the values of her family's patriarchal culture.

If we cannot pinpoint her cultural perspective in the parodies, we can ascertain her aesthetic preferences. Austen's humorous portraits of the courtship novel as a jumble of techniques, themes, and codes implies her commitment to standards, not only of literary realism but also of organic form. To be sure, the desire for a unity of parts in the novel does not conform with late twentieth-century critical values. Few critics today assert the superior claims of harmony and wholeness in literature. But contemporary values should not lead us to overlook Austen's remarkable achievement in the parodies of a sustained, sophisticated critical view, one that would direct her subsequent innovative efforts to develop and extend fictional realism.

Two of her later, nonparodic juvenilia, explored in this chapter after the parodic works, should tell us more about Austen's disposition toward the domestic ideology. Unlike the earlier juvenilia, whose overt, mocking intertextual play serves as criticism, the later "Catharine or the Bower" and the third letter in "A Collection of Letters" revise many of the familiar conventions of the courtship novel. These surprisingly accomplished efforts at literary realism, which include fresh representations of heroines and their female friendships, should inscribe a cultural perspective on the domestic ideology. But in these works, too, such a cultural perspective remains elusive. The representations themselves are ambiguous; in both "Catharine" and "Letter the Third," depictions of the heroines and their female friendships are partly shaped by the domestic ideology and partly, it would appear, by Austen's women's culture. More importantly, these pieces are impossible to pin down because they are incomplete. "Letter the Third" and "Catharine" testify to the power of one particular set of mediating fictional conventions—narrative endings—precisely because they do not end. Without resolutions, these two pieces neither confirm social and sexual hierarchies nor endorse the values of the women's culture.

"Letter the Third" and "Catharine" constitute an important stage in Austen's development. In these initial works of realism, Austen first evinced an interest in representing the women's culture. At the same time, she also expressed in these multivalent and inconclusive fictions her unwillingness to relinquish the values of the gentry's culture. In subsequent works, because of this cultural duality, she would wrestle with the desire to move out of the shelter of indeterminacy, and she would come remarkably close to subverting the courtship novel with the perspective generated exclusively and privately by women.

2

Novelist Samuel Richardson is widely known to have promoted the ideology of domesticity in eighteenth-century courtship fiction, but he was not alone.[9] In the second half of that century many writers, including Frances Brooke, Frances Sheridan, Susanna Keir, Eliza Parsons, Charlotte Smith, Sophia Lee, Frances Burney, and Elizabeth Inchbald, industriously carried on that advocacy in the courtship novel. Whether these women writers were genuinely committed to the ideology or, as some recent feminist critics have contended, felt and even subtly expressed conflicts about it, they followed Richardson in making the domestic ideology a crucial concern of the courtship novel and helping to fashion the literary conventions that represented it.[10] They tended to make their female protagonists, for example, bearers of the precepts of domestic femininity, and because novelists (and critics of the day as well) were not confident that mixed portraits would inspire virtue, they usually constructed exemplary heroines.[11]

Some of Austen's parodies mock the heroines' clichéd language and flawless conduct as such.[12] But many of them consider what happens to representations of exemplary heroines in the medium of the courtship novel, and they show that several other conventions of this novel form clash with those that convey models of domestic femininity. Parody, as several critics have noted, generally implies a standard of realism,[13] and Austen's early parodic works are no exception. They suggest that when perfectly feminine virtue is yoked with quite different literary conventions, it is made implausible—rigid or incoherent and, inevitably, strange and silly. They also suggest that, because virtue is made implausible in the courtship novel's inconsistent medium, its moral function is undercut.

The parodies call attention to the moral inefficacy of fictional representations of the domestic ideology, but to what end? Austen may have been implying that the novel should more suitably—more smoothly and subtly—house the ideology. Or she may have wished to excise it from the courtship novel. If she wanted to rid the novel of the ideology of domesticity, it may have been because she thought it had a more appropriate place in some other prose form; on the other hand, she may have been expressing dislike for the ideology in itself. However acute their analysis of the uncomfortable fit between the domestic ideology and the courtship novel, the parodies do not provide us with evidence to choose any one of these motives for that analysis.

Unfortunately, we possess too little historical evidence about her life during this period to wrest motives from it, either. Austen wrote the extant juvenilia during approximately six years of her adolescence, beginning at the age of eleven (she turned twelve at the end of 1787). We might suppose that in the first half of this period, before she had reached the age of fifteen, she would have been more securely attached to and more comfortable with the gentry's patriarchal culture than at any later time in her life. We might suppose, then, that she meant no disrespect for the domestic ideology itself in her early, parodic writings. But we should also note how very useful the ambiguity of parody would be for someone already developing loyalty to two cultures: whether chosen intentionally for this reason or not, parody would have enabled her to avoid committing herself to one position or another.

However implausible this fiction may have seemed to Austen, the eighteenth-century courtship novel was not itself devoid of conventions for expressing realism. Indeed, it helped to pioneer concrete and commonplace descriptions of bourgeois or "middling" life. Such descriptions, as critic George Levine notes about nineteenth-century realism, are "exuberant with details"—"the clutter of furniture, the cut of clothing, the mutton chop and the mug of hot rum."[14] Sometimes Austen's parodies mock the conventions of literary realism in themselves, for overrepresenting the minutiae of day-to-day life.[15] More often, however, they show that conventions that create literary realism clash in the courtship novel with those representing domestic femininity. When perfect female characters are brought into conjunction with depictions of a socially and materially imperfect reality, they come to seem wooden and out of place.

An implausible femininity, as some of Austen's parodies indicate, is often created in novels by the abstract tributes that introduce the heroine into an otherwise concrete and prosaic social world. Austen relies on hyperbole to call attention to these torrents of praise, although, to be sure, her exaggerated imitations hardly exaggerate. Susanna Keir's heroine in *The History of Miss Greville*, for example, has "that simplicity of manner, which needs no ornament to render it attractive; that affability, which flows directly from the heart; that humility, which is equally secure from giving or taking offence; and that total forgetfulness of self, in promoting the enjoyment of others, which, without courting the admiration of any, secures the favour of all."[16] In addition to hyperbole, Austen also relies on the parodic device of deflation to emphasize and ridicule the contrast between ideal traits of character and other, physical, material, and sometimes trivial concerns in fiction's ordinary world. One of the characters in the epistolary "Lesley Castle," for example, provides both lavish and undermined praise of her niece, Louisa. The niece is "as handsome as tho' 2 & 20, as sensible as tho' 2 & 30, and as prudent as tho' 2 & 40" though she is, in fact, just—two. "That she already knows the two first letters in the Alphabet, and that she never tears her frocks" stand as proofs of her virtues (6:111).

Austen's introductions to exemplary heroines lampoon such formulaic descriptions in the courtship novel; her representations of their behavior similarly mock their good conduct in that novel tradition. Some of Austen's heroines can bring their great virtues to bear only on pedestrian matters. In "Frederic & Elfrida," Rebecca elicits her companions' "admiration," as they tell her, for "sentiments so nobly expressed on the different excellencies of Indian & English Muslins, & the judicious preference you give the former" (6:6). Moreover, the heroine constructed out of excessive and all too familiar praise is herself sometimes "all talk." Hopelessly tendentious, she does not fit comfortably into the everyday life generally created by the courtship novel, a point made in "The Female Philosopher," one of Austen's "Scraps."

The piece emphasizes the contrast between paragon Julia Millar's nonstop delivery of "wisdom" and the more commonplace fictional furniture of drawing rooms and carriages. With her father and sister Charlotte, Julia has come to call on Arabella Smythe and her father. Julia has "a countenance in which Modesty, Sense & Dignity are happily blended," according to deadpan narrator Arabella, and "a form which at once presents you with Grace, Elegance & Symmetry." During the brief half hour in which the Millars stay, "the sensible, the amiable Julia uttered Sentiments of Morality worthy of a heart like her own." Roaming from one somber cliché to another, she embarks finally on the doctrine "that all earthly Joys must be imperfect" and is about to prove it "by examples from the Lives of great Men when the Carriage came to the Door and the amiable Moralist with her Father & Sister was obliged to depart" (6:171).

The clash of flawless heroines with other technical and thematic conventions—even a formal rather than thematic device like first-person narration—may rob exemplary female characters of credibility and moral sincerity. In some courtship novels the heroine herself, rather than the narrator or another character, introduces and explains her virtues. Self-characterization is not uncommon in eighteenth-century novels, given the popularity in that century of fictionalized memoirs and correspondences. Pamela-like, the heroine may represent her virtues in letters by reporting to her correspondent the praise accorded her by others. She may also more directly, if ingenuously, volunteer her own admirable traits. In a letter to a friend, the protagonist of Frances Sheridan's *Memoirs of Miss Sidney Bidulph*, for example, explains her indifference to Mr. Faulkland, to whom she had been engaged. "Time," she notes, "joined to my own efforts, must, without any other help, have intirely subdued my inclination, which was always restrained by prudential motives and rendered subservient to my duty."[17] Austen's parodies indicate that such avowals of self-restraint in first-person narration tend to make characterizations not so much stiff and strained as contradictory.

The epistolary "Lesley Castle" exaggerates the self-display in first-person accounts of feminine virtue in order to call attention to the immodesty of announcing one's modesty. The incoherence of heroines made to give such testimonies is amplified in the frenetic, babbling Margaret Lesley, who provides this description of herself and her sister, Matilda, to a friend: "We are handsome . . . very handsome and the greatest of our Perfections is, that we are entirely insensible of them ourselves" (6:111). Margaret bestows on herself the valorized position in the moral and geographical dichotomy common to conduct books and courtship novels: her new stepmother, Susan, is the avaricious, pleasure-seeking cosmopolitan, while she and her sister, the exemplars of domestic femininity, reside happily in rural retirement. But this conventional dichotomy, voiced by the "modest" Margaret, repeatedly breaks down. Arriving in London, for example, she begins a stereotypical lament in a letter to a female correspondent: "Ah! my dear Freind I every day more regret the serene and tranquil Pleasures of the Castle we have left, in exchange for the uncertain & unequal Amusements of this vaunted City" (6:135). It is not cosmopolitan life to which she objects, however, but the impact she claims to have on men. Although she complains of it, "Dislike" and "Aversion" are a vehicle for self-congratulation: "It is my sensibility for the sufferings of so many amiable Young Men, my Dislike of the extreme Admiration I meet with, and my Aversion to being so celebrated both in Public, in Private, in Papers, & in Printshops, that are the reasons why I cannot more fully enjoy, the Amusements so various and pleasing of London" (6:135).[18]

"Lesley Castle" shows that the self-contradictions that first-person narration facilitates may undercut both plausibility and propriety in the courtship novel. Other parodies suggest that conventions of sensibility (conveying histrionic displays of emotion and liberal moral and political perspectives) may have a similarly compromising effect when combined with representations of domestic femininity.[19] Her sensibility usually takes even the flawless heroine outside the bounds of appropriately feminine conduct, and her divergences are not often acknowledged. The heroine's bold behavior, Austen's juvenilia suggest, is unconvincingly rationalized by the moral and political codes of sensibility, conventionally dramatized by a benevolent, feeling individual situated in a heartless and often corrupt world. All on the grounds of sensibility, the heroine of "Love and Freindship" defies her husband's family, travels several hundred miles by coach with her friend Sophia, helps to persuade another young woman to defy parental authority and elope, steals banknotes from Sophia's cousin, and offers only the medical care of extravagant (albeit daily) emotional outbursts to the dying Sophia: "I had wept over her every Day—had bathed her sweet face with my tears & had pressed her fair Hands continually in mine—" (6:102).

Austen has her heroine periodically encounter characters who are, at least sometimes, not under the influence of sensibility at all. These interactions highlight the bizarre and indecorous conduct of heroines created by the fusion of sensibility and domestic femininity. One such encounter occurs between heroine Laura and her friend Isabel, who holds to an ideal of proper feminine conduct unadulterated by sensibility. When Laura tells all her "Misfortunes & Adventures" to Isabel, she expects to evoke tears and praise. Isabel instead reproaches her. Laura's outrage at her friend's disapproval, which she conveys to Isabel's daughter, Marianne, intensifies Austen's implicit critique of this heroine's odd and inappropriate conduct:

Pity & Surprise were strongly depictured in your Mother's Countenance, during the whole of my narration, but I am sorry to say, that to the eternal reproach of her Sensibility, the latter infinitely predominated. Nay, faultless as my Conduct had certainly been during the whole Course of my late Misfortunes & Adventures, she pretended to find fault with my Behaviour in many of the situations in which I had been placed. As I was sensible myself, that I had always behaved in a manner which reflected Honour on my Feelings & Refinement, I paid little attention to what she said. (6:104)

Romantic and melodramatic conventions, too, may subvert representations of domestic femininity in the eighteenth-century courtship novel.[20] As incredible as a perfectly virtuous heroine might seem, courtship novels often make her more so by adding the enhancements of wealth and beauty. Such wish-fulfilling attributes are highlighted in the parodies through the technique of reversal. The amiable Lucy in "Jack & Alice" is the daughter of a Welsh taylor, albeit a "capital" one (6:20). And in "Frederic & Elfrida" the not only exemplary but "lovely & too charming" Rebecca possesses a "forbidding Squint," "greasy tresses" and a "swelling Back" (6:6). The flawless heroine is also typically a magnet for the gratifications and excitements of marriage proposals. The main character of Burney's *Cecelia; or, Memoirs of an Heiress* receives at least six; Keir's Miss Greville receives four. Austen has a wealthy Duke propose to Lucy in "Jack & Alice" within two weeks of meeting her at Bath; Edward proposes to Laura in "Love and Freindship" when they first meet (this heroine of sensibility immediately accepts, of course); and Mr. Cecil quickly transfers his affections from another woman to the heroine of "Henry and Eliza" and is able to marry her in secret because the chaplain, "being very much in love with Eliza himself, would . . . do anything to oblige her" (6:35).

Austen's parodies also call attention to the courtship novel's tendency to ignore the erratic behavior of flawless female characters who have "Adventures." They do so in two instances by presenting characters who, unlike Isabel in "Love and Freindship," show no reaction to the heroine's unconventional conduct. In "Letter the Second" from "A Collection of Letters," the narrator's opinion of Miss Jane—"charming," "lovely," and "so sweet, so mild in her Countenance, that she seems more than Mortal"—is unchanged by the discovery of Miss Jane's secret marriage (6:153). And in "Jack & Alice," Lucy makes a "bold push" for the hand of Charles Adams, writing to him repeatedly and then finally setting out alone from Wales to pressure him in person (6:21). Adams may not wish to marry this heroine, but she is immediately loved and esteemed by everyone else that she meets.

The experience of Charlotte, a character in "Frederic & Elfrida," encapsulates many of the odd, incoherent results of representing domestic ideology in the courtship novel. She is an exemplar, as the narration repeatedly notes, of a key trait of domestic femininity, "an earnest desire to oblige every one" (6:8). What opportunities did the courtship novel make available to a heroine who wished to practice this virtue? In the concrete and ordinary world of such fictions, Charlotte manifests it by buying one friend a bonnet and complimenting another on her complexion. She also receives two marriage proposals from gentlemen she has never met before, one right after the other, and, exercising "the natural turn of her mind to make every one happy," she accepts both (6:8). Because she is an exemplar of sensibility as well as a model of feminine deference, when she remembers "the double engagement she had entered into," Charlotte drowns herself— behavior hardly recommended by conduct books (6:9).[21]

Austen's earliest, extant compositions suggest that she recognized the courtship novel as a peculiar medium not only for flawless heroines but also for perfectly didactic female friendships. Eighteenth-century courtship novels depict the female protagonist's relationship with a female mentor—an acquaintance, a mother, an aunt, or, occasionally, a governess. Such friendships, built around the moral project of "feminizing" the young protagonist, appear frequently in the courtship novel. Prescribed by the ideology of domesticity, these friendships also gave eighteenth-century novelists a context for articulating precepts of domestic femininity. The relationships served, in effect, as a textual emblem for the pedagogical relationships that novelists may have wished to have with their readers. Focusing on the transmission of advice central to the didactic friendship, Austen's parodies launch attacks against such relationships. As with their mockery of model heroines, the parodies imply criticism of the effects of juxtaposing these idealized friendships and other fictional conventions, but they do not indicate Austen's views on didactic female friendships in themselves.

According to the parodies, perfectly didactic friendships, like perfect heroines, are often neither believable nor inspirational within courtship fiction. Mentors are given to lecturing, commanding, and warning, and, more incredibly, the recipients of advice eagerly submit. "To follow your instructions, and practise what you teach both by precept and example, shall be the daily study of Your affectionate Niece," writes Lucy Herbert to her aunt Helen Maria Stanley in *The History of Miss Greville*.[22] Some heroines don't just intend to follow advice; they quickly and readily succeed. For example, the protagonist of

Memoirs of Miss Sidney Bidulph admits: "I have been accustomed from my infancy to pay an implicit obedience to the best of mothers; the conforming to this never yet cost me an uneasy minute, and I am sure never will."[23] The female monitor's insistent and stilted preaching and the young heroine's automatic and easy submission push these representations outside the realm of pedestrian realism.

The juvenilia's parodies usually turn to deflation to call attention to the mixing of morally improving female friendships with fictional representations of more flawed and mundane social experiences. "Letter the First" in "A Collection of Letters" mocks the convention of a young woman's social debut, typical of novels such as Burney's *Evelina; or, The History of a Young Lady's Entrance into the World.* In the process, however, it also makes fun of the preparatory instruction young women receive from their mothers. Mother and daughters make dutiful speeches to one another just prior to the daughters' coming out into adult social life. "My dear Girls," says the mother, "the moment is now arrived when I am to reap the rewards of all my Anxieties and Labours towards you during your Education. You are this Evening to enter a World in which you will meet with many wonderfull Things; Yet let me warn you against suffering yourselves to be meanly swayed by the Follies & Vices of others" (6:151). The daughters assure their mother, as she tells a friend, "that they would ever remember my advice with Gratitude, & follow it with Attention" (6:151). Mother and daughters then go off to "the World," represented in the comically reductive form of tea with neighbor Mrs. Cope and her daughter. The momentous rhetoric of the mentoring relationship, as "Letter the First" suggests, is incompatible with fictional representations of ordinary genteel life.

A few of Austen's parodies specifically target and deflate idealized dramatizations of the impact of instruction. In many courtship novels a mentor typically tells her life story to her less experienced friend. The dutiful recipient listens carefully to the impressive tale and inevitably profits from it. Just such a life story is elicited by Alice Johnson in "Jack & Alice": "You mentioned," she tells Lady Williams, "something of your having yourself been a sufferer by the misfortune [first love] you are so good as to wish me to avoid. Will you favour me with your Life & Adventures?"(6:16). But Lady Williams's account comes to an abrupt halt when she and her friend begin to quarrel over a matter of greater concern to them—whether a woman can have too much color in her cheeks.

Although Margaret and Matilda Lesley have a penchant for recounting the "Life & Adventures" of their brother, that life story serves the same function of moral exemplum in "Lesley Castle." (The brother's unhappy marriage may be a parodic adaptation of Lord Elmwood's disastrous domestic history in Elizabeth Inchbald's *A Simple Story*.) Margaret and Matilda's sister-in-law, Louisa, has "wantonly disgraced the Maternal character and . . . openly violated the conjugal Duties," by leaving her husband and daughter and taking a lover. The Lesley brother, sinking into "melancholy and Despair," has gone off travelling, leaving his little girl and his sad story in the hands of his sisters (6:110). "Lesley Castle" ridicules the powerful effect such stories have in courtship novels by endowing the sisters with a mechanistic compulsion to narrate and by depicting the resistance—in levity or boredom—of the female recipients. Charlotte Lutterell, in response to Margaret's letter containing her brother and sister-in-law's history, politely thanks her for the story, noting that it "has not the less entertained me for having often been repeated to me before" (6:119). Margaret's new stepmother is even less moved. As she tells Charlotte Lutterell, with whom she, too, corresponds, about her arrival at Lesley Castle: "I found a little humoured Brat here who I believe is some relation to them [Margaret and her sister Matilda]; they told me who she was, and gave me a long rigmerole story of her father and Miss *Somebody* which I have entirely forgot" (6:123–24).

Some of the parodies also attack the generally sententious and sober style of the advice central to ideal female friendships, for that wisdom often seems out of place in the context of the heroine's everyday experience. In "Jack & Alice" the very "last words" of her governess, which Lady Williams has ever remembered and now repeats tearfully to Alice Johnson, mock the sage style of advice because they are insistently mundane: "My dear Kitty she said, Good night t'ye" (6:17). The parodies often turn the warnings and aphorisms of advice into nonsense, thus calling attention to the artificiality of this discourse in the courtship novel's social world. "That one should receive obligations only from those we despise," Lucy piously offers in "Jack & Alice," "is a sentiment instilled into my mind by my worthy aunt, in my early years, & cannot in my opinion be too strictly adhered to" (6:27). And Lady Williams volunteers similarly silly counsel to Alice Johnson: "Preserve yourself from a first Love," she urges, "& you need not fear a second" (6:16).

Other fictional conventions besides those for the representation of the ordinary may, when brought into play with didactic female friendships, destabilize the mentor's characterization. "Love and Freindship," for example, suggests that female friendships may become opportunities for self-promotion when combined with conventions of sensibility. Laura's pedagogical motive for writing her life story to her friend's daughter does not conceal the narcissism of her sensibility: "May the fortitude with which I have suffered the many Afflictions of my past Life, prove to her a useful Lesson for the support of those which may befall her in her own" (6:77).

"Love and Freindship" indicates, in addition, that courtship novels are often more concerned with the youth and beauty of mentors than with their credibility and moral authority. One novel that was popular in the late eighteenth century, Charlotte Smith's *Emmeline, The Orphan of the Castle*, bestows on the young Mrs. Stafford, herself in a bad marriage, the role of mentor to the heroine, Emmeline; Emmeline, in turn, is counselor to the pregnant and intermittently insane Lady Adelina Trelawny. In that role Emmeline accompanies her friend to Bath and attends at the birth of her illegitimate child. In "Love and Freindship"'s hardly more sensational depiction of female friendship, the authority and wisdom of young mentors are called into question. According to its heroine, Laura, her friend Isabel had a right to the role of her instructress because she was three years older and "had seen the World," that is, "she had passed 2 Years at one of the first Boarding schools in London; had spent a fortnight in Bath & had supped one night in Southampton" (6:78). Isabel's advice mixes the clichés of domestic ideology with the firsthand knowledge gained from her "wide experience" of the world: "Beware of the insipid Vanities and idle Dissipations of the Metropolis of England; Beware of the unmeaning Luxuries of Bath & of the Stinking fish of Southampton" (6:78–79).

Laura's complaint about this advice points to the awkward combination of moral instruction and melodramatic adventures in courtship novels. Although heroines of such novels ostensibly wish to be quiet, prudent, and modest, "Love and Freindship" suggests that that wish covers a lust for adventure—which must be satisfied if the novel is to be a novel. "Alas!" exclaims Laura in response to Isabel's warnings, "how am I to avoid those evils I shall never be exposed to? What probability is there of my ever tasting the Dissipations of London, the Luxuries of Bath or the stinking Fish of Southampton? I who am doomed to waste my Days of Youth & Beauty in an humble Cottage in the Vale of Uske" (6:79).

Sophia's "sage" deathbed advice to Laura calls attention once more to the odd marriage of domestic ideology, sensibility, and melodrama in many courtship novels. The *form* is familiar—a ponderous warning issued to restrict conduct. But the advice points to the liberal allowances novels actually make for female behavior, as well as to the nonsensical results of this liberality. "Take warning from my unhappy

End," says Sophia, "& avoid the imprudent conduct which has occasioned it . . . beware of fainting-fits. . . . A frenzy fit is not one quarter so pernicious; it is an exercise to the Body & if not too violent, is I dare say conducive to Health in its consequences—Run mad as often as you chuse; but do not faint." Laura, of course, is very willing to comply. In perfect imitation of the facile dutifulness of recipients of advice, she intones, "these were the last words she ever addressed to me. . . . It was her dieing Advice to her afflicted Laura, who has ever most faithfully adhered to it" (6:102).

The treatment of domestic femininity in Austen's parodies shows her to have been, even as an adolescent, an astute critic with a particular, if implicit, aesthetic program. Thirty-five years ago critic Ian Watt in his landmark book on realism, *The Rise of the Novel*, singled out Austen's achievement of organic form, praising her novels for combining "into a harmonious unity the advantages both of realism of presentation and realism of assessment." He noted as well their profound impact on later nineteenth-century novelists, particularly the French Realists.[24] His view is compatible with and, in effect, reinforced by the criticism of the courtship novel conveyed by Austen's parodies—which is also based on a strong preference for organic form.

Much recent literary criticism does not endorse organicism. Scholars are currently more interested in the inconsistencies of literary texts. Terry Eagleton, for example, has recently maintained that Samuel Richardson's *Pamela* is "too morally discursive" and "too fantastic" to be realist but "too realist to be read simply as symbolic wish-fulfillment or moral fable."[25] Rather than ascribing this mix to Richardson's supposed technical inability to sustain realism, he finds in the novel's inconsistencies an important locus of meaning. "The fissuring of 'formal realism' in *Pamela*," he argues, "is determined, in part, by an historical conflict between two essential yet disparate styles: the emergent metalanguage of bourgeois morality, and a still resilient popular speech."[26] Because he does not see all fiction through the restrictive lens of literary realism, Eagleton is open to a wider range of forms and techniques in the novel, providing insight into the social circumstances that produced them. But current trends in literary criticism should not prevent us from recognizing the remarkable critique that the adolescent Austen formulated. Her early juvenilia, however playful, are deeply informed responses to the often unwittingly amusing composite productions that she understood eighteenth-century courtship novels to be.

3

After 1790 Austen occasionally turned away from parodying the courtship novel to try to revise and improve on it. Two of the pieces from this period—"Letter the Third" in "A Collection of Letters" and "Catharine or the Bower"—offer us a glimpse of the courtship novel Austen was beginning to fashion, and they manifest, among their many formal innovations, efforts to transform the novel's customary renderings of domestic femininity.

Both works make one tendency within the courtship novel tradition—literary realism—much more dominant, in part by excluding other thematic and stylistic conventions that might undercut it. Austen self-consciously avoided melodrama, for example. Instead of traveling hastily through the British Isles on a path strewn with adventures, the heroine's experience in both works is restricted to home and neighborhood, arenas in which she must cope with prying neighbors, the need for dance partners, the irritating prattle of visitors, and her own feelings. The small scale of female experience, expressed in candles and cold weather, hair powder and toothaches, is charged with meaning.[27] Sensibility, too, though not completely abolished, is diminished, confined to the youthful fantasies and illusions of one of the characters. To reduce what she viewed as discord in the courtship novel's conventions, Austen also infused representations of the female with a new plausibility: neither the heroine, her female monitors, nor her responses to their counsel are exemplary.

It is not enough, however, to say that Austen extends the use of literary realism in "Letter the Third" and "Catharine." George Levine has suggested about later literary realist writers that "no major Victorian novelists were deluded into believing that they were in fact offering an unmediated reality; but all of them struggled to make contact with the world out there."[28] In Austen's case we need to ask, which world? Or rather, which culture? What do Jane Austen's revisions of the female in these two later works tell us about her cultural affiliations at that time? In Jane Austen's extant letters, which begin in 1796, she voiced the ideology of domesticity when she wanted to endorse her wider community's patriarchal values. When she wanted to object to these same values, she turned to the culture exclusive to women, for the locus of dissent in Austen's social world was their same-sex bonds. We have seen both affirmations of and opposition to the domestic ideology in the letters, where these positions generate opposing views of female identity and female friendship. Assuming that both cultural resources were available to her when she was writing the later juvenilia, which did she choose?

The representations of heroines and their female friendships in "Letter the Third" and "Catharine" often give voice to the perspective of the gentry's culture by endorsing, though not idealizing practices of, the domestic ideology. Far from perfect, both heroines find it difficult to live up to the standard of domestic femininity, but they try. In "Letter the Third," Maria Williams, "A young Lady in distress'd Circumstances," acknowledges that she is repeatedly provoked by the snobbery and intrusiveness of her neighbor, Lady Greville. She is frequently driven into "a great passion" by the older woman's insulting treatment, although she is striving to be quiet and submissive (6:160). "Catharine" revises not just the heroine's characterization but also the simplistic town/country dichotomy in which she is often situated. Although Camilla Stanley, the protagonist's foil, lives in London only six months a year, her fashionable tastes, superficial education, transient affections, and selfishness are all town-marked. The country-bred Kitty,[29] by contrast, is intellectually curious, sensible, and well read, capable of deep feeling, and, perhaps most important, capable of "Resignation & Patience" (6:208). This portrait of Kitty extends beyond the flat, conventional dichotomy without destroying the structure of values it conveys. The narrative suggests that, because Kitty is also inexperienced, high-spirited, prone to vanity, and to understanding experience in the terms of sentimental fiction, she does not always easily adopt the feminine conduct to which she subscribes.

The representations of female friendship in "Letter the Third" and in "Catharine" also both de-idealize yet sustain their didactic function. "Letter the Third" features the guidance provided to the letter-writer, Maria Williams, by her mother. "I dare not be impertinent," Maria writes, "as my Mother is always admonishing me to be humble & patient if I wish to make my way in the world. She insists on my accepting every invitation of Lady Greville, or you may be certain that I would never enter either her House, or her Coach, with the disagreable certainty I always have of being abused for my Poverty" (6:157). Maria's letter shows that it is always easier to give than to take advice. It also suggests that the ideology of domesticity is more easily adhered to by a mother who "never goes out" than by a daughter repeatedly provoked in the social world (6:155). Still, Maria does try to follow her mother's counsel.

In "Catharine" Mrs. Percival views herself as moral guide to the heroine, her niece. She articulates the goals of her instruction at a moment when she is particularly distressed by Kitty's behavior: "All

I wished for, was to breed you up virtuously; I never wanted you to play upon the Harpsichord, or draw better than any one else; but I had hoped to see you respectable and good; to see you able & willing to give an example of Modesty and Virtue to the Young people here abouts" (6:232). "Catharine" dramatizes the rigid tendentiousness of this monitor's role. Like Maria Williams's mother, she occupies a marginalized position in relation to the social world. With an irrational fear of her niece's socializing with gentlemen, whenever possible she avoids company or any venturing away from home. She also magnifies her niece's small infractions, responding to them with a "harangue" (6:232). "Catharine"'s depiction of the heroine and her experiences underscores the wooden artificiality of this didactic friendship. Mrs. Percival's moral instruction does not make allowances for her niece's youth, inexperience, and high spirits or for the possibility of small but unexpected occurrences—teeth may stop hurting, gentlemen may suddenly arrive at the door or kiss a lady's hand. Kitty finds exact, inflexible compliance to a conduct code, particularly when faced with the unexpected, extremely difficult, although she does try not to annoy her aunt or to "offend against Decorum" (6:219).

"Letter the Third" and "Catharine," then, do express the domestic ideology, albeit a more realistic version. The heroines have a difficult time realizing the values of femininity, whether or not they are imparted by a mentor, but their labors indicate that they think the values are worthwhile. And yet, sometimes, these two pieces register a different perspective. Sometimes the heroines wish *not* to comply with domestic femininity. Moreover, they have friendships in addition to those with a mother or guardian that are not shaped by the didactic function of mentoring. These bonds with other female characters seem to be constructed by the private discourse that Austen and her female friends and kin used with one another. These fictional portraits of character and relationship have some affinities with the exclusive culture women generated among themselves.

What are we to make of this? Because letters written by Austen have not survived from the early 1790s, it is impossible to say from sources outside her fictions whether she was at that time finding same-sex associations especially meaningful. At best, we can only generate hypotheses about the social experience influencing her writing, working backward from the distinctive, textual features of Austen's later juvenilia. It certainly would *appear*, based on the characterizations of women and their relationships in these works, that within a supportive community of family and friends Austen was developing a distinctly different or separate set of allegiances to women. That Austen was just reaching adulthood lends support for this hypothesis, for pressures to conform to domestic ideology would have been increasing at this time. She might have found a women's culture especially useful in this transitional period.

The heroines of "Letter the Third" and "Catharine" strive to conform to proper feminine conduct but sometimes feel rebellious. Drawn to two opposing codes of conduct, they often experience ambivalence. Once, Maria Williams refuses to keep silent and firmly contradicts Lady Greville's rude suppositions about her family. She is left feeling neither wholly triumphant nor wholly remorseful. As she explains to her correspondent: "I was half delighted with myself for my impertinence, & half afraid of being thought too saucy" (6:158). Kitty is also tempted to indulge in an unladylike discourse. Impertinent rejoinders readily occur to her, although she suppresses them for the most part (6:210, 211, 223). (Austen herself also suppressed a few such replies, erasing two in her manuscript that R. W. Chapman, editor of the standard edition of her works, was able to read and so to include in the text in brackets.[30]) Overly familiar remarks Kitty doesn't always keep back (6:216). And when forced by Edward Stanley to barge indecorously into the Dudleys' ballroom, Kitty is "half angry & half laughing" (6:220). The narrator, too, is ambivalent about Kitty's lapses in proper conduct, admiring and sympathizing with the cause of these lapses: "the natural Unreserve & Vivacity of her own Disposition" (6:216).

In addition, each heroine has one or more female friends to whom she can convey the difficulties of assuming domestic feminine conduct and from whom she receives not instruction but sympathy. These more egalitarian friendships, in enabling the expression of complaints, provide opportunities for the rejection, albeit momentarily, of feminine modesty and self-effacement. In "Letter the Third," Maria Williams's two friends—her correspondent and Ellen Greville—offer an alternative to her didactic tie to her mother. Maria's addressee does not, of course, respond to Maria's sentiments, but her existence permits Maria to voice her social difficulties and her discontent. To this friend she readily owns her "impertinence." To Ellen, she cannot speak frankly because it is Ellen's mother, Lady Greville, about whom she would complain. But Ellen dramatizes the solidarity and sympathy that Maria's correspondent does not. Ellen frequently defends Maria when her mother is particularly rude (6:156, 157, 159), and she prefers her friend's company to that of her mother (6:158). Although she does not say so, Maria knows that she "felt for me" (6:156).

A similar bond appears in "Catharine" between the heroine and the

Wynne sisters. Although the Wynnes have left the neighborhood, the bower that the sisters and Kitty built in Mrs. Percival's garden remains a symbol of their ties. The fiction initially presents the bower as a symbol of sentimental friendship: "In those days of happy Childhood, now so often regretted by Kitty this arbour had been formed, and separated perhaps for ever from these dear freinds, it encouraged more than any other place the tender and Melancholy recollections of hours rendered pleasant by *them*" (6:194). But that conventional version of female friendship rapidly gives way in "Catharine" to an innovative rendering of women's bonds. The bower comes to symbolize the sufferings caused by women's social and economic dependence and the mutual sympathy, support, and expressiveness of female friends.[31] Moreover, to the extent that this portrait was shaped by Austen's own experience of a culture generated by women, the female-constructed bower may be seen as a symbol of her unconventional revisions of female friendship in "Letter the Third" and "Catharine."

The bower evokes the sufferings of women because "Catharine" provides extended descriptions of the Wynnes' unpleasant fates. Genteel and well-educated, they were left penniless after the death of their mother and clergyman father. Cecilia Wynne has taken "the only possibility that was offered to her, of a Maintenance; Yet it was *one*, so opposite to all her ideas of Propriety, so contrary to her Wishes, so repugnant to her feelings, that she would almost have preferred Servitude to it, had Choice been allowed her." One of her cousins paid her way to the East Indies where she got "splendidly, yet unhappily married" (6:194). Her sister, Mary, has had to hire on as companion and poor relation to the daughter of some distant kin. The bower is also associated with female solidarity and expressiveness; Kitty goes to it when she is distressed. It is the only place where she can freely experience anger, which she feels in particular toward those who would make the Wynnes unhappy. She runs out to it in order to "indulge in peace all her affectionate Anger against the relations of the Wynnes, which was greatly heightened by finding from Camilla that they were in general considered as having acted particularly well by them—. She amused herself for some time in Abusing, and Hating them all, with great spirit" (6:207).

The letters exchanged between Kitty and the Wynnes give voice to what the bower symbolizes. They are a medium for mutual revelation and for comfort. The "world" may think the Wynnes well treated, but their private communications tell a different story. Cecilia's letters to Kitty do "not openly avow her feelings, yet every line proved her to be Unhappy. She spoke with pleasure of nothing, but of those Amusements which they had shared together and which could return no more" (6:194). The tone of Mary Wynne's letters—"she wrote usually in depressed Spirits" (6:195)—conveys her misery too, a bit more openly. And Kitty herself writes "her Misfortunes to Mary Wynne" (6:212). These letters indicate that expressions of unhappiness and discontent are exclusive to women's communications.

Austen's treatments of women and their friendships in "Letter the Third" and "Catharine" are not only innovative; they are provocative. They affirm feminine propriety, but they also raise questions about its desirability by depicting female characters who are sensitive to social or economic oppression. The characters struggle to mute themselves, but they yearn as well to break with domestic femininity, at least now and then, and to voice their anger and discontent, especially to one another. Still, the images of female identity and relationship in these works are no more subversive than they are conformist, and not just because these opposing representations neutralize one another.

The perspective of these works is indeterminate primarily because both are unfinished. "Letter the Third" is a slice of a fiction, a few scenes, while "Catharine" has a distinct beginning, proceeds through a series of incidents, delineates a group of characters, provides the basis for the heroine's change and growth, and then abruptly halts. Renderings of character may be multivalent, but they are in the courtship novel situated in plots whose conventions of ending usually enforce a particular ideological view. Indeed, some critics have recently drawn attention to narrative endings as the most important sites of ideology in fiction. As Joseph Boone, drawing on the work of neo-Marxist theorists, explains, "ideological 'solutions' to social contradictions become, in a profound sense, the 'resolutions' offered in traditional fiction."[32] And Rachel DuPlessis has similarly suggested not only that ideology is "coiled" in narrative structure but that "narrative outcome is one place where transindividual assumptions and values are most clearly visible, and where the word 'convention' is found resonating between its literary and its social meanings."[33]

Granted that the ending is the site of the novelist's "official" ideological position, features of the text, including some within the resolution itself, may undermine that formal summing-up. The ending is crucial, because of the perspective it articulates and because it enables us to identify the impact of other aspects of the text. We can recognize representations influenced by Austen's women's culture or by domestic ideology without the ending. But we cannot determine which representation is supportive and which subversive of the novel's concluding and, at least ostensibly, conclusive perspective unless we know what that perspective is.

What if "Catharine" were to close with happy, satisfying marriages for the heroine and perhaps Mary Wynne? What if Cecilia Wynne were to die, or to elope, or to be reconciled to her marriage? Such traditional resolutions of courtship novel plots—even when tragic—express conservative, patriarchal values, promoting, in Boone's words, the "culture's valorization of hierarchy and order within social (and sexual) relations."[34] But what if Kitty, Mary, and Cecilia were to run away in order to live together under a larger, more permanent bower? Such an ending conveys a very different vision of women's lives and of marriage. Representations of women's painful awareness of subordination or expressions of their discontent take on very different valences in the context of these diverse plot resolutions, subtly undermining traditional courtship resolutions and overtly contributing to endings that officially endorse women's egalitarian bonds and their separations from men. Conversely, representations of domestic femininity would contribute to the trajectory of traditional plots but undercut plot endings that enable women to be together without men.

Austen may have preferred writing fragments when making her first forays into serious comedy, in order to avoid the necessity of inventing a plot resolution bearing either cultural perspective. Certainly, she was aware by this time that narrative endings were freighted with such significance. "The Beautifull Cassandra," one of her earlier parodic juvenilia, reveals that awareness by playfully rejecting conventions of the courtship plot and its patriarchal resolution. The heroine encounters a viscount "no less celebrated for his Accomplishments & Virtues, than for his Elegance & Beauty," but she falls in love only with "an elegant Bonnet" (6:45). Resisting the conventions of courtship—she "curtseyed & walked on" (6:45)—Cassandra has several distinctly unromantic adventures and happily returns in the final chapter to the arms of her mother. We cannot, however, say with certainty that, by leaving "Letter the Third" or "Catharine" unfinished, Austen was *refusing* to choose for her "official" ending between the values of the gentry's or women's culture. It is possible, for example, that she had simply not yet mastered all the technical difficulties of developing as well as ending plots—whether with marriage or with an alternative fate for women.

Austen would eventually develop her own distinct versions of the courtship novel's comic conclusion, compatible with her wider community's patriarchal values. But we have no record of that achievement until 1811, almost two decades later, when she published *Sense and Sensibility*. Between the early 1790s and 1811 she embarked on several fictions, though only a few texts have survived. They are crucial to any history of Jane Austen's literary development, however. Informed by Austen's experience of female friendships and the culture they generated, these fictions offer even more assertive, unconventional portraits of women and their same-sex relationships than we have encountered in "Letter the Third" and "Catharine." They also evince Austen's further struggles with narrative endings, suggesting, in fact, that she was tempted to depart from traditional—and patriarchal— resolutions. Produced in an often overlooked, underappreciated period of her creative life, these works are the most daring and experimental of her career.

CHAPTER 7

The "Middle" Fictions:
Visible Conflicts

1

STUDIES of Jane Austen's fiction conventionally place her earliest writings in the category of juvenilia and label her six novels as her "mature" productions. The writings of the period of more than fifteen years between the early fragments and published novels have been more difficult to classify, and for an understandable reason. Although Austen may have written other works of which we have no record during this period, we have conclusive evidence about her composition of only five manuscripts. She wrote *Lady Susan* in 1793–94; "Elinor and Marianne" in 1795; "First Impressions" between October 1796 and August 1797; another draft of "Elinor and Marianne" in the fall of 1797; and "Susan" in 1798–99. She may have done more work on "Susan" during the next four years. In 1804–5 she drafted approximately 17,500 words of a novel, *The Watsons*.[1] Of these works, however, only the first, *Lady Susan*, and the last, *The Watsons*, have survived.

Because the works produced between *Lady Susan* and *The Watsons* were destroyed and we have been left with a mysterious ten-year gap between them, the two extant fictions have rarely been linked in critical studies of the novelist. Indeed, at first glance they do not seem to have much in common. The earlier work is epistolary; the later is a third-person narration. Literary critics have considered the mood that *Lady Susan* creates to be cool, sprightly, maliciously clever; they have sometimes likened the novel to Choderlos de Laclos's *Les Liaisons*

Dangereuses and its main character to the "merry widows" of earlier eighteenth-century fiction and drama.[2] By contrast, most critics have perceived enervation and depression in *The Watsons*.[3] Certainly *Lady Susan*'s female characters have an unusual ability to manipulate their social world, while *The Watsons'* female characters are often stymied.

Despite these differences, however, the two works have some intriguing similarities that suggest that Austen may have had a typifiable "middle" period. Both *Lady Susan* and *The Watsons* contain elements of conventional courtship novels that dramatize the ideology of domesticity. *Lady Susan* offers the standard dichotomy of persons and places: virtuous women residing in the country and vicious, fashionable women who prefer life in town. *The Watsons*, too, juxtaposes characters who are models of domestic femininity and those who, while not urban sophisticates, refuse the traits marked out by the domestic ideology. But both fictions undermine these moral and pedagogical oppositions.

Both pieces call attention to the problem Austen first began to probe in "Letter the Third" from "A Collection of Letters" in 1791 and in "Catharine or the Bower" in 1792: women's social and economic dependence in a socially hierarchical and patriarchal world. *Lady Susan* and *The Watsons* suggest that *all* female behavior, whether exemplary or depraved, is a response to women's social and economic vulnerability. And both fictions feature the relationships women form with one another as a particularly important response to this vulnerability. These bonds are neither didactic and idealized nor sentimental. Like some of the female ties represented in "Letter the Third" and "Catharine," they satisfy women's desires for solace and for opportunities to vent anger and frustration about their dependence.

But in *Lady Susan* and *The Watsons* these bonds do more, and thus mark a distinctive and previously ignored stage in Austen's development; female friends voice an awareness of their differences from males and some antagonism toward them. Because all adult women in *Lady Susan* form such bonds, the dichotomy of female virtue and vice is superseded by one based simply on male and female. In *The Watsons* only the heroine and one of her sisters sustain such a friendship over time. In this work, then, women's ties do not efface distinctions between female paragons and their flawed foils. Still, they throw the opposition out of alignment by radically altering one of its two terms: domestic femininity. They make women who are committed to domestic virtues and family life also strikingly independent of, and impatient with, men.

These two fictions are stunning in their bold, innovative critiques of male power. So strong are those critiques that they challenge the comic courtship plot, which inscribes patriarchal social arrangements in romantic and heterosexual unions. *Lady Susan* and *The Watsons* do not dismantle that plot, but they shift the focus away from its structure. Although their narrative techniques differ, both styles of narration render female alliances more important than heterosexual relationships.

Evidence about the period of time during which Austen wrote these works shows that she was coming to rely increasingly on female friendship as a crucial intellectual and emotional support for her social life and literary endeavors. Although we have none of Austen's letters before 1796 (two years after she wrote *Lady Susan*), the surviving letters from the second half of the 1790s suggest that her sister Cassandra and Martha Lloyd were key and enthusiastic readers of her fiction. They show as well the importance of women's alliances at a time when Austen was expected to marry and then, particularly in the early years of the nineteenth century, when she was beginning to experience the marginalization of the aging single woman. It is not surprising, then, that during this period Austen should draw on the culture of her close female friends in constructing not only female characterizations and relationships but also plot, a crucial locus of a work's cultural perspective.

Nevertheless, though *Lady Susan* and *The Watsons* are daring, they register as well Austen's doubts about diverging from standard fictional conventions, particularly of plot. In what I am calling Austen's "middle" period, she first evinced the desire to write for the public. Her father's efforts to sell "First Impressions" in 1797 (she was then twenty-one) to the publishing firm of Cadell & Davies testify to that wish, of course, as does the sale of her novel "Susan" to Crosby & Co. in 1803. More fundamentally, she expressed that desire in her writing itself. She was not now generating bits of parodic, playful fiction; neither was she devoting herself only to the private letter with its intermittent *sotto voce* comments meant for women's ears alone. Instead, she was attempting, along with writing her double-voiced letters, sustained, carefully plotted works of fiction whose very generic identity implies serious authorial intention and a wide audience of male and female readers. When in *Lady Susan* and *The Watsons* she represented heroines and other female characters as assertive, sometimes protesting women and depicted the power and appeal of female bonds, Austen was, in effect, preparing to offer for public consumption criticism of the patriarchal values expressed by modest and submissive heroines, their didactic female friendships, and their marriages. Features of both these texts indicate that she had second thoughts about doing so.

Both demonstrate a hesitancy about shifting attention away from the comic resolution of marriage. Both refuse to follow through on this shift. Moreover, they also evince subtle, protective guises intended to offset the impact of such refocusing. In these compensatory strategies, *Lady Susan* and *The Watsons* thus express Austen's efforts to accommodate, if not a large reading public, then her male as well as female friends and kin. Ambivalent about her cultural allegiances and literary intentions, she gave voice to and then attempted to muffle her women's culture.

We can only hypothesize about the lost manuscripts of the second half of the 1790s—"Elinor and Marianne," "First Impressions," and "Susan." But we can and should pay more attention to the works composed just before and just after these productions. They are, as we shall see, remarkably experimental within a highly formulaic form. Linked together, they provide coherent testimony about a crucial and conflict-ridden stage of Austen's development.

2

Lady Susan has many of the ingredients of a conventional late-eighteenth-century courtship novel, one that might have been entitled "The History of Frederica De Courcy." (Austen herself probably did not choose the name *Lady Susan*; her nephew, who gave the work that title when he first had it published in 1871, is the more likely source.) The fiction has a young and innocent heroine, Frederica, and it establishes the economic and social necessities for her marriage. She is dependent on a mother, Lady Susan, whose poverty and amorality make her an inadequate, indeed dangerous, guardian for the young girl. Frederica is also supplied with suitors: one, a wealthy baronet, who is a silly "rattle"; the other, a sensible gentleman of good family. Frederica manages to avoid marriage to the rattle and is heading toward marriage to the sensible gentleman when the work closes. Following a particular tradition of courtship novels, *Lady Susan* is also pedagogical in its presentation of the domestic ideology. Frederica inhabits a fictional world organized by the familiar dichotomy of domestic/provincial and fashionable/urban life. She is primed to learn from characters who have one or the other set of values and experiences.

Her mother, Lady Susan, and her mother's friend, Alicia Johnson, shun affective family ties, self-effacing feminine duties, and a quiet, private home life. Lady Susan describes her daughter, Frederica, to Alicia as "a stupid girl" with "nothing to recommend her," while Alicia advises her friend to "think more of yourself, & less of your Daughter" (6:252, 295). Both lament, when Alicia's husband is attacked with gout, that Alicia will have to take care of him. "To have you confined, a Nurse in his apartment!" exclaims Lady Susan in horror (6:298). And they view the prospect of domestic and rural retirement as a "penance" (6:294). By contrast, Catherine Vernon and her mother, Lady De Courcy, cultivate affectionate relations with all their family members. Catherine is also quick to adopt the roles of mother and mentor to Frederica, which Lady Susan rejects. She sees not "a stupid girl" but one who has all the makings of a good domestic woman: "There cannot be a more gentle, affectionate heart, or more obliging manners, when acting without restraint. Her little Cousins are all very fond of her" (6:273). Her vision of a comfortable life for her niece consists of staying at home and "at peace" with "regular employments, our Books & conversation, with Exercise, the Children, & every domestic pleasure in my power to procure her" (6:297).

This description of the novel, of course, misrepresents it. The work *could* have been organized around Frederica—the ingredients of such a story are all present—but Austen diverged from the fictional formulas of her predecessors and contemporaries by choosing not to focus on the young girl's subjectivity. We are, in fact, given only brief, sporadic access to it; she is for much of the novel prevented from contributing to the novel's web of social discourse. Hence, we are never witness to her embarrassments or dread when she is brought into company with Sir James; we do not follow along with her when she panics and runs away from school; we are unable to watch and empathize with her progress in becoming, despite the "dreadful example of Levity in her Mother" (6:273), a model domestic woman; and we do not experience with her the gratifications of receiving finally the tribute of the sensible gentleman Reginald De Courcy's love. On the few occasions when we do have access to her thoughts and feelings, we see only her marginality in relation to the social world. As the title he used indicates, James Edward Austen-Leigh viewed the character Lady Susan as the focus of the piece. But the novel might more appropriately have been named after a group; it focuses not on Frederica and not only on Lady Susan but on all the adult female characters.[4]

Surprisingly, the novel calls attention to the similarities among characters who are, following a popular convention, set in opposition to one another. Both domestic and fashionable female characters are keenly aware of the social and economic vulnerability of unmarried women, of the lurking twin destinies of poverty and humiliation. Hence, they all appreciate the crucial importance for their sex of marriage to prosperous men, and they, rather than just Frederica, are all vitally involved in marriage "plotting," manipulations that situate them *against* men. Finally, because of their interconnectedness they are quite effective at this plotting. Austen built both their ties and the effectiveness of them into the structure of her text—through her use of epistolary form.

The world of *Lady Susan* is made up in letters, which are the particular province, indeed, the genre of women. Of the forty-one that constitute the fiction, the majority—thirty—are written by one woman to another. Letters thus affect our perceptions of the characters, calling our attention to not domestic wives and mothers *or* dissipated sophisticates but female affiliations, in general. We encounter women primarily and not as isolated individuals but always within relationships. They appear to have not subjectivities but intersubjectivities, created not only because of the letter form but also because there is no mediation by a third-person, omniscient narrator. The interactions of Lady Susan and Catherine Vernon, when Lady Susan visits the Vernons' country estate, are, in effect, the interactions of two networks of women, not of this pair alone. Lady Susan discusses her experiences with Alicia Johnson. Catherine Vernon, Lady Susan's sister-in-law, does the same with her mother, Lady De Courcy. Although only these female relationships are extensively dramatized, references to another female bond in the text—between Mrs. Manwaring and her sister-in-law— suggest that the two friendships are representative.

If the letters in *Lady Susan* offer direct access to the meeting of women's minds, they also call our attention to the nature and importance of their discourse. The narratives of the domestic as well as the fashionable women are scheming, aggressive, pragmatic, and *powerful*. They manage a comic reversal within the patriarchal social world of the fiction, placing, in historian Natalie Zemon Davis's words, "women on top."[5] In a world that offers them few resources independent of men, women with very different attitudes and perceptions recognize a common goal: marriage to men of fortune. Their letter narratives produce the flattering self-representations that are their primary means of attracting such men. They band together around favorable images of themselves and of other women they wish to see married, and they successfully prompt marriage proposals from men who come to believe in the images.

Women develop such imagery in their correspondences or they repeat it in letters to their friends after they have tried it out on a man.

The linguistic exchanges that constitute women's bonds, then, serve the important function of generating and validating the self-representations crucial to attracting husbands. The letter form highlights the collaborative context of these representations. As Janet Altman in her study of *Epistolarity* reminds us, "the interpersonal bond basic to the very language of the letter . . . necessarily structures meaning in letter narrative."[6]

Because men of fortune are relatively scarce in this world, the female characters' networks, as their letters reveal, are also teams in competition with one another. If Lady Susan, with the help of her partner, Alicia, is an obvious competitor, so are the female members of the Manwaring family, who Lady Susan complains "are united against me" (6:244). And so is Catherine Vernon, who with the aid of her mother champions the cause of Lady Susan's daughter; Catherine attempts to draw her brother, Reginald De Courcy, away from Lady Susan and to Frederica.

Their competitions are enacted as feuds between alternative versions of the self. In the struggle over Reginald, for example, his sister attempts to enforce her view of Lady Susan, lamenting "the badness of her disposition" (6:256). But Lady Susan seeks, as she tells Alicia Johnson, "to persuade Reginald that she [his sister] has scandalously belied me" (6:254). That Lady Susan portrays herself as a paragon of domestic femininity only helps to break down the dichotomy between the domestic and the fashionable common to many courtship novels. She likes, for example, to speak with "tenderness & anxiety" about her daughter, "lamenting . . . the neglect of her education" and to take one of Catherine Vernon's children on her lap (6:251).

Each women's network tries to censor the opposition. Because Lady Susan is the more talented verbal artist, she can often make her stories more persuasive than those of others. Reginald rapidly comes to believe that "her prudence & economy are exemplary" and that "as a Mother she is unexceptionable" (6:265). When she presents to Catherine an attractive picture of marriage between her daughter and Sir James, she even manages to silence her sister-in-law. As Lady Susan confides to Alicia, "I . . . told my story with great success to Mrs. Vernon who, whatever might be her real sentiments, said nothing in opposition to mine" (6:280). By contrast, Catherine's more defensive strategy is either to try to remove the object of the rivalry, Reginald, out of earshot of Lady Susan's stories—she asks her mother to urge Reginald to come home—or to offer Reginald a replacement for Lady Susan.

The career of the person of liminal status, the adolescent Frederica, highlights the nature of female adulthood in this world. Frederica's immaturity is initially enforced by her mother's ban on her discourse. Lady Susan fears that were her daughter free to speak, she would "tell tales" (6:268) about herself and her mother and join an opposing network. Nonetheless, if she does, Lady Susan writes to Alicia, "I trust I shall be able to make my story as good as her's" (6:268). When Frederica does venture to express herself in a letter—by admitting her dislike of Sir James and asking Reginald to intervene with her mother—her linguistic inexperience is apparent. By contrast to the improvisational eloquence of her mother, Frederica writes slowly, providing only a brief and hesitating portrait of her feelings, punctuated by several self-effacing apologies. Because Catherine Vernon encourages Frederica, however, urging her, above all, to talk and to write, we understand that she will someday reach social and linguistic maturity as part of the Catherine Vernon–De Courcy network.

In *Lady Susan* women elicit marriage proposals not simply by producing attractive images of themselves and of their friends but also by creating themselves as effective agents. They assume authority by representing themselves with it in their letters. "I . . . advise you by all means to marry him [Reginald]" (6:256), goes a letter of Alicia Johnson's to Lady Susan. "I beleive I owe it to my own Character, to complete the match between my daughter & Sir James, after having so long intended it" (6:294), Lady Susan writes Alicia. The construction of such assertive selves by Alicia Johnson and Lady Susan may not be surprising. But the model of domestic femininity, Catherine Vernon, depicts herself in the same way. "When I next write, I shall be able I hope to tell you that Sir James is gone, Lady Susan vanquished, & Frederica at peace. We have much to do, but it shall be done" (6:285), Catherine Vernon tells her mother. Such commanding declarations are not only the means to power through marriage; they *are* power. Women's linguistic creativity in itself compensates for their economic dependence.

That compensation is made so successful that it frequently preempts the initiative of men. Although no network of women achieves all of its desires, the teams divide the men among them. Lady Susan and Alicia lose Reginald to the Catherine Vernon–Lady De Courcy–Frederica Vernon network. Lady Susan marries the wealthy Sir James. The Manwaring women lose Sir James, but they at least prevent Lady Susan from winning Reginald. What we never see in the resolution of these struggles is the active participation of a man who determines for himself whom and whether to marry.

Men in the social world of *Lady Susan* have comparatively little

power. Although wealth and property ought to make men commanding, inheritance practices alone severely limit their power. Reginald
has hardly any authority because he does not come into possession of
his father's estate until his father dies. His father has little authority
over his son because the estate is entailed; it will pass to his son
regardless of what his son does. But in *Lady Susan* men also lack power
because, unlike women, they have no adequately developed same-sex
relationships or correspondences through which they can be realized.
Consequently, they have no practice in generating and sustaining imagery counter to that produced by the women's networks. Reginald,
for example, refuses to accept his father's representation of Lady Susan
not only because his growing attraction to her is stronger than his tie
to his father but also because his father's linguistic skills cannot match
those of the women. In his letter to his son warning him against marrying Lady Susan, Sir Reginald conveys the image of Lady Susan
created within the Catherine Vernon–Lady De Courcy network, but he
does not know how to use it to dominate alternative images of her. Nor
does he represent himself as a masterful figure. He admits that "it is
out of my power to prevent your inheriting the family Estate"(6:261),
and, even worse, he gives Reginald a chance to defend Lady Susan. As
such linguistic modesty should indicate, men are unequipped to enter
the social world's representational feuds and, in fact, can only be their
victims, dupes of any compelling imagery presented to them.

Without the ability to use language as women do, to command, men
are reduced to objects. They are often metonymically identified in
Lady Susan as property. To Alicia Johnson, "M^r De Courcy may be
worth having" (6:256). To Catherine, lamenting Lady Susan's influence over her brother, Reginald "is more securely her's than ever"
(6:291). Men seem almost to have no subjectivity in this world. That
impression is reinforced for the reader by the dearth of letters written
by them—only five. We are given little direct access to the perspectives
of men, viewing them usually from the hostile vantage point of the
women. When men occasionally act or express their wills, women, in
their letters, find them ineffectual or irrationally contrary. Lady Susan
and Alicia hide their relationship from her husband because he disapproves of it. "Since he will be stubborn," she tells Alicia, "he must
be tricked" (6:249). Similarly, Catherine is frustrated by what she per-
ceives as her husband's almost perversely passive behavior when he
chaperones Frederica from London. He "was too fearful of distressing
her," Catherine writes to her mother, "to ask many questions as they
travelled. . . . I think I should have discovered the truth in the course
of a Thirty mile Journey" (6:271).

[163]

With her youthful ignorance of the social world, Frederica, again, calls our attention to the nature of manhood in it. She asks Reginald to persuade her mother not to marry her off to Sir James. Her choice of Reginald reveals that she romanticizes the male, an attitude which, her mother implies, she has learned from the novels she reads (6:283, 290). The young girl imagines Reginald with powers to protect and command that he does not possess, for he will, as the text reveals, always be a captive of women's discourse. Although he tries to represent Frederica's views, Lady Susan eventually overpowers him with her account of the matters at hand until he reverses himself, concluding that he has "entirely misunderstood Lady Susan." Frederica, he explains to his sister, "does not know her Mother—Lady Susan means nothing but her Good—but Frederica will not make a friend of her. Lady Susan therefore does not always know what will make her daughter happy. Besides I could have no right to interfere—Miss Vernon was mistaken in applying to me" (6:287).

Reginald finally rejects Lady Susan's version only when he finds another woman's story, that of Mrs. Manwaring, more persuasive. In the correspondence that concludes their relationship, Lady Susan demands another hearing. He can defend himself against the power of her discourse, however, only by refusing to listen to her anymore. He returns to the Vernon–De Courcy affiliation—to the net of their discourse—only to encounter a mother and sister ready to catch him for Frederica. "When Reginald has recovered his usual good spirits," Lady De Courcy writes to Catherine, "we will try to rob him of his heart once more" (6:309).

The domination of women in *Lady Susan* does not transform the patriarchal structure of the social world. *Lady Susan*'s world is no feminist utopia like the one depicted in Charlotte Perkins Gilman's *Herland*. Power, in Austen's work, is still based on property, and only men generally have direct access to it. Women acknowledge and accept their sole social recourse, to marry men of property. They do not change the structure of the social world, but the female characters reverse the distribution of power in it, reducing men to the status of mere prizes of their competitions. They also manage to reverse the impact of the gender-marked genres of their society—the public courtship novel and the private and primarily female discourse of letter-writing. Frederica, whose selection of a male to be her protector is based on the romantic, heterosexual models offered by the novels she reads, is unable to compete with her mother, whose letters construct versions of reality that triumph over the life-models of the patriarchal novel. If Frederica is to become an effective member of this social

[164]

world, so the text suggests, she must learn to write letters to other women. Rather than imitating the histories of novel heroines, she must compose her own history in conjunction with the female friends to whom she would write.

These reversals are possible, again, because women have formed relationships with one another within their larger social world. The domination of *Lady Susan*'s female characters is the outcome of a *system* of women. *Lady Susan*'s institution of women's networks and its expression in the epistolary form renders acts—otherwise isolated and arbitrary—politically effective.[7]

This vision of power does not, of course, replicate Jane Austen's experience of her women's culture. Although devoid of the sentimentality, melodrama, and wildly implausible trappings of plot that were pervasive in contemporary courtship novels, the more realistic *Lady Susan* still endows women's networks with more power than they had in Austen's actual life. At the heart of the novel lies the fantasy that the discourse of one woman to another has magic power: women writing and speaking to one another are doing and becoming. As a consequence of both their own and, particularly in Frederica's case, their friends' powerful discourse, the female correspondents in *Lady Susan* have married or are moving toward marriages with men of property. Because Austen and her female friends and relatives kept their implicit and explicit criticism of patriarchal authority private, however, their discourse did not turn the social relations of the wider genteel community upside down; in fact, it had no impact on those relations. But their culture did have an effect on the emotional and conceptual responses of its participants, and it prompted one of its most imaginative participants—Jane Austen—to reenvision the social world, if only in the play of her writing. Although Jane Austen and her female friends produced a ghettoized, confidential discourse, the tendency of these women, among themselves, to put their own desires and experiences first and to express critical, discontented feelings fueled *Lady Susan*'s fantasies of reversal.

A particular trait of Austen's letters, however, suggests a closer and more specific creative link between the discourse of her women's culture and *Lady Susan*. Although Austen wrote *Lady Susan* before 1796, when her surviving letters commence, it is worth noting that many of the letters she wrote to Cassandra contain short, comic sex-reversal fantasies. They emerge in so many letters and over so many years that they appear to be an habitual expression to her most intimate confidante of opposition to the inequality in her society's gender relations.

These reversals imply a resentment over women's subordination to and dependence on men. Austen likes to predict or direct, with all the confidence of a Lady Susan or a Catherine Vernon, the desires and behavior of men. Moreover, she enjoys inventing women desirable to men and men vulnerable to rejection. "I rather expect to receive an offer from my friend in the course of the evening," she playfully confides to Cassandra in 1796; "I shall refuse him, however, unless he promises to give away his white coat."[8] She informs Cassandra in another letter, "I took an opportunity of assuring Mr. J. T. that neither he nor his Father need longer keep themselves single for You."[9] "I propose," she writes in 1809, "being asked to dance by our acquaintance Mr. Smith, now *Capt*ⁿ Smith, who has lately re-appeared in Southampton—but I shall decline it."[10] In the following passage Austen reverses the distribution of power in her society not only in expressions of agency but also in her metaphoric use of a legalistic jargon that invests her actions with the authority of the usually male will-writer and turns men into property: "Tell Mary that I make over Mr. Heartley and all his estate to her for her sole use and benefit in future, and not only him, but all my other admirers into the bargain wherever she can find them, even the kiss which C. Powlett wanted to give me, as I mean to confine myself in the future to Mr. Tom Lefroy, for whom I do not care sixpence."[11] In communications to her sister, Austen had a tendency to imagine in the shape of these brief reversals, and they may have inspired the extended sexual reversal of the first of the novels of her "middle" period.

Lady Susan was not the first of Jane Austen's fictions to express the discourse of her women's culture. "Letter the Third" and "Catharine" register her initial, tentative expressions of it in their characterizations of women and their friendships. But *Lady Susan* goes further, amplifying the culture's oppositional impulses and imaginings, so much so that they affect the plot: the "end" of marriage seems nominal, consistently overshadowed by the "means" of women's affiliations. This greater emphasis on the oppositional power of women's bonds, however, apparently troubled Austen. She did not sustain it through the work, did not allow the fiction to close with "women on top." The work's "Conclusion" brings the plot established in the letters to a logically consistent termination. We learn that Lady Susan, having returned to London and having lost Reginald De Courcy, manipulates Sir James into marrying her. Because she needs her daughter out of the way, she is glad now to send her back to the Vernons' country estate and into the Vernon–De Courcy network. There Frederica has only to wait until Reginald falls in love with her. However, the technique used to convey this ending—the "Conclusion" is not in epistolary form but in third-person narration—alters the impact of this material.

Some critics have suggested that Austen switched narrative forms for the ending of *Lady Susan* because she could not adequately guide her readers' moral responses to her characters by using the letter form. Without such guidance the cosmopolitan Lady Susan, who should serve to highlight the virtues of the domestic characters, is just too compelling. Mary Poovey argues, for example, that "the epistolary form generates moral anarchy. . . . there is no moral authority because there is no narrative authority. In the laissez-faire competition the epistolary *Lady Susan* permits, the reader will identify with whatever character dominates the narration or most completely gratifies the appetite for entertainment. In *Lady Susan* this character is, of course, the dangerous heroine."[12] We can see, however, that it is not only Lady Susan whose power and stature are diminished in the "Conclusion"; the criticism of Lady Susan that the third-person narrator can and does offer contributes to a more general reperception of women and their relationships.

Morally anarchic though it may be, the letter form is in *Lady Susan* the terrain of women's networks and of their power. As long as the story is told in letters, most of them written by the female characters, the reader has the opportunity to identify with, to seem to be "inside," women's intersubjectivities. The invention of an omniscient narrator—simply the narrator's presence—diminishes this identification, for the narrator, situated outside of these intersubjectivities, distances the reader from them, too. If that distance is metaphorically spatial, it is literally temporal. The female correspondents tell their stories in what Janet Altman has called the "pivotal" present tense, which "looks out toward past and future," thus giving readers a sense of the stories' immediacy. By contrast, the narrator completes the female characters' stories only in a past tense, which seals them off from the readers' present.[13]

In addition, the narrator offers criticism of women's networks in subtle alterations of its own vantage point. Although the following passage, which opens the "Conclusion," conveys the typically intense conspiracies and competitions within women's relationships, we are asked to see the letters that express them from the perspective of "Post office" and "State":

> This Correspondence, by a meeting between some of the Parties & a separation between the others, could not, to the great detriment of the Post office Revenue, be continued longer. Very little assistance to the State could be derived from the Epistolary Intercourse of Mrs Vernon & her neice, for the former soon perceived by the stile of Frederica's Letters, that

they were written under her Mother's inspection, & therefore deferring all particular enquiry till she could make it personally in Town, ceased writing minutely or often. (6:311)

The narrator's hyperbolic language—"great detriment"—reinforces a narrative viewpoint that indicates of what small importance these relationships actually are.

The narrator subtly diminishes the importance of women's relationships again by reeling off in rapid and clipped succession their typical activities: "Frederica was therefore fixed in the family of her Uncle & Aunt, till such time as Reginald De Courcy could be talked, flattered & finessed into an affection for her" (6:313). However, having pulled back from and caused the reader to pull back from women's networks, the narrator does not now embrace the conventions of comic plot endings. Frederica even in the "Conclusion" is not brought center stage. We are given no evidence in these last pages that *she* wishes to marry Reginald. His desires receive more attention in the ending section, but the narrator refuses to treat them with the admiration or piety often reserved for the hearts of heroes in post-Richardsonian courtship novels. His love for Frederica, the narrator goes on to announce,

allowing leisure for the conquest of his attachment to her Mother, for his abjuring all future attachments & detesting the Sex, might be reasonably looked for in the course of a Twelvemonth. Three Months might have done it in general, but Reginald's feelings were no less lasting than lively. (6:313)

At the end of the "Conclusion" the narrator disavows the power of women's networks by pretending to acknowledge it. The narrator becomes an "I" whose perspective, rather than distancing it, embraces the viewpoint of women. But because the narrator is generally omniscient and not one of the characters in the social world of the fiction, "her" increasingly biased perspective and extreme diction render ridiculous not just her but the characters whose perspective she simulates. The narrator offers the following ironic but unambiguous observations about Lady Susan. Though adopting the "I" persona and seemingly limited powers of knowing, she does have some authority here because of her secure moral standards:

Whether Lady Susan was, or was not happy in her second Choice—I do not see how it can ever be ascertained—for who would take her assurance of it, on either side of the question? The World must judge from Probability. She had nothing against her, but her Husband, & her Conscience. (6:313)

The narrator then sheds the objectivity of her moral standards along with her omniscience. Who has suffered, she asks, from Lady Susan's conduct? Sir James, certainly. "I leave him therefore," says the narrator, "to all the Pity that anybody can give him" (6:313). And then she declares and simultaneously undercuts *her* concerns, in her recognition and exaggeration of the dramas of women's networks:

> For myself, I confess that *I* can pity only Miss Manwaring, who coming to Town & putting herself to an expence in Cloathes, which impoverished her for two years, on purpose to secure him, was defrauded of her due by a Woman ten years older than herself. (6:313)

The "Conclusion," then, undermines the subversive vision that the epistolary form made possible.

Although the interrupted and radically altered narrative form of *Lady Susan* testifies to Austen's discomfort with the subversive vision she had created by means of epistolary form, she did not cease to work in that form after *Lady Susan*. Indeed, she made considerable use of it in the second half of the 1790s when she was drafting three of her novels for the first time. Literary critic B. C. Southam has persuasively argued that Austen composed two of them, "First Impressions" and "Elinor and Marianne," in epistolary form.[14] Because none of these early drafts has survived, we can only speculate about their visions of domesticity and her motives for rewriting them in third-person narrative before publishing them.

A. Walton Litz offers reasons for Austen's change in form shaped by an evolutionary paradigm. He views the young Austen, the Austen of the juvenilia and the longer, slightly later works such as *Lady Susan*, as an experimenter with "the range of the conventional forms." According to Litz, Austen found that she was "unable to express her maturing view of the world completely in any one of them" and had to develop "a narrative method of her own." In the context of such an evolution *Lady Susan* is "a dead end, an interesting but unsuccessful experiment in a dying form," which Austen attempted to salvage with the third-person narrative she was beginning to use.[15] But did Austen encounter difficulties with a limited narrative form or with the paradoxes of her worldview? Perhaps "First Impressions" or, more likely, "Elinor and Marianne," by offering unmediated access to women's narratives, also endowed their discourse with a desirable power.[16] It may be, too, that Austen recognized in the power of women's discourse challenges to patriarchal literary as well as social conventions and that she did—and did not—want to represent such challenges. That is the conflict that *Lady Susan*, in its sudden shift in narrative voice, expresses, and it is the conflict to which *The Watsons*, though without a shifting narrative, testifies as well.

3

Although incomplete, *The Watsons* (also named not by Austen but by James Edward Austen-Leigh) was to have been structured by a comic courtship plot and to forward the domestic ideology. Traces of a conventional plot, recognizable to readers familiar with other courtship novels, emerge initially in the establishment of the unmarried Emma Watson as heroine, in the interest that Lord Osborne takes in her, and in Emma's attraction to the "sensible, unaffected" clergyman, Mr. Howard (6:335). The ideology of domesticity quietly informs the work's conventional characterizations: Emma is a model of domestic femininity who has several foils in the vain and self-serving behavior of other female characters. The courtship plot hinted at in the manuscript fragment was confirmed by Cassandra Austen after her sister's death. According to James Edward Austen-Leigh, she told her nieces that "Mr. Watson was soon to die; and Emma to become dependent for a home on her narrow-minded sister-in-law and brother. She was to decline an offer of marriage from Lord Osborne, and much of the interest of the tale was to arise from Lady Osborne's love for Mr. Howard, and his counter affection for Emma, whom he was finally to marry."[17]

What *The Watsons* was *meant* to be, however, is not exactly what it is in the surviving manuscript. If we read it in light of what it was supposed to become, we may be unable to perceive fully what Austen was actually representing in the pages of the work she wrote. Although elements of a courtship plot do appear in the work, much of the fiction constructs a social world in which heterosexual ties are hard to establish and female friendship serves as an alternative to marriage and, inevitably, to the courtship plot.

Like *Lady Susan, The Watsons* portrays a patriarchal world in which women's social and economic vulnerability determines and simultaneously threatens to frustrate their desires. When their families do not supply them with portions or legacies, they need to find husbands. But because they lack economic resources of their own, their quest is very difficult. The imperative to marry is underscored in the first scene of *The Watsons*. Because women must venture out of their homes and families to seek spouses, Elizabeth Watson is driving her youngest sister, Emma, to the Edwardses, old family friends who will take her to their town's first winter assembly. Elizabeth herself, past her prime and needed at home, is not going to the ball.

Information about the Watson family's material circumstances, which emerges during the drive, further emphasizes the imperative. The widowed Mr. Watson has a very small income. His ill health only makes the situation of his four unmarried daughters more precarious; they could be thrust into destitution at any moment. Although Emma has been raised by a prosperous uncle and aunt with expectations of receiving from them a considerable portion, the death of her uncle and the remarriage of her aunt have thrown her back on the very limited resources of her immediate family. The Watsons' "poor Father and . . . great wash," though seemingly disparate responsibilities, are justly linked as emblems of the family's impoverished material life (6:321). They signify a family running down and using up, a family without enough servants to enable ready and rapid renewal. Other emblems that emerge in the scene also point, if indirectly, to the insufficient resources of the Watsons' establishment. The Watsons' chaise with its old mare makes a poor contrast to the Edwardses' roomy carriage, and Elizabeth's focus on the "comfortable soup" that the Edwards family has after every ball calls attention to the less than abundant stores available at their own house (6:315).

The Watsons sustains an analysis of the detrimental effects that women's social and economic dependence can have on their feminine identities. Two of the Watson daughters, the novel suggests, have been deformed by the imperative to marry. Although Jane Austen stopped writing the novel before she could bring one of them, Penelope, before the reader, Elizabeth attests to her spoiled character: "She thinks everything fair for a Husband" (6:316). So competitive is she that she had once even attempted to capture Purvis, at the time courting Elizabeth. "I trusted her," Elizabeth explains, "she set him against me, with a veiw of gaining him herself, & it ended in his discontinuing his visits & soon after marrying somebody else" (6:316). Emma's response to the story indicates that Penelope has violated the norms of conduct, at least within families: "Could a sister do such a thing?—Rivalry, Treachery between sisters!" (6:316). Penelope's efforts to find a husband take her from home quite often, and the return of Emma, whom she has not seen in several years, has not attracted her away from her current efforts to further a match with a rich elderly doctor in Chichester.

Another Watson sister, Margaret, is also away when Emma returns and does not choose to hurry home on her account. She too is attempting to catch a husband, by trying with her absence to make a local gentleman, Tom Musgrave, long for her. In the pages Austen wrote of the novel, Margaret does return home in the company of Robert, one of the two Watson brothers, and Robert's wife, Jane. Margaret then demonstrates a disturbing doubleness of character shaped by her desire and efforts to marry. In company, she adopts the supposedly appealing pose of sensibility; she exhibits a gentleness, a delicacy of feeling worthy of a novel heroine. But when she is alone with her family she is "fretful & perverse" (6:319). The husband hunt has even affected her appearance. Although she is pretty, the narrator informs us that "the sharp & anxious expression of her face made her beauty in general little felt" (6:349).

Penelope and Margaret's unpleasant traits and behaviors ruin the texture of the Watsons' home life. Their frequent desertions leave household tasks such as the "great wash" to fewer hands—specifically Elizabeth's—and their discontent and sharp preying impulses have murdered family affection (6:321). Thus, when Emma receives an invitation to visit her brother and sister-in-law, Elizabeth advises her to go. "You do not know," she tells her, "what you have to bear at home" (6:362).

Penelope and Margaret's contributions to "family Discord" do not, of course, augur well for their success as wives and mothers (6:361). Women's economic subordination and the consequent *necessity* of their marriages have destroyed their dispositions and, so we can infer, will make impossible the affectionate, comforting domesticity they are expected to create as married women. Even those women entering the marriage market with a portion—Robert Watson's wife was one—are not untainted by the mercenary cast of the quest for spouses. She has never moved beyond the triumph of having had £6,000 to bring to a husband, and her conceit and materialism outweigh, or rather give new meaning to, motherly care. When Elizabeth laments that the couple have left her niece behind, her sister-in-law blithely responds: "I assure you it went very hard with Augusta to have us come away without her. I was forced to say we were only going to Church & promise to come back for her directly.—But you know it would not do, to bring her without her maid, & I am as particular as ever in having her properly attended to" (6:350).

Not all female characters, however, are deformed by their social and economic vulnerability. Elizabeth and Emma Watson can sustain the modesty and generosity of a feminine identity because, for different reasons, they refuse to respond to the marital imperative with Penelope and Margaret's single-minded desperation. Elizabeth, denied her one love, Purvis, still enjoys company but no longer appears to be capable of a sharp wish for any particular man. And Emma, as Elizabeth tells her, is "very refined" (6:318). She has a moral delicacy that makes her loathe mercenary marriage despite the insecurities of her social and economic situation. Ironically, they often demonstrate feminine virtues precisely when they put aside any efforts to fulfill the feminine "destiny" prescribed by the ideology of domesticity. In a properly feminine display of deference each, for example, expresses a willingness to stay home from the ball so that the other sister may attend.

At the ball Emma also demonstrates an unselfish concern for others when at one point she gives up the possibility of dancing with any prospective suitor to be the partner of ten-year-old Charles Blake. He has been disappointed of his own partner, Miss Osborne, who has broken her promise to the little boy in order to dance with a military officer. Emma's nurturing feelings outweigh her desire to circulate, and though her compassion wins her the admiration of more than one man at the ball, that is not her intention. She enjoys pleasing the boy and his mother and in response to Mrs. Blake's thanks, "Emma with perfect truth could assure her that she could not be giving greater pleasure than she felt herself" (6:331).

Rather than devoting themselves to the quest for husbands, Emma and Elizabeth Watson confide to one another reservations about such quests, women's need to engage in them, and the single men who are their objects. In reflecting on women's prospects in general and their own in particular, Elizabeth and Emma voice their discomfort with the inequalities of gender. Such sentiments are part of a women's culture. "You know we must marry," Elizabeth tells her younger sister, though she would at this point be happy not to: "I could do very well single for my own part—A little Company, & a pleasant Ball now & then, would be enough for me, if one could be young for ever, but my Father cannot provide for us, & it is very bad to grow old & be poor & laughed at" (6:317). And Emma proclaims: "I would rather be Teacher at a school (and I can think of nothing worse) than marry a Man I did not like" (6:318). The two sisters are also critical of Tom Musgrave, an eligible man in their neighborhood, who takes advantage of his superior social and economic position by being insincere to women. "It is a hard thing for a woman to stand against the flattering ways of a Man," Elizabeth declares (6:343).

If Austen's long-range solution to women's need for marriage was to have been one exemplary union—of Emma Watson and Mr. Howard—*The Watsons* proposes another, more immediate solution in the relationship of Emma and Elizabeth. Indeed, the pages of the novel actually written do not make Mr. Howard a key character. He dances with Emma at the ball, wins her approbation, and appears briefly in Mr. Watson's narrative as a fine-sermon giver and a kind escort when the ailing man must climb a steep flight of stairs. But Mr. Howard otherwise remains offstage. Much more in evidence is the close, considerate friendship of the two sisters, which functions as a viable alternative to the heterosexual love and esteem offered by courtship novels with comic endings.

Emma and Elizabeth enjoy "tranquil & affectionate intercourse" (6:348). The sisters are also said to look alike (6:324), and their physical similarity is an emblem of their similar tastes. Both prefer and, therefore, when alone with their father enjoy "serenity" at home (6:348). Without men or a desperate desire for them, Emma and Elizabeth can successfully adhere not only to feminine virtues but to the feminine role. They are able to create a harmonious domestic life, filled with comfort, calm, and concern for their father.

Their preference for a quiet domestic life together is not, of course, without a tax. Without the financial resources of husbands, they must severely restrict their own consumption. Careful female economy and the etiquette of their status group necessitate, for example, that they deprive themselves at precisely their most enjoyable moments—when home alone—in order to provide generous hospitality to guests and their more demanding siblings. Still, they prefer scant resources if they can be enjoyed in intimate harmony. After one "quietly-sociable little meal," Elizabeth "could not help observing how comfortably it had passed. 'It is so delightful to me . . . to have Things going on in peace & goodhumour. Nobody can tell how much I hate quarrelling. Now, tho' we have had nothing but fried beef, how good it has all seemed'" (6:343). When Margaret and Robert and his wife arrive to put an end to "almost all that had been comfortable in the house," Elizabeth and Emma still attempt to carve out a tranquil space for themselves in the increasingly crowded house, choosing to share a bedroom and to give Margaret the material luxury of one to herself (6:348).

Elizabeth and Emma's relationship is represented in a narrative which, though not epistolary, has features especially suited to convey both their intimacy and their discontented feelings. Although the novel is narrated in the third person, the narrative voice does not intervene in their relationship or distance it from the reader with intrusive commentary. In representing dialogue, for example, Austen rarely lets her narrator interrupt the characters' exchanges. She often assigns to the narrator only the obligatory "she says" and "he says" and sometimes not even those explanatory tags of the discourse. One character's statements are separated from another's by quotation marks alone. Thus when Emma and Elizabeth converse—and their tête-à-têtes are among the longest represented in this novel—they create a sense of intimacy at least equivalent to that generated by the letter-writing women friends in *Lady Susan*. Here is a sample of their talk as it appears in the text:

> —'And so, you really did not dance with Tom. M. at all?—But you must have liked him, you must have been struck with him altogether.'—'I do *not* like him, Eliz:—. I allow his person & air to be good—& that his manners to a certain point—his address rather—is pleasing.—But I see nothing else to admire in him.—On the contrary, he seems very vain, very conceited, absurdly anxious for Distinction, & absolutely contemptible in some of the measures he takes for becoming so.—There is a ridiculousness about him that entertains me—but his company gives me no other agreable Emotion.' 'My dearest Emma!—You are like nobody else in the World.' (6:342)

Moreover, the narrative voice has none of the irony and cool wit of those Austen created for her six subsequent novels. Rather, it is closely aligned with Emma's point of view. It sympathetically assesses Emma's change in life-style: from "the expected Heiress of an easy Independance, she was become of importance to no one, a burden on those, whose affection she c^d not expect, an addition in an House, already overstocked. . . . It was well for her that she was naturally chearful;— for the Change had been such as might have plunged weak spirits in Despondence—" (6:362). The narrator introduces or restates the heroine's impressions of the "inferior minds" of family members Robert, Jane, and Margaret (6:362). It also shares Emma's critical view not of Robert alone but of all the males who make appearances in this social world.

So closely identified is the narrator with the heroine that unattractive descriptions of men, which Emma and Elizabeth would be likely to convey only to one another, also appear outside their discourse. These severe representations show men to be unappealing precisely because of the way they treat women. If single, they refuse to commit themselves. The narrator dramatizes a point of view whose province is a women's culture, when, for example, introducing Lord Osborne: "He was not fond of Women's company, & he never danced" (6:329-30). He comes to the ball only in order to "gape without restraint" (6:332). The narrator portrays Tom Musgrave as equally inaccessible, although his style is different. An inveterate flirt, he desires only to be desired. As a single man of independent means, he believes himself to be a valuable resource and offers himself as dance partner or coach driver to needy women in order to capture affections he has no intention of returning. He makes several pointed efforts to attract Emma but is also happy, when trying to cultivate her interest, to serve simultaneously as Lord Osborne's surrogate. He cannot even promise to come to dinner when Margaret prompts Elizabeth to invite him, saying yes and then "possibly" and then "I . . . must not engage—You will not think of me unless you see me" (6:360).

The narrator also offers unflattering portraits of married men who show insensitivity towards women. Although both Mr. Edwards and Robert Watson are described or shown as civil and occasionally even kind-hearted, they are not so when speaking of Emma's aunt and, in the process, of women in general. No one thinks the aunt was wise to remarry, but Watson and Edwards are insulting. "When an old Lady plays the fool," says Mr. Edwards, "it is not in the course of nature that she should suffer from it many years" (6:326). And Robert Watson brusquely asserts, "A woman should never be trusted with money. . . . I hope the old woman will smart for it. . . . you know every body must think her an old fool" (6:351-52). Watson is subsequently shown behaving with yet more disrespect for women. Although he has ignored his wife's entreaties that he powder his hair before dinner, he excuses his appearance to unexpected caller Tom Musgrave with the explanation that "we got here so late." Surprised by this sudden show of vanity and by his courtesy toward male acquaintances though not toward the females of his own family, "Emma [like the narrator] could not help entering into what she supposed her Sister in law's feelings at that moment" (6:357).

The narrator's representation of the visit of Lord Osborne and Tom Musgrave to Emma and Elizabeth is also shaped by a perspective that belongs to the private culture of women. The scene calls attention to women's distance and difference from men. The two men are hardly the first unwanted suitors to call on novel heroines. It is difficult to think of a contemporary courtship novel that doesn't depict an aggressive, obnoxious suitor taking the heroine by surprise in her garden, her drawing room, or even, as in *Emmeline*, in her chamber. But when Tom Musgrave and Lord Osborne come to call on the Watson sisters, they appear as not only unpleasant but, by virtue of their gender and status, as alien intruders. The men are interrupting a specifically female domestic harmony, attended, of course, by inelegant thrift: the women are about to begin an unfashionably early, less-than-sumptuous dinner, serving themselves informally in the parlor.[18]

The polarity the narrator highlights between male and female is based on social and economic power. The two men's very entrance into the Watsons' home testifies to their superior position. Dominance is emblematically reinforced by their knock on the door with "as smart a rap as the end of a riding-whip c^d give" (6:344). The women are unable to turn their visitors away: Lord Osborne is too superior in status to be denied and, in any case, there are not enough servants or hallways and rooms intervening between doorway and parlor to give the insiders adequate control over meetings with outsiders. Emma and Elizabeth can only receive their guests with dismay and embarrassment. But Emma is also annoyed at the visit, finding "quite as much Impertinence in it's form as Goodbreeding" (6:348).

Her resentment of the power of men is expressed in the conversation that follows. Lord Osborne, as usual, would rather "gape" than make efforts to please in conversation, and Emma is consequently "not inclined to give herself much trouble for his Entertainment" (6:345). She becomes animated only when he suggests that she ride horseback. Relying on a misogynistic cliché Lord Osborne supposes that women have only to desire and "the means w^d soon follow." Emma responds by calling attention to the different perspectives of men and women— "Your Lordship thinks we always have our own way.—*That* is a point on which Ladies & Gentle^n have long disagreed"—and then her plain, serious talk forces on him recognition of the genuine limitations of female desire. "There are some circumstances," she insists, "which even *Women* cannot controul.—Female Economy will do a great deal my Lord, but it cannot turn a small income into a large one" (6:346).

Expressions of the wide gap between men's and women's perceptions, of men's power and their disrespect, and of women's resentment—whether voiced by one female character to another or, on a larger scale, depicted by the narrator—do not point toward the heterosexual resolutions of comic courtship novels. Instead, they prompt us to consider whether a conventional, comic courtship plot could manage to override or outweigh the effect achieved by these expressions. This speculation leads to another: could the perspective of a women's culture, rendered in *The Watsons*, be related to the novel's unfinished state? In order to probe this possibility, we need to turn to the growing debate over the question of *The Watsons'* incompleteness.

Most critics, musing about why Austen never finished *The Watsons*, have fashioned biographical explanations. They have reeled off a series of depressing personal experiences, most notably the death of Austen's father in January 1805, to show that Austen might have lost heart for writing. This was a time, James Heldman has suggested, "of disruption, dislocation, disappointment, frustration, alienation, anxiety, loss, grief, and uncertainty about the future."[19] Such reasoning may explain why Austen stopped writing, but it does not explain why she refused to pick up *The Watsons* again at a later date. Heldman, however, maintains further that the work itself took shape from Austen's unhappiness and that she did not go back to the project because she was reluctant to encounter the distress reflected in it: "She could not—or would not—return to *The Watsons,* and especially to the plight of a heroine who was so much like herself, without recalling and suffering more unpleasantness and pain than she was willing to endure."[20] Another critic, basing her argument upon Austen's personal experience also, has similarly suggested that the writer did not return to *The Watsons* when her life was said to take a more secure, settled form at Chawton because she could not bear to confront the painful memories evoked by the work. According to Margaret Drabble, "when she felt like writing again, the melancholy associations of the manuscript were too much for her, and she put it aside."[21]

But Joseph Wiesenfarth has cast doubt on the biographical approach to the problem by calling attention to the circularity of these claims: "Jane Austen's life shows why *The Watsons* is a fragment and why it is lacking in power; *The Watsons* shows that the pressure of circumstances in Jane Austen's life affected her creative powers." And he notes in addition a small, dissenting band of critics who have praised the "heightened" rather than diminished "creative power" of the text.[22]

A few commentators have sought aesthetic explanations for *The Watsons'* incompleteness. James Edward Austen-Leigh, for example, in offering the fragment to the public for the first time in 1871, maintained that Austen ceased to work on it because she came to see "the evil of having placed her heroine too low, in such a position of poverty and obscurity as, though not necessarily connected with vulgarity, has a sad tendency to degenerate into it." The portrait of Fanny Price's Portsmouth visit in *Mansfield Park,* however, indicates that Austen was subsequently willing, contrary to what Austen-Leigh claims, to place her heroine in "circumstances likely to be unfavourable to the refinement of a lady."[23] B. C. Southam has suggested that because the heroine of *The Watsons* is at the start of the novel already "sensitive, intelligent, spirited, charitable, affectionate and high principled, the possibilities for her development are limited."[24] But it is hard to see why Austen's nearly flawless heroines Fanny Price and Anne Elliot do not serve as an adequate rebuttal for this view. Finally, Juliet McMaster, combining the biographical with the aesthetic, focuses on Cassandra's claim that *The Watsons* was supposed to depict Mr. Watson's death. McMaster notes that Austen was "chary of representing death," choosing to kill characters off before or after the novel's action or offstage. Moreover, McMaster hypothesizes that while Austen was preparing to represent Mr. Watson's demise, her own father died, and she must have felt "a surge of guilt, strong though irrational" which made her stop work on the book for good.[25]

McMaster—as well as Austen-Leigh and Southam—does not take into account Austen's habits of revision. The surviving original draft of *The Watsons* testifies to her tendency to scrutinize and alter her writing primarily at the level of the word or phrase. Moreover a comparison of the surviving draft chapters ten and eleven of *Persuasion* with the radically rewritten version of this section in the published novel reveals more extensive revisions at the level of plot structure, characterization, narrative tone, theme, and setting.[26] Given that Austen revised heavily, what would have prevented her from altering her representation, allowing Mr. Watson to survive, endowing the Emma Watson character with more potential for growth, or even painting the Watson household as a bit less "vulgar"?

Joseph Wiesenfarth provides a different kind of aesthetic explanation for Austen's decision not to finish *The Watsons*, compelling because it attributes to Austen a penchant for a particular kind of revision. He argues that the novels Austen went on to publish recreate and in many cases improve on the most interesting characters and scenes of *The Watsons*. Thus, for example, the characterizations of Jane Fairfax and Anne Elliot are closely related to the portrait of Emma Watson, Mr. Darcy is a not very distant variation on Lord Osborne, and the assembly ball rendered early in *Pride and Prejudice* is similar to the ballroom scene in *The Watsons*. Austen, Wiesenfarth contends, did not like to repeat herself and, consequently, after she wrote six novels, there was little left in *The Watsons* new enough for her to say.[27] Yet why *after* she wrote six novels? Why didn't Austen choose to finish *The Watsons* before writing, for example, *Emma* and *Persuasion*? Wiesenfarth's argument does not explain why *The Watsons* did not preempt one or more of the later novels instead of the other way around.

We would be on firmer ground, in fact, if we switched the focus of Wiesenfarth's argument, looking not at character traits or scenes Austen reused in the six novels but rather at those she did not attempt again. Even those of the six novels that depict quite intimate female friendships—such as *Pride and Prejudice*—do not, as we shall see, suggest that such friendships have a compensatory function, standing in lieu of efforts to bring desperate women together with noncommittal men. If the six novels Austen went on to publish do not include such an unqualifiedly assertive and alienated perspective, it is fair to suppose that she felt that she could not portray that vision in any completed, publishable version of *The Watsons*, either. Austen may have seen that her representation of female friendship would ultimately be incompatible with the courtship plot and, if allowed to reshape that plot, would be not altogether appropriate for either her own community or a general audience.

To be sure, the compensatory relationship of Emma and Elizabeth echoes the great value Austen attributed to the companionship of women in her letters before 1805 and anticipates the appreciation she would continue to voice for it after that date. Elizabeth and Emma's "quietly-sociable little meal," for example, although they eat "nothing but fried beef," bears similarities to Austen's 1808 assessment of her home life. "The pleasures of Friendship, of unreserved Conversation, of similarity of Taste & Opinions," as she wrote to Cassandra, "make good amends" for the inelegance of homemade wine.[28] Austen's observation, however, was not a publicly proclaimed solution to the subordination of women; the expression was intended for Cassandra's ears alone.

Still, what I have suggested about the critical views of McMaster, Austen-Leigh, and Southam applies to my own argument too. By habit an extensive reviser, Austen could have radically rewritten *The Watsons*, adding to it an ironic narrator (similar to that in the novels she went on to publish) who would have helped to downplay the intimacy between the sisters by literally coming between them and who would have established a more distanced, ambiguous relationship to her heroines. The narrative could also have softened the portraits of Lord Osborne, Tom Musgrave, Robert Watson, and even Mr. Edwards, eradicating any traces of misogyny. Austen could have done these things, but she chose not to.

She may possibly have opted not to finish *The Watsons* because she was reluctant to efface those features drawn from a women's culture. The work gestures toward a conventional courtship plot, but it stops before the female characters are drawn inexorably into the heterosexual unions of the courtship comedy. With the form of a fragment she could retain those representations. Its fragmentary nature declares the work's forever-in-progress status, which helps to mute the sentiments it preserves.

The physical manifestation of this declaration is, of course, the heavily corrected extant manuscript itself. Austen never made a fair copy of it, as she did of the juvenilia and even *Lady Susan*. As long as *The Watsons* was not made up of last, authoritative words, as long as it was not made presentable and readable as fair copy, it could be circulated widely among and approved by Austen's family members. When the text was published in 1871, its editor James Edward Austen-Leigh compensated for its presentable appearance with reminders of its unfinished form and with Cassandra's summary of its plot. This is the frame, of course, that still greets readers of *The Watsons* (most editions provide Cassandra's summary) so that we are invited to add to and thus to offset *The Watsons'* representations of women's culture.

———

Lady Susan and *The Watsons* go beyond Austen's later juvenilia in depicting women in friendships forceful or nourishing enough to challenge the patriarchal courtship plot. But the middle works also exceed the juvenilia in manifesting Austen's uncertainties over portraying this subversive material. In the early and later juvenilia, indeterminacy may have provided the textual solution for Austen's divided loyalties. By contrast, *Lady Susan* and *The Watsons* inscribe that division, giving textual representation to Austen's sincere and somewhat incompatible allegiances.

Austen expressed both her women's culture and her contradictory cultural commitments in the work she turned to after *Lady Susan* and *The Watsons*. But they have subtler manifestations in her subsequent fictions, the novels published in the second decade of the nineteenth century. My last chapter considers the impact of publication on Austen's opposing views and values. At the same time, it assesses the concept so crucial to this biographical study—cultural duality—as a feminist interpretive frame for understanding Austen's fictions.

CHAPTER 8

Pride and Prejudice: Cultural Duality and Feminist Literary Criticism

1

"**I** HAVE finished the Novel called *Pride & Prejudice*, which I think a very superior work," wrote Anne Isabella Milbanke to her mother in May 1813. "It depends not on any of the common resources of Novel writers, no drownings, nor conflagrations, nor runaway horses, nor lapdogs & parrots, nor chambermaids & milliners, nor rencontres and disguises. I really think it is the *most probable* fiction I have ever read." After praising the book, Milbanke, who was to marry Lord Byron in 1815, began to wonder about its writer. "I wish much to know who is the author or *ess* as I am told."[1] Milbanke's opinions and curiosity—the responses of a woman outside of Jane Austen's family and community—underscore another stage in Austen's development as a writer. Her long apprenticeship as a writer of private fictions had come to an end. Finally, in the last decade of her life, she had begun to publish the six novels on which her subsequent reputation rests.

In turning now to the best known of these published and public works, *Pride and Prejudice*, I focus again on fictional conventions that concerned me in the discussions of Austen's juvenilia and her "middle" works: the heroine and female friendships. *Pride and Prejudice*, like Austen's other fictions published between 1811 and 1818, evinces her continuing efforts to revise the implausible conventions, including female characterizations and relationships, that generally purveyed domestic femininity in the eighteenth-century courtship novel. The novel shows as well that, in seeking to render these conventions with more verisimilitude, Austen drew on the cultures of both her female friends and her wider community.

I explore, too, the perspective expressed by the novel's plot resolution. *Pride and Prejudice*, and Austen's other novels as well, affirm patriarchal values with the resolution of marriage. None offers the heroine a refuge from marriage under the bower of female friendship. Nevertheless, her comic endings are not all the same. Some convey more conviction than others. Moreover, certain aspects of the ending itself, as well as other conventions in the novel, may subtly confirm or pull against the cultural perspective of its conclusion. I examine the comic ending of *Pride and Prejudice*, then, in order to weigh its investment in patriarchal values.

Because I also wish to talk about the process of interpreting while making an interpretation of Austen's work in this chapter, I concentrate on a single novel rather than discussing all six. I make explicit the kind of criticism that the concept of cultural duality has enabled me to produce for Austen's middle fictions and for this examination of *Pride and Prejudice*. Although my use of the term *cultural duality* has its origins in feminist scholarship outside of the discipline of literary studies, when used as a framework for interpreting Austen's fiction, it coincides to a large degree with the strategies and premises of American feminist literary criticism.[2] Because scholars have produced several rich American feminist interpretations of *Pride and Prejudice*, that novel makes an especially appropriate subject for a self-conscious discussion of feminist methodology.

Not just consistent with American feminist interpretations of the novel, the framework of cultural duality both enhances them and exposes their limitations. It shows that Austen created novels that are largely but not entirely accessible to an American feminist critical approach. In highlighting the area of inaccessibility, I call attention to historically specific and local influences on Austen's novels and to Austen as an author different, in part, from her feminist critics' vision of her. In doing so, I hope to make a case for a literary criticism that is both feminist *and* historically grounded.

2

In 1816 Austen penned "Plan of a Novel," a parodic outline for a courtship novel. It strings together technical and thematic conventions that she had encountered in novels or that kin and acquaintances particularly admired. The "Plan" gives us a glimpse of some fictional conventions that amused her not in the late 1780s and early 1790s but in the second decade of the nineteenth century and that she revised for the novels she was publishing in this later period. There are some differences between the targets of the parodic juvenilia and of the "Plan," which attest in part to changes in literary tastes over those two decades.[3] But there is continuity as well: in particular, the 1816 sketch, like Austen's earliest parodies, mocks domestic femininity as it was typically conveyed in the medium of the novel.

Because Austen made notes in the margins of the "Plan," identifying the kin or acquaintance whose tastes provoked some of the parodic conventions that compose it, we know that she was making fun not only of idealized heroines but also of her niece Fanny's preference for them when she proclaimed: "Heroine a faultless Character herself—, perfectly good, with much tenderness & sentiment." And with a nod to her cousin Mary Cooke's wishes, she also imagined her heroine without "the least Wit." Austen does not directly ridicule the other key vehicle for the expression of domestic femininity, the didactic female friendship, although she does have the heroine draw back from one potential companion unlikely to seek moral improvement through female friendship: "The heroine's friendship to be sought after by a young Woman in the same Neighbourhood, of Talents & Shrewdness, with light eyes & a fair skin, but having a considerable degree of Wit, Heroine shall shrink from the acquaintance" (6:428, 429). Austen offered this depiction in mock deference again to her cousin Mary who, we may assume, found wit as inappropriate in the characterization of a female friend as in a heroine.

Published in the same decade, *Pride and Prejudice*, like some of Austen's earlier, private works, revises stereotypical representations of heroines and their female friendships. But what perspective on womanhood do the revisions convey? Critical commentary about Elizabeth Bennet, the heroine of the novel, reveals disparate conceptions of her. The early nineteenth-century critic found the female protagonist's characterization consistent with contemporary, patriarchal norms. "Elizabeth's sense and conduct," claimed the *Critical Review*'s anonymous commentator in March 1813, two months after the book appeared, "are of a superior order to those of the common heroines of novels. From her independence of character, which is kept within the proper line of decorum, and her well-timed sprightliness, she teaches the man of Family-Pride to know himself." The reviewer goes on to single out for approval the novel's instructional value: "An excellent lesson may be learned from the elopement of Lydia:—the work also shows the folly of letting young girls have their own way."[4]

Critics, however, have not always made judgments based on a standard of propriety. Many twentieth-century commentators, particularly in the rich post–World War II decades of Austen criticism, have praised the heroine's liveliness, wit, intelligence, charm, or physical vitality, while evincing little concern for an ideal of feminine decorum.[5] But recently scholars have begun once again to evaluate Elizabeth Bennet's propriety, although they are drawing conclusions different from those of the writer for the *Critical Review* in 1813. Claudia Johnson suggested in 1988, for example, that "Austen's conviction that Elizabeth was 'as delightful a creature as ever appeared in print' was well-founded, for, as she could not have failed to realize, no heroine quite like Elizabeth Bennet had 'ever appeared in print' before. . . . Standing where we do, we tend either to overlook or to underestimate Elizabeth's outrageous unconventionality which, judged by the standards set in conduct books and in conservative fiction, constantly verges not merely on impertinence but on impropriety."[6]

Critics have viewed the heroine of *Pride and Prejudice* so differently over time because their perceptions have been influenced by the changing context of literary criticism and the social ideologies that influence that criticism.[7] The *Critical Review*'s commentator sounded no alarms about Elizabeth Bennet because his investment in patriarchal ideology very likely made it hard for him to see anything in her character that did not fit his particular vision of womanhood. Claudia Johnson's outlook, by contrast, is informed by American feminist criticism, itself propelled and influenced by the women's liberation movement, which began in the late 1960s. That criticism first tended to identify patriarchal "images of women" in the literary works of writers of both genders. By the mid 1970s, however, feminist critics had turned to identifying and applauding departures from patriarchal social and literary conventions by women writers and their representations. They have considered those divergences as the expression of a specifically female experience, view, or voice, and have treated that experience, view, or voice as either essentially female or socially constructed.

This second phase of American feminist criticism has made visible aspects of Elizabeth Bennet's character that were not perceptible to

[185]

earlier generations of critics. It does not single out only the heroine's vigor, her "critical energies," or her "vivacity of thought and communication,"[8] for most of these features have been cited and admired repeatedly by twentieth-century nonfeminist critics. Rather, feminist criticism also stresses the unconventional (because unladylike) character of these attributes. In keeping with this feminist critical activity and as a first step toward exploring cultural duality in this novel, I want to call attention to one such unconventional trait: not Elizabeth's wit in particular but rather the expressive range of her talk in general. That talk is a particularly literal rendering of the "female voice" so central to feminist criticism. Moreover, when other characters in the novel comment on her talk, *Pride and Prejudice* treats the female voice thematically. "You give your opinion very decidedly for so young a person," remarks Lady Catherine, for example, with some surprise (2:165–66). And in response to Elizabeth's verbal liberties at Netherfield, her mother warns her not to "run on in the wild manner that you are suffered to do at home" (2:42).

Confident in conversation and sure of her opinions, Elizabeth does not hesitate to convey either her certainty or her views. She decides on and tells Mr. Darcy of his main character flaw after being in his company only a few times: "*Your* defect is a propensity to hate every body" (2:58). Similarly, she insists soon after that they have little in common: "I am sure we never read the same [books], or not with the same feelings" (2:93). She also readily shares her assessment of Mr. Darcy with Mr. Wickham: "I have spent four days in the same house with him, and I think him very disagreeable." Quite certain as she is of her conclusions, she will offer her views to anyone. "I say no more *here*," she assures Mr. Wickham, "than I might say in any house in the neighbourhood, except Netherfield [Mr. Bingley's residence]" (2:77).

Under the cover of irony she sometimes assumes a dictatorial persona. Irony, because it is play, gives her license to dominate, but it does not nullify the impact of her assertive, indeed aggressive verbal behavior. Dancing with Mr. Darcy at the Netherfield ball, Elizabeth orders him to speak: "It is *your* turn to say something now, Mr. Darcy.—*I* talked about the dance, and *you* ought to make some kind of remark on the size of the room, or the number of couples" (2:91). To his courtly response, she adopts a queenly air. "Very well.—That reply will do for the present.—Perhaps by and bye I may observe that private balls are much pleasanter than public ones.—But *now* we may be silent" (2:91).

In her playfully domineering role, she refuses the silence and subordination marked out for women; she also assigns desires and sentiments to Darcy, preempting the expression of whatever his own may be. When he asks, "Do not you feel a great inclination, Miss Bennet, to seize such an opportunity of dancing a reel?" she sketches for him a melodramatic scene of an arrogant Darcy victimizing a bravely defensive Elizabeth: "You wanted me, I know, to say 'Yes,' that you might have the pleasure of despising my taste; but I always delight in overthrowing those kind of schemes, and cheating a person of their premeditated contempt. I have therefore made up my mind to tell you, that I do not want to dance a reel at all—and now despise me if you dare" (2:52).

In playfully switching roles with Mr. Darcy and assuming his dominance, Elizabeth implicitly challenges his power. In other interactions, with Colonel Fitzwilliam as well as Mr. Darcy, she is explicitly critical. She objects to his willfulness, to the "great pleasure" he takes "in the power of choice." As she tells Colonel Fitzwilliam, "I do not know any body who seems more to enjoy the power of doing what he likes than Mr. Darcy" (2:183). Everyone, as the Colonel replies, likes to have his or her own way, but Elizabeth, and Colonel Fitzwilliam to some degree as well, are aware of the fact that some are more able to exercise their wills than others. Elizabeth knows that being a man in itself creates opportunities for "the power of choice" that women do not have, and in response to this inequality her recourse is, again, talk.

She watches Mr. Darcy demonstrate power based specifically on gender at a neighborhood ball. Because only gentlemen are endowed with the power to ask women to dance, as only they are empowered to propose marriage, Elizabeth has no option but to wait, partnerless, while Mr. Darcy relishes his power to decide to dance or not. "He walked here, and he walked there," says Mrs. Bennet of his behavior at the ball (2:13), and while she is not in general a reliable witness, she captures nicely Mr. Darcy's tendency at the ball to flaunt his power to choose by exhibiting himself detached and free. Single women like Elizabeth, who are not dancing, by contrast remain seated. Elizabeth suffers the embarrassment of his rejection but then challenges his power with verbal mockery, transforming the incident into a story which she tells "with great spirit among her friends" (2:12).

In or out of marriage, as Elizabeth notes, willful gentlemen like Mr. Darcy have particular advantages due to gender, and again she articulates and criticizes these advantages explicitly. The wife of such a man is very much "at his disposal," she informs Colonel Fitzwilliam. "I wonder he does not marry, to secure a lasting convenience of that kind. But, perhaps his sister does as well for the present, and, as she is under his sole care, he may do what he likes with her" (2:184).

Gentlemen also have some opportunities for the exercise of their wills due not specifically to their gender but to the social and economic independence that more generally falls to them because of it. Elizabeth articulates this advantage, broadening her critique to men other than Mr. Darcy. If everyone likes to have his own way, as Colonel Fitzwilliam tells Elizabeth, Darcy does have "better means of having it than many others, because he is rich, and many others are poor." He wishes to contrast himself to Darcy: "I speak feelingly. A younger son, you know, must be inured to self-denial and dependence" (2:183). But Elizabeth, accustomed to the greater and much more widespread dependence of gentlewomen, refuses to sympathize or to remain politely silent: "In my opinion, the younger son of an Earl can know very little of either. Now, seriously, what have you ever known of self-denial and dependence? When have you been prevented by want of money from going wherever you chose, or procuring any thing you had a fancy for?" (2:183). She expresses similar irritation at the freedom of choice possessed by Mr. Bingley because of his wealth: "If he means to be but little at Netherfield, it would be better for the neighbourhood that he should give up the place entirely," she insists to Mr. Darcy. "But perhaps Mr. Bingley did not take the house so much for the convenience of the neighbourhood as for his own, and we must expect him to keep or quit it on the same principle" (2:178).

Bothered by men's social and economic advantages over women, she is quick to identify with Mr. Wickham, the least prosperous and independent gentleman of her acquaintance. In so doing, she reveals the social limits of her sense of injustice: her concern does not extend to women or men beneath the status of the gentry. Mr. Wickham rapidly elicits Elizabeth's sympathy because, as he represents it, his position is similar to that of a marginally *genteel* woman. His father began life, as he tells the heroine, as a country attorney just like her mother's father and her uncle, Mr. Philips. Promised a clerical living by the elder Mr. Darcy, he finds himself, after the deaths of both his own father and the elder Mr. Darcy, dependent on the heir who, so he claims, has without cause elected not to honor his father's promise.

Elizabeth chastises Mr. Darcy for victimizing Mr. Wickham, calling attention to his overbearing and unjust agency, in her repetitions of the second person pronoun: "You have reduced him to his present state of poverty, comparative poverty. You have withheld the advantages, which you must know to have been designed for him. You have deprived the best years of his life, of that independence which was no less his due than his desert. You have done all this!" (2:192). She attacks Mr. Darcy on Mr. Wickham's behalf as well because she has been attracted to Mr. Wickham and believes that, in arbitrarily controlling the fates of other men, Mr. Darcy controls those of women, too. It is *"that* abominable Mr. Darcy" (2:144), Elizabeth thinks, who has blocked the possibility of her courtship by Mr. Wickham, just as it is Mr. Darcy who has separated Mr. Bingley from her sister Jane.

To convey awareness of sexual inequality and subtle and overt expressions of its unfairness, then, the heroine speaks with a female voice. But again it is important to note that that voice has, in effect, a limited register. If Elizabeth's sympathies do not extend to those without genteel social status, neither in her view does Mr. Darcy's oppression. She is preoccupied with his power only over those with whom she socializes. Not until she visits Pemberley does Elizabeth begin to realize the wide social range on which Mr. Darcy may impose his will: "As a brother, a landlord, a master, she considered how many people's happiness were in his guardianship!—How much of pleasure or pain it was in his power to bestow!" (2:250–51). But she comes to appreciate the extensive reach of his power just at the moment when Mr. Darcy's housekeeper persuades her of his benevolent use of it among social inferiors.

3

American feminist criticism encourages us to recognize Austen's expression of a divergent, "improper" female voice within *Pride and Prejudice*. It also typically teaches us to see women writers curbing representations of that voice in response to the power of patriarchal ideologies. With its dual foci of expression and restraint, this feminist critical tradition, according to political theorist Kathy Ferguson, "always has to balance the ability of power to distort the worldview of the powerless with the ability of the oppressed to comprehend and transcend their confinement."[9] In practice, however, balance has been difficult to achieve.

The work most responsible for developing and popularizing American feminist criticism, Sandra Gilbert and Susan Gubar's *Madwoman in the Attic*, demonstrates this difficulty. It generally shifts in one direction or the other, giving more weight sometimes to female expression and sometimes to patriarchal restraint. In places it implicitly views the woman writer's divergences from "femininity" as conscious and denies any pervasive power to patriarchal ideologies. Indeed, its crucial palimpsest metaphor tends to make patriarchal ideologies into mere "façades." The metaphor likens the literary text to a series of sheets whose "surface designs" of conservative ideology conceal subversive "levels of meaning": the woman writer's expressions of rage and rebellion.[10] But elsewhere, particularly in the introductory, theoretical section of their study, Gilbert and Gubar attribute considerable power to patriarchal ideologies, including the power to shape subjectivity, and they offer, consequently, a sustained examination of the forceful ideological constraints on women and their expressiveness.[11] Although tilted in different directions, these two positions within American feminist criticism still rely on the same twofold interpretive procedure.

Feminist critics, then, have called attention not only to Elizabeth Bennet's unconventionality but also to the ways in which Austen simultaneously qualified or contained it. One scholar has argued that the vulgar and defiant Lydia Bennet serves as "a decoy who attracts the disapproval to which Elizabeth herself could otherwise be subject."[12] The displacement, I would note, is verbal as well. When the heroine complains to her father about Lydia's wild behavior, for example, her championship of feminine self-restraint diverts attention from her own usually unrestrained talk (2:231). Other critics have claimed that Elizabeth's perception and treatment of Mr. Darcy are all bluster. One motive for her "rebelliousness," according to Judith Newton, is "self-defense; she wants to resist intimidation and to deny Darcy's particular assumption of control over her." In doing so, "she is also defending herself against a desire to please Darcy and to enjoy the benefit of his positive attentions."[13] And a third strategy for qualifying Elizabeth Bennet's unconventional talk has been located in the heroine's repudiation of her own conduct, including her assertive and critical discourse. When she receives Mr. Darcy's letter, she begins to regret her earlier behavior. Becoming more self-reflective and self-critical, Elizabeth wishes "that her former opinions had been more reasonable, her expressions more moderate!" (2:376).

Although I concur with the feminist critical emphasis on identifying qualifying strategies as well as the unconventional representations of womanhood that they limit, textual evidence does not support unambiguously all the strategies of constraint that critics have located in *Pride and Prejudice*. For example, if Elizabeth's bold remarks to or about Mr. Darcy are defensive, she is just as self-confident and assertive on other topics and with other people—with her sister Jane, Lady Catherine, and even Mr. Bingley. "I understand you perfectly," she informs him, although she has known him for only a few weeks (2:42).[14] But more important, none of the constraining strategies that critics have pinpointed takes us to the crucial site in *Pride and Preju-dice* where the subversiveness of Elizabeth's talk is most effectively limited. We can locate that site only with a biographical approach to the novel and only if we are familiar with Austen's social and cultural contexts.

To understand how Austen qualified her heroine's unconventional talk, we need to look to the source of Elizabeth Bennet's characteri-zation, and it is knowledge of Austen's dual cultural allegiances that directs us to it. Feminist and nonfeminist critics alike who have con-sidered the question of source usually have pointed to similarities between Elizabeth Bennet and Jane Austen, implying that the novelist stamped her heroine with her own personality.[15] But how do we know Jane Austen? Identifications of Austen as Elizabeth Bennet are more textually based than critics have generally acknowledged. Access to Austen is mediated by the written testimonies of her relations and, more importantly, by her own letters. The self she conveys in her letters, as we have seen in earlier chapters, varies, depending on wheth-er she was writing as a member of her community or as a member of her small band of intimate female friends. Her self-representation is closest to Elizabeth Bennet's assertiveness when it is created by the discourse she directed exclusively to these female friends. Although Austen's letters are generally more incisive and witty than those of her female neighbors and kin, it is important to remember that other women's letters also produced unconventionally assertive female iden-tities.

The Austen constructed by this woman-to-woman discourse, like *Pride and Prejudice*'s heroine, makes quick, confident, unqualified pro-nouncements. "I am quite tired of so many Children," Austen writes to her niece Fanny in 1817, after announcing the pregnancies of anoth-er relative and a neighbor.[16] She issues such opinions only to a few confidantes. "A Widower with 3 children has no right to look higher than his daughter's Governess," she tells her sister in 1807.[17] The self who emerges from this private women's discourse sometimes also ex-presses a playfully ironic awareness that she wants to dominate. And, as with Elizabeth Bennet, the irony does not negate the aggressiveness of her verbal behavior. "Make everybody at Hendon admire Mansfield Park," she cheerfully commands her niece Anna in 1814.[18] A letter to Cassandra, who was visiting Mrs. Knight in 1807, not only imagines that the two women will have "a great deal of unreserved discourse" but orders them to "abuse everybody but me."[19] Finally, the self creat-ed by the letter's same-sex discourse can also be critical of men's priv-ileges and power: the tendency of oldest brothers to dominate their siblings; fathers to ignore their daughters; husbands to boss their wives or to "sneer" at their unmarried sisters-in-law; and arrogant male acquaintances to assume their visits invariably welcome.[20] This criticism, like Elizabeth Bennet's, addresses the gender inequality only of elite men and women.

Female friends, then, not only tolerated but created and encouraged a self whose voice is confident, imaginative, and critical, although the criticism is not aimed at male domination outside their own social group. But if Austen made use of the key resource of her women's culture in constructing the "voice" of *Pride and Prejudice*'s heroine, she also muted in a crucial way in the novel the relationships that produced that female voice. She placed the most powerful curb on her heroine's unconventionality in the way she depicted the bonds among female characters. [21]

Affectionate female friendships, to be sure, are dramatized in this novel, and there are more of them than critics have generally noticed.[22] Emotional intimacy and frankness characterize the relationship of Elizabeth with Jane, Elizabeth with Charlotte Lucas, the two sisters with their aunt, Mrs. Gardiner, and Elizabeth with Georgiana Darcy, though this last tie is only asserted at the end of the novel and not dramatized. These women are quick to empathize with one another. Elizabeth can even read Jane's feelings in the subtle play of her manners and expressions in a crowded ballroom (2:95). The friendships thrive best in privacy; women alone together are more open with one another than they generally are with others. Elizabeth tells "all her griefs to Charlotte Lucas" during a few minutes of quiet talk that they manage at the Netherfield ball, but friends also look for opportunities to converse out of public view (2:90). "When Jane and Elizabeth were alone, the former," according to the narrator, "who had been cautious in her praise of Mr. Bingley before, expressed to her sister how very much she admired him" (2:14). And "when alone with Elizabeth," her aunt "spoke more on the subject" of Jane's relationship with Mr. Bingley (2:140).

Nevertheless, we cannot determine the moral and political valence Austen assigns to female relationships in *Pride and Prejudice* simply by showing that close female friendships appear in the novel. Our knowledge of Austen's affiliations with two cultures enables us to see the limitations of this position. Female friendships, to be sure, were the linchpin in Austen's women's culture: they both generated and were represented by that culture. But the gentry's domestic ideology also constructed a version of female friendship. To determine, then, whether female ties in *Pride and Prejudice* express the perspective of the patriarchal culture of Austen's wider community or of the alternative culture of her female friends, we need to explore their functions.

What ends do the frank interchanges of female friends serve? They rarely fulfill the didactic function represented by the ideology of domesticity. Once, Mrs. Gardiner does attempt to advise Elizabeth, imparting a view espoused by that genteel ideology; she urges her niece not to cultivate affection for Mr. Wickham because he has no fortune. But the narrator's subsequent stress on the atypicality of Elizabeth's response reminds us that Austen was in *Pride and Prejudice*, as in the juvenilia, reacting against the courtship novel's stereotype of perfectly didactic female friendships: "Elizabeth having thanked her for the kindness of her hints, they parted; a wonderful instance of advice being given on such a point, without being resented" (2:145). In depicting friendship functioning to transmit instruction in domestic femininity, Austen distances her representation from the model version of this fictional convention. For the most part, however, she does not attempt transmissions of advice in *Pride and Prejudice* even when deidealized with narrative commentary.[23] "We all love to instruct," the heroine tells her sister Jane, "though we can teach only what is not worth knowing" (2:343; see also 333). In general, didactic communications are mocked in the novel—left to Mary Bennet, who pompously and ineffectually lectures her sisters on "thread-bare morality" (2:60).

More often, intimate friends in *Pride and Prejudice* engage in *some* of the behavior productive of and nourished by the women's culture. They discuss one another's romantic desires. To be sure, these interactions are male-centered, a point which has led Nina Auerbach and some other feminist scholars to criticize these relationships. Still, when friends talk to one another about their relationships with men, they are also providing one another with a context for the admission and nurturing of their desires. When Jane, for example, grows despondent over Mr. Bingley's departure for London, Elizabeth "forcibly" insists not that Jane should subdue her feelings but that Mr. Bingley will return to propose. As a result, Jane "was gradually led to hope . . . that Bingley would return to Netherfield and answer every wish of her heart" (2:120).

In acknowledging and encouraging one another's desires, these friends parallel Austen and her female kin and neighbors, when participating in their women's culture. But the fictional ties lack the bite, the subversiveness, that was also an important part of the women's culture. Elizabeth, as we have seen, speaks out boldly, but the novel does not locate her voice specifically within a community of women. Elizabeth is more likely to be verbally aggressive with Mr. Darcy, Mr.

Bingley, or Lady Catherine than with intimate female friends. She does not hesitate to express criticism of men to other men, complaining about Mr. Darcy to Colonel Fitzwilliam and about Mr. Bingley to Mr. Darcy. Although her forceful talk may betray a striking sense of autonomy, she does not make autonomy a topic of conversation with Jane or Charlotte or her aunt, nor do these female characters encourage one another to express dissent. No one complains to a female friend about the necessity of fulfilling female "duties" or wishes for more liberty and authority, as Austen and her female friends and neighbors did.

The limitations Austen placed on her heroine by obfuscating the source of her unladylike discourse become particularly apparent when we compare aspects of *Pride and Prejudice* to Austen's middle fictions. For *Lady Susan,* Austen had drawn on the women's culture for a fantasy of empowerment, of "women on top," achieved through female solidarity. *Pride and Prejudice* avoids such a vision, as a comparison of Elizabeth Bennet and Charlotte Lucas's relationship to that of female friends in *Lady Susan* makes clear. Whereas in *Lady Susan* women band together to achieve the goal of marriage to men of fortune, Charlotte Lucas's purely economic motives for marrying alienate Elizabeth and weaken their bond. When Charlotte, in one of their private conversations, argues in favor of an insincere behavior intended to catch an affluent husband regardless of his character, Elizabeth does not believe she is in earnest. When Charlotte proceeds to act on her beliefs, Elizabeth feels "the pang of a friend disgracing herself and sunk in her esteem" (2:125). Elizabeth believes that women should marry for love and not just a competence, and she is also disturbed by Charlotte's blunt concern for her own economic dependence and by her efforts to do something about it. Jane urges Elizabeth not to acknowledge and accept the mercenary motive behind Charlotte's marriage but to "be ready to believe, for every body's sake, that she may feel something like regard and esteem for our cousin" (2:135). But Elizabeth cannot bring herself to believe Jane's rosy interpretation, and Charlotte's engagement introduces a "restraint" between them. "Elizabeth," the narrator notes, "felt persuaded that no real confidence could ever subsist between them again" (2:127, 128).

The Watsons, the other "middle" work, portrays candid discussions between two sisters about the economic subordination of women. Despite this concern for female poverty, it proffers, albeit in its unfinished state, close female friendships as a preferable alternative to marriage. This perspective *Pride and Prejudice* eschews as well, as a comparison between scenes from each work demonstrates.

On one of Mr. Darcy's visits to Elizabeth at the Collins's parsonage, he suggests, referring to Mrs. Collins, that fifty miles is not far for a woman to travel to visit her family. His remark is similar to one made by Lord Osborne when he and Tom Musgrave come to call on the Watson sisters. Any woman, the nobleman unthinkingly assures Emma Watson, can get exercise on horseback if she desires it. Elizabeth Bennet and Emma Watson make similar points in response, reminding their visitors that financial resources must underwrite travel or horseback riding and that financially independent men and women dependent on not-very-affluent male relatives will understandably often have different perspectives on what is possible. "The far and the near," Elizabeth corrects Mr. Darcy, "must be relative, and depend on many varying circumstances. Where there is fortune to make the expence of travelling unimportant, distance becomes no evil. . . . I am persuaded my friend would not call herself *near* her family under less than *half* the present distance" (2:179). Although Emma Watson's answer is like Elizabeth Bennet's, her blunter tone betrays her greater psychic distance from men: "Female Economy will do a great deal my Lord, but it cannot turn a small income into a large one" (6:346). But there are even more significant differences in the two scenes.

Both heroines experience their unexpected callers as intruders, but only in *The Watsons* are the men shown to break in on women alone together in an alternative, solacing domestic society that they have created for themselves. When the gentlemen arrive, Emma and her sister are about to sit down to the nourishments of companionship and an informal dinner. In *Pride and Prejudice*, by contrast, female society is merely alluded to—Elizabeth Bennet is writing to her sister when Mr. Darcy enters the room. Moreover, Emma Watson is not just surprised and ashamed when the men call but also resentful, while Elizabeth Bennet feels only "very great surprise" at Mr. Darcy's entrance (2:177).[24]

Although *Pride and Prejudice*, then, does offer a series of female friendships, we may construe those alliances as a sisterhood of women only if we mean by sisterhood the affection and support that women give other women. The novel does not portray sisterhood as a political constituency, showing women aware of themselves as a distinct, egalitarian group united in the context of their discontent with patriarchal and hierarchical social relations. *Pride and Prejudice*'s sisterhood is neither antithetical nor alternative to marriage. Elizabeth may be critical of men's privileges and power, but sisterhood does not generate this critique.

With a feminist approach, we identify a female expressiveness—in

Pride and Prejudice, Elizabeth's conversation—and we expect to find it qualified or mediated. But awareness of Austen's context, specifically her dual cultures, enables us to see that in this novel expression is itself also restraint. The "female voice" is its own mediation. Elizabeth Bennet's bold talking stands in for a community of female voices—and points us toward its absence.

4

The plot that incorporates Elizabeth Bennet's complex characterization ends with her marriage to Mr. Darcy. Austen's long-term views and previous experience of writing plot resolutions suggest that we should pay particular attention to *Pride and Prejudice*'s ending. Some of her earliest juvenilia, works such as "Frederic & Elfrida," ridicule novels that conclude with trite, implausible, or overly sentimental marriages, and Austen's 1816 "Plan of a Novel" confirms that she remained critical of cliché and melodrama in comic resolutions in the decade when she was publishing novels. The heroine, so the "Plan" declares, "at last in the very nick of time, turning a corner to avoid him [the Anti-hero], runs into the arms of the Hero himself. . . . The Tenderest & completest Eclaircissement takes place, & they are happily united" (6:430). Moreover, parodic juvenilia such as "The Beautifull Cassandra" show awareness of endings as expressions of a cultural perspective, and *Lady Susan* and *The Watsons*, as the framework of cultural duality enabled us to see, manifest her conflicts over the perspective she wanted her plot endings to convey. That framework will make it possible for us to probe the ending of *Pride and Prejudice* as well. The resolution depicts the heterosexual and hierarchical union that constituted, so the gentry believed, the destiny of feminine women. But does the novel consistently, uniformly endorse that destiny?

The answer, as with commentary on the novel's heroine, depends on the social and literary views of the critics responding. Austen's contemporaries assumed that the plot resolution unilaterally affirmed patriarchal values because they themselves subscribed to those values. Although none of the 1813 reviews specifically singles out *Pride and Prejudice*'s ending for analysis, we can infer their authors' attitudes toward the ending from the lengthy plot summaries usually included in these essays. The anonymous writer for the *British Critic*, for example, saw nothing in the text to undermine the stability and pleasure of the concluding marriage. "Explanations of the different perplexities and seeming contrarieties, are gradually unfolded, and the two principal performers are happily united."[25] And a writer for the *Critical Review* expressed similar complacency about the resolution (and condescension toward women writers) when praising "the considerable ingenuity" of "the fair author" for her "mode of bringing about the final *eclaircissment* between her [Elizabeth Bennet] and Darcy."[26]

Critics' satisfaction with the marital fate of the heroine was expressed throughout the nineteenth century and well into the twentieth century. Many modern critics have just celebrated the ending more overtly, praising the marriage as the desirable end point in the personal developments of both Elizabeth Bennet and Mr. Darcy. "Their story," according to Stuart Tave, "comes to a happy ending earned by two properly humbled people who have learned to bear mortification and to rise under it with love."[27] *Pride and Prejudice,* suggests Joseph Wiesenfarth, "ends not only with the total individual development of each character but also with his total social development, because personal love is satisfied in marriage and harmonized with society."[28] Some critics have also viewed the marriage as a metaphor for the harmonious union of antithetical, though often stereotypically gendered, social meanings. Thus for Lionel Trilling, "the relation of Elizabeth Bennet to Darcy is real, is intense, but it expresses itself as a conflict and reconciliation of styles: a formal rhetoric, traditional and rigorous, must find a way to accommodate a female vivacity, which in turn must recognize the principled demands of the strict male syntax."[29] And for Tony Tanner, the marriage is a metaphor for the union of "playfulness and regulation—energy and boundaries."[30]

Feminist critics, who have commented on the novel's close in recent years, have expressed a much less cheerful view of the marital resolution. Often reminding readers that the nineteenth-century institution of marriage enforced women's legal, economic, and social subordination, they have reperceived Elizabeth and Mr. Darcy's union as a deflating, even degrading fate for the heroine.[31] They disagree, however, over Austen's attitude toward the marriage. Assuming Austen's commitment to it, Mary Poovey, for example, laments that the ending of *Pride and Prejudice* and Austen's other novels serves to "disguise the inescapable system of economic and political domination." "Romantic love," she explains, "seems to promise to women in particular an emotional intensity that ideally, compensates for all the practical opportunities they are denied."[32]

Other feminist critics have challenged the assumption that Austen was committed to the novel's resolution, and they have had to marshal what is usually quite subtle textual evidence in support of their view. This critical approach, once again, *suspects* the representation and looks in or around it for evidence of another perspective, the "female voice." Carolyn Heilbrun, for example, refers to the "perfunctoriness of the endings of Jane Austen's novels."[33] Susan Lanser sees in the courtship plot of Pride and Prejudice and the other novels Austen's "legacy of covers and silences."[34] And Karen Newman has argued that Austen's novels "reveal the gap between sentimental ideals and novelistic conventions on the one hand, and the social realities of sexist prejudice, hypocrisy, and avarice on the other." Pride and Prejudice, according to Newman, both satisfies and undercuts the reader's expectations with concluding details marked with "self-consciousness and parody."[35]

A close look at the comic resolution does reveal some subtle, self-conscious divergences from the conventions of comic endings. It is not a glamorous or melodramatic coincidence but the ordinary gossip of Mr. Darcy's aunt that unites the hero with the heroine. Hearing that her nephew and Elizabeth Bennet are on the verge of matrimony, Lady Catherine visits Elizabeth in order to make her refute this gossip. But in carrying back to her nephew an account of Elizabeth's refusal to deny the report, Lady Catherine unwittingly makes her own gossip the catalyst for Mr. Darcy's second and successful proposal.

In addition, however "tender" and "complete" their éclaircissement, it is followed by Elizabeth's concerns about the vulgarity of the treatment that Mr. Darcy receives from her neighbor Sir William Lucas and from her mother, Mr. Collins, and Mrs. Philips. As the narrator suggests, "though the uncomfortable feelings arising from all this took from the season of courtship much of its pleasure, it added to the hope of the future; and she looked forward with delight to the time when they should be removed from society so little pleasing to either, to all the comfort and elegance of their family party at Pemberley" (2:384). The narrator also provides a synopsis of their postdenouement married life in which the "pleasures" of Pemberley are frequently interrupted. The insincere Miss Bingley and the condescending Lady Catherine make visits. Lydia repeatedly sends requests for money and comes to stay when her husband goes off to London or Bath. Mr. Bennet, too, though beloved, keeps showing up unexpectedly at Pemberley.

But these details, though they are undermining, work only to soften the implausibility of the closure. "A rebellion against the dictates of love-plotting in the name of greater fictional realism," as critic Joseph Boone has suggested, "does not necessarily guarantee a radical move against the love-plot's conservative sexual ideology."[36] By describing, however briefly, Elizabeth and Darcy's discomforts before and after marrying, the narrative strives for greater verisimilitude against the all-too-neat convention of happy endings. While deflating details may correct the illusion of perfection in marriage, they do not undercut the desirability of the heroine's fate, nor do they make that fate seem less hierarchical. The narrator lodges with the heroine, for example, awareness of the discomforts belonging to "the season of courtship." Elizabeth tries to "shield" Mr. Darcy from her vulgar neighbors and relatives; she is "ever anxious" about their contacts with him. The society of home and neighborhood is "so little pleasing to either," but she is displeased because he is (2:384).

In addition to endorsing marriage as a patriarchal institution, *Pride and Prejudice*'s plot resolution confirms that Elizabeth Bennet's "impertinence," rather than being part of a collective response to a social situation, is unique to her personality. Because it is unique, the heroine's feisty talk has made her lovable. This point is articulated toward the close of the novel when Elizabeth explains to Mr. Darcy why he fell in love with her. The rarity of assertiveness in a young, marriageable woman has attracted him, she insists. Although she assumes again a mockingly dominant role, the novel never casts doubt on the account she offers:

> "Now be sincere; did you admire me for my impertinence?"
>
> "For the liveliness of your mind, I did."
>
> "You may as well call it impertinence at once. It was very little less. The fact is, that you were sick of civility, of deference, of officious attention. You were disgusted with the women who were always speaking and looking, and thinking for *your* approbation alone. I roused, and interested you, because I was so unlike *them*." (2:380)

If the comic resolution makes Elizabeth Bennet's impertinence lovable because it is unique, the ending also makes it unique because it is lovable. Although other women in the novel view Mr. Darcy as a desirable mate, he is attracted to Elizabeth only. *Pride and Prejudice* heightens the heroine's individuality, by making her Mr. Darcy's sole choice. During the course of the novel his passion for her is frequently in evidence—in his blushes, silences, absentmindedness, "odd unconnected questions" (2:182), and, most commonly, his stares. Indeed, passion is registered in his very presence—in his frequent, surprising appearances wherever she may be: at Rosings, at her cousin's parsonage, at Pemberley, in the town of Lambton, at Longbourne. These signs point toward and culminate in the plot resolution which, with Elizabeth's marriage to Mr. Darcy, asserts her singularity.

The assertion is striking because while it too suppresses the collective source for the heroine's "female voice," such suppression is not necessary. Austen's representation of female friendship in the novel in itself effectively mutes the subversive aspects of her women's culture. *Pride and Prejudice* can be said not just to draw on but also to *exploit* the comic plot's focus on an individual woman and her union with a suitor in the interest of denying potentially disruptive female bonds. The resolution's gratuitous emphasis on individuality, combined with its rendering of the pleasures, however imperfect, of marriage, thus makes for a more emphatic endorsement of patriarchal values than either *Lady Susan* or *The Watsons* evinces.

It should be clear by now that I do not think we can find the explanation for this difference between the middle works and *Pride and Prejudice* in Austen's personal experience. Such an account would depend on a comparison of her life when writing *Lady Susan* and *The Watsons* to her experience while living at Chawton, during which time she revised and published *Pride and Prejudice*. Although her female circle at Chawton fostered her writing, she may, as some feminist critics have suggested, nonetheless have felt discontented with her all-female household and blamed her female housemates, ironically, for making it possible for her to choose celibacy.[37] But her letters from the second decade of the nineteenth century, as I have shown, suggest, on the contrary, that she was satisfied with the choice she had made and continued to cherish intimacies with a few female friends and kin.

The difference can be attributed more persuasively to Austen's shift from private to public writing. I have suggested that Austen's middle works, in both representing strong female bonds and seeking to offset or muffle them, inscribe Austen's ambivalence, her genuinely divided loyalties. *Pride and Prejudice*, while showing traces of her attachment to two cultures, evinces less ambivalence, less conflict over her cultural commitments. In writing for publication, Austen had a strong sense of her audience. Her six novels assume readers familiar with the many novel conventions to which she alluded in subtle and occasionally overt revisions of them. Her novels also assume a public readership with patriarchal values. For that audience, we can assume, she muted the most subversive signs of her women's culture.

Pride and Prejudice also works to suppress evidence of her conflicting loyalties in order to avoid representing contradictions. Some critics have recently called attention to the novel as an ideological act, which seeks through formal means to resolve social contradictions.[38] But we need not implicitly transfer all agency to the genre itself or view Austen as only the unconscious medium of ideology. Austen knew that her perceptions and values were at times in opposition, and, as an exponent of organic form, she would have sought to avoid (un-self-reflexive) renderings not only of ridiculously incompatible novel conventions but also of overtly conflicting cultural perspectives. Haste, spontaneity, and contradiction were conventions of the genre of private letters, in which women communicated with one another; the novel, as Austen was constructing it, did not share these conventions. It did not endorse the forms of that verisimilitude.

Still, in her efforts to defer to the expectations of a public readership and to construct an apparently nondiscordant or seamless fiction, Austen need not have so enthusiastically celebrated the relationship of hero and heroine. She curtailed her portrait of the women's culture in this novel much more than in *Lady Susan* and *The Watsons*. Moreover, she amplified the hierarchical and heterosexual bond that closes the published work. Austen made it particularly attractive by emphasizing the desirability of the hero—his wealth, family connections, good looks, and estimable character—and the gratifications of his passionate and unwavering desire for, his "heart-felt delight" in, Elizabeth (2:366). Because feminist critics have had difficulty coming to terms with this compelling portrait of patriarchal marriage, their responses will help us to see the limitations of perceiving the novel through the lens of American feminist criticism.

The difficulty lies in the asymmetrical duality at the heart of this critical tradition. I have already described two positions within feminist criticism that make for unequal binary oppositions. One position gives more power to the female voice than to oppressive patriarchal ideologies; the other tilts the balance in the opposite direction. But though they differ on the issue of power, both positions agree on and enact another more crucial inequality: whatever power they ascribe to the female voice, both value it more. Feminist critics generally not only locate the "female voice" in literature by women; they prize that voice over other expressions in a literary work, consciously reversing the particular hierarchy of value that has given to the male priority over the female. In addition, the female voice is often not as apparent in the text as are patriarchal values, or, if overt, it has nevertheless gone undetected. Because feminist critics generally enact the discovery of an obscured female voice, they tend to understand that voice to be more meaningful or "real" than the views and values that the text makes particularly accessible and that critics' social ideologies have hitherto made recognizable.[39]

The discovery process implicit in feminist criticism works well, when we seek in Austen's novels evidence of her women's culture. The fit between the criticism and Austen's literary representations is fairly close in these instances, and it doesn't matter whether one views the identity generated by the women's culture as naturally female or, as I have suggested, as a social construction. But feminist criticism has difficulty in confronting particularly ebullient expressions of the gentry's culture in Jane Austen's novels. It is suspicious of appearances: could the woman writer really mean to endorse dominant, conventional values? Surely, they are merely the surface sheet of the palimpsest. Her more genuine sentiments are, so we are urged to assume, tucked away under or within the text's patriarchal appearance. Alternatively, the critic, supposing that the woman writer did really intend allegiance to the gentry's culture, disapproves of a loyalty not in her own interests (since the ideology she represented prescribed her subordination). The critic uses evidence of the woman writer's allegiance to a patriarchal ideology to call attention to the power of the dominant culture's ideology to mystify and harm women. Feminist criticism thus tends either to trivialize Austen's commitment to her more dominant culture or to translate it into a version of false consciousness.

Can reading Austen's work with the framework of her two cultures avoid these same limitations? After all, the concept also has its origins in feminist scholarship, though in the work of historians of American women. It, too, relies on an asymmetricality, placing more value on the women's than on the gentry's culture. But the framework's duality of cultures, because of a subtle difference from feminist criticism's duality of female voice/dominant ideology, bears the *potential* for perceiving in another way Austen's enthusiastic textual endorsements of patriarchal values.

The binary opposition of feminist criticism isolates gender—the female voice, view, or experience—from other aspects of social identity and experience. But the framework of women's and gentry's cultures, while highlighting the conflicts between these cultures, also situates one within the other. It thus calls attention to the inextricable connection between gender and other features of experience, particularly social rank, for Austen and her female friends and kin. To say that Austen and her circle identified themselves by gender *and* social rank is insufficient. If the gentry's culture produced gender as a high status identity—"genteel femininity"—the women's culture's construction of female identity, though partly in opposition, was also circumscribed by status concerns drawn from the gentry's culture. These concerns, as we have seen, limit Elizabeth Bennet's awareness of and anger over female subordination to the community of genteel persons just as they prevent a more devastating, more radical portrait of male domination across social ranks.

[202]

The framework of cultural duality, then, may enable us to recognize Austen and her female circle's dependence on and perceived need for the gentry's culture, as a feminist criticism oblivious to social rank or class as aspects of female identity cannot. The framework may enable us to appreciate that, whether or not *we* admire the gentry's culture, it was in their interests not as women but as gentlewomen in a hierarchical society to identify with and prize that culture. It may also enable us to see that, when writing for publication, Austen at times could downplay conflicting representations of her two cultures with strong and sincere endorsements of the gentry's dominant culture and not only out of concern for her public's expectations or seamless representations. She could and would want to do so in her public work because the women's culture was, paradoxically, not just "against" but "within" the gentry's patriarchal culture.

The framework may make it possible for us to do these things, that is, if we are prepared to acknowledge that Austen's *Pride and Prejudice* is not always and everywhere subtly, obliquely subversive. Literary critical approaches function in part to make the writer and his or her work familiar because cast in terms recognizable to a contemporary community of readers. *Pride and Prejudice* does fit the familiarizing paradigm of feminist criticism, but not completely. And what of Austen's other novels? Although it is not possible to examine them here, I want to offer a few generalizations about what we can expect to find when approaching them within the framework of cultural duality.

Like *Pride and Prejudice*, the other novels published between 1811 and 1818 express and simultaneously restrain a perspective drawn from Austen's women's culture. Like *Pride and Prejudice*, they do so only *sometimes*, for these works also intermittently advocate, without destabilizing qualifications, the patriarchal perspective of the gentry's culture. In these ways *Pride and Prejudice* is representative of Austen's other published fictions. It differs, however, as all the novels do one from another, in the way it combines these varying representations.

Whereas Austen turned to her women's culture for her representation of Elizabeth Bennet and then obfuscated the source and subversiveness of that culture in her depictions of *Pride and Prejudice*'s female friends, the characterizations of some of the other novels' heroines bear no influence of the women's culture. Austen's comments about her female protagonists reveal her awareness of their diversity. Although she knew that her niece Fanny Knight and cousin Mary Cooke and some other female friends and kin preferred model heroines, "pictures of perfection," as she was to assure Fanny in 1817, "make me sick &

wicked."[40] Because her own tastes differed from those of some in her female circle,[41] she believed, as her nephew James Edward Austen-Leigh attests in his memoir of the novelist, that the outspoken, playful Emma Woodhouse was "a heroine whom no one but myself will much like."[42] *Persuasion*'s quiet, somber Anne Elliot she viewed quite differently, informing her niece Fanny, "You may *perhaps* like the Heroine, as she is almost too good for me."[43]

Unlike *Pride and Prejudice, Mansfield Park*, which was published just after it, depicts a heroine untouched by Austen's women's culture; moreover, it provides an extended representation of a didactic female friendship, an unambiguous move that, like the ending of *Pride and Prejudice*, gratuitously champions the patriarchal values of the gentry's culture. The narrative shows Fanny Price, while at Portsmouth, introducing her younger sister to the habit of reading and study and helping her to manage her bad temper. This is not a novel in which "we can teach," as Elizabeth Bennet remarks, "only what is not worth knowing," although in illustrating and endorsing the didactic function of female friendship, *Mansfield Park* does also render it plausible by showing the mentor, while teaching her sister self-control, struggling to master her own desire for her cousin Edmund Bertram.

Areas other than the plot resolution can, in Austen's other novels, convey warm, unambiguous endorsements of patriarchal values. Conversely, the plot resolutions of the other novels may not, as in *Pride and Prejudice*, express such a strong commitment to those same values, although they all unite the heroines and heroes in marriage. The ending of *Northanger Abbey*, for example, subtly undercuts the perspective of the gentry's culture. With its sudden and belated manufacture of a husband for Eleanor Tilney, that novel slyly mocks marriage as the always necessary and all-too-conventional fate for women.

Austen's six novels express and obscure aspects of the women's culture, *and* they unequivocally endorse patriarchal ideology, but they do not offer these differing representations in the same places or in the same proportions from one novel to the next. *Pride and Prejudice*, then, does not illustrate an exact pattern to which the other novels conform. We may never know the specific reasons for these variations—Austen's surviving letters from the second decade of the nineteenth century provide few hints. But we do know that the women's culture's paradoxical relationship to the gentry's culture, partly dissenting from and wholly dependent on it, made possible inconsistencies of perspective within the novels and variations among them. Those of us who are feminists need to acknowledge these inconsistencies and variations and, difficult as it may be, relinquish some of our intimacy with

Austen's novels. With an interpretive approach that is both feminist and responsive to Jane Austen's social and cultural contexts, we can expect to find her published works sometimes hospitable and sometimes resistant, sometimes familiar and sometimes strange. The framework of cultural duality makes her six published novels only partially ours.

NOTES

NOTES ON THE REFERENCES

The following manuscript collections have been abbreviated:

A-L	Austen-Leigh
CKS U624	Harris (Centre for Kentish Studies, Maidstone)
CKS U951	Knatchbull (Centre for Kentish Studies, Maidstone)
CKS U1015	Papillon (Centre for Kentish Studies, Maidstone)
HRO 20M64	Bramston, Hicks, Beach, and Chute (Hampshire Record Office, Winchester)
HRO 31M57	Chute (Hampshire Record Office, Winchester)
HRO 63M84	Heathcote (Hampshire Record Office, Winchester)
JAH	Caroline Gore Diaries (Jane Austen's House, Chawton)
LF	Lefroy
NMM AUS/101-9	Charles John Austen, Journals and Diaries (National Maritime Museum, Greenwich)
PL	Powlett
PML MA4500	Gordon N. Ray (Fanny Palmer Austen Letters) (Pierpont Morgan Library, New York)

I have retained spelling and punctuation as they appear in these unpublished sources.

Two published sources cited in this text have also been given abbreviations:

AP   *Austen Papers, 1704–1856*, ed. R. A. Austen-Leigh (Colchester: Ballantine Press, 1942)

JAL   *Jane Austen's Letters to Her Sister Cassandra and Others*, ed. R. W. Chapman, 2nd ed. (1952; rpt. Oxford Univ. Press, 1979)

Volume and page numbers in parentheses in text refer to Austen's fiction as it appears in the Chapman editions: R. W. Chapman, ed., *The Novels of Jane Austen*, 3rd ed. (1932; rpt. London: Oxford Univ. Press, 1973): vol. 2, for citations of *Pride and Prejudice*, and R. W. Chapman, ed., *The Works of Jane Austen* (1954; rpt. London: Oxford Univ. Press, 1972): vol. 6, for citations of the Juvenilia, *Lady Susan, The Watsons*, and "Plan of a Novel."

INTRODUCTION

1. Poems of Anne Lefroy, LF. The Duchess was probably planning the production in late 1786 or early 1787, for Lady Catherine Paulett (also spelled "Powlett"), married in September 1787.
2. By *ideology* I mean those ideas and beliefs about social relations and experience that explain, naturalize, and legitimate (but do not by themselves create) the domination of one social group over others. Social groups may be formed by class or rank but also by other social categories such as gender. For useful discussions of variations in its meaning, see Terry Eagleton, *Ideology: An Introduction* (London: Verso, 1991) and Raymond Williams, *Marxism and Literature* (Oxford: Oxford Univ. Press, 1977).
3. See the letters referring to the Austen family's 1787 theatrical in *AP*, 123–29. Philadelphia Walter, assumed by many to be the real-life progenitor of *Mansfield Park's* Fanny Price, did not object to women acting or to home theatricals. When she turned down the Austens' invitation to participate in their home entertainment, she may have given feminine propriety as one of her own reasons, but she did not marshal the domestic ideology in the service of a blanket condemnation of genteel women taking acting parts. Eliza de Feuillide's unpublished holograph letters in A-L provide a bit more evidence of Philadelphia Walter's concern for feminine decorum.
4. Virginia Woolf, *A Room of One's Own* (New York: Harcourt Brace, 1929); Tillie Olsen, "Silences: When Writers Don't Write," *Harper's Magazine*, Oct. 1965, 153–61; Elaine Showalter, *A Literature of Their Own: British Women Novelists from Brontë to Lessing* (Princeton: Princeton Univ. Press, 1977); Sandra Gilbert and Susan Gubar, *The Madwoman in the Attic: The Woman Writer and the Nineteenth-Century Literary Imagination* (New Haven: Yale Univ. Press, 1979); Mary Poovey, *The Proper Lady and the Woman Writer: Ideology as Style in the Works of Mary Wollstonecraft, Mary Shelley, and Jane Austen* (Chicago: Univ. of Chicago Press, 1984). Although Poovey's complex view of ideology sets her book off from the other works listed above, *The Proper Lady and the Woman Writer* does bear the influence of American feminist criticism.
5. Gilbert and Gubar, 71.
6. Park Honan, *Jane Austen: Her Life* (New York, St. Martin's Press, 1987).
7. Historians of American women have also borrowed. They have been influenced not only by studies of African American slave cultures but also by feminist anthropological studies of culture. For a discussion of the concepts of women's culture and cultural duality in history, anthropology, and literary studies in the 1970s and early 1980s, see Ellen Carol DuBois et al., *Feminist Scholarship: Kindling in the Groves of Academe* (Urbana: Univ. of Illinois Press, 1985), 38–67.
8. Compare, for example, Carroll Smith-Rosenberg, "The Female World of

Love and Ritual: Relations between Women in Nineteenth-Century America," *Signs* 1, no. 1 (1975): 1–29, and Nancy F. Cott, *The Bonds of Womanhood: "Woman's Sphere" in New England, 1780–1835* (New Haven: Yale Univ. Press, 1977) with Suzanne Lebsock's more recent study, *The Free Women of Petersburg: Status and Culture in a Southern Town, 1784–1860* (New York: W. W. Norton, 1984).

9. Ellen DuBois et al., "Politics and Culture in Women's History: A Symposium," *Feminist Studies* 6, no. 1 (1980): 52. See also two earlier Gerda Lerner essays, "Placing Women in History: Definitions and Challenges" and "The Challenge of Women's History," in *The Majority Finds Its Past* (New York: Oxford Univ. Press, 1979), 145–59, 168–80.

10. For a useful assessment of studies of women's cultures in the past decade, see Nancy A. Hewitt, "Beyond the Search for Sisterhood: American Women's History in the 1980s," in *Unequal Sisters: A Multicultural Reader in U.S. Women's History*, ed. Ellen Carol DuBois and Vicki L. Ruiz (New York: Routledge, 1990), 1–14. See also the discussion of research on women's cultures and the ideology of separate spheres in Linda K. Kerber, "Separate Spheres, Female Worlds, Woman's Place: The Rhetoric of Women's History," *Journal of American History* 75, no. 1 (1988): 9–39.

11. The preface to Judith Lowder Newton's *Women, Power, and Subversion: Social Strategies in British Fiction, 1778–1860* (Athens: Univ. of Georgia Press, 1981), which refers to women's culture, exhibits the benefits of crossing disciplines. In literary studies, researchers have, for the most part, used the term *women's culture* to refer to the collective experience and traditions of women *writers*. See especially Elaine Showalter's "Toward a Feminist Poetics" and "Feminist Criticism in the Wilderness" in *The New Feminist Criticism: Essays on Women, Literature, and Theory*, ed. Elaine Showalter (New York: Pantheon Books, 1985), 125–43, 243–70. See also her more recent essay, "A Criticism of Our Own: Autonomy and Assimilation in Afro-American and Feminist Literary Theory," in *The Future of Literary Theory*, ed. Ralph Cohen (New York: Routledge, 1989), 347–69.

12. For a discussion of the split within feminist theory between subject-centered and subject-problematizing positions, see Kathy E. Ferguson, "Interpretation and Genealogy," *Signs* 16, no. 2 (1991): 322–39. See also Mary Poovey, "Feminism and Deconstruction," *Feminist Studies* 14, no. 1 (1988): 51–65.

13. I think particularly of the way some literary studies have drawn on the work of Michel Foucault. See Judith Newton, "History as Usual?: Feminism and the 'New Historicism,'" *Cultural Critique* 9 (Spring 1988): 101–4 for a discussion of feminist objections to the work of Foucault.

14. A few historians have recently proposed approaches influenced by postmodern critical theories that challenge or at least deemphasize subjectivity and agency. But their positions are much more in the minority in the discipline of history than are postmodern approaches in literary studies. See, for example, Joan W. Scott's "On Language, Gender, and Working-

Class History" and the responses to this essay in *International Labor and Working Class History*, no. 31 (Spring 1987): 1–36.

15. Raymond Williams, *The Country and the City* (New York: Oxford Univ. Press, 1973), 166.

16. Quoted in William Austen-Leigh and Richard Arthur Austen-Leigh, *Jane Austen: A Family Record*, revised and enlarged by Deirdre Le Faye (London: The British Library, 1989), 79–80. This book is a substantial rewriting of the Austen-Leighs' *Jane Austen: Her Life and Letters*, published in 1913. Le Faye has included much valuable, additional information though without making many alterations in the Austen-Leighs' interpretive commentary.

17. Rev. James Wiggett to William Wiggett, 3 Nov. 1818, HRO 31M57/962.

18. "To Cassandra Austen," 28 Dec. 1798, Letter 16, *JAL*, 47; ibid., 8 Jan. 1799, Letter 17, *JAL*, 52; ibid., 1 Nov. 1800, Letter 24, *JAL*, 80.

19. David Spring, "Interpreters of Jane Austen's Social World: Literary Critics and Historians," in *Jane Austen: New Perspectives, Women & Literature*, n.s., 3, ed. Janet Todd, (New York: Holmes & Meier, 1983), 59–63.

20. Spring, 61.

21. The Rev. Charles Powlett was one of those exceptions, no doubt, because he identified with and longed for the favor of his aristocratic relatives at Hackwood. An 1806 letter that he wrote to his wife about Tory M.P. William Chute notes, "I had a very pleasant Journey yesterday; Chute was one of my Companions, we of course did not touch upon Party" (PL).

22. Increasingly over the course of the eighteenth century, women were allotted other forms of property. The substitution of jointures for dower rights, for example, which during that century became commonplace, was one means by which widows were denied access to landownership. See Susan Staves, *Married Women's Separate Property in England, 1660–1833* (Cambridge: Harvard Univ. Press, 1990).

23. Lawrence Stone, *The Family, Sex and Marriage in England 1500–1800* (New York: Harper & Row, 1977), 9.

24. "To Fanny Knight," 30 Nov. 1814, Letter 106, JAL, 419.

CHAPTER 1

Genteel Domesticity

1. William Chute to Henrietta Hicks Beach, 16 June 1793, HRO 31M57/951.

2. "Rev. James Austen to Frank Austen," 30 Jan. 1805, *AP*, 236.

3. Most of the relevant literature on this issue responds directly or indirectly to Lawrence Stone's *The Family, Sex and Marriage in England, 1500–1800* (New York: Harper & Row, 1977). See, for example, E. P. Thompson, "Happy Families," *Radical History Review* 20 (1979): 42–50; and Alan Mac-Farlane, *Marriage and Love in England: Modes of Reproduction 1300–1840* (Oxford: Basil Blackwell, 1986). MacFarlane would argue that at least cer-

tain aspects of the ideology of domesticity were not only practiced but promulgated in print long before the seventeenth century (see, for example, 182–83).

4. For discussions of eighteenth-century conduct books for women and their history, see Joyce Hemlow, "Fanny Burney and the Courtesy Books," *PMLA* 65 (1950): 732–61; Mary Poovey, *The Proper Lady and the Woman Writer: Ideology as Style in the Works of Mary Wollstonecraft, Mary Shelley, and Jane Austen* (Chicago: Univ. of Chicago Press, 1984); and Nancy Armstrong, *Desire and Domestic Fiction: A Political History of the Novel* (New York: Oxford Univ. Press, 1987).

5. For studies of groups that put this ideology into practice, see Stone, *The Family, Sex and Marriage*; and Randolph Trumbach, *The Rise of the Egalitarian Family: Aristocratic Kinship and Domestic Relations in Eighteenth-Century England* (New York: Academic Press, 1978).

6. Hester Chapone, *Letter to a New-Married Lady* (1777; published with *A Father's Legacy to His Daughters* (London: John Sharpe, 1828), 109.

7. By showing that many aristocrats adopted at least some aspects of domesticity in the eighteenth century, Trumbach's work helps us to remember that the ideology of domesticity's images of aristocrats were just that— images.

8. Thomas Gisborne, *An Enquiry into the Duties of the Female Sex*, ed. Gina Luria (1797; rpt. New York: Garland, 1974), 317.

9. Charles Powlett to Anne Temple, 19 March 1791, PL.

10. Ibid.

11. "To Cassandra Austen," 1 Dec. 1798, Letter 13, *JAL*, 36.

12. Charles John Powlett, "Abstract" of family papers, 1903, PL.

13. Raymond Williams, "Base and Superstructure in Marxist Cultural Theory," in his *Problems in Materialism and Culture* (London: Verso, 1980), 38.

14. Quoted in Charles John Powlett, "Abstract" of family papers, 1903, PL.

15. Lady Sarah Pennington, *A Mother's Advice to Her Absent Daughters*, ed. Randolph Trumbach (1817, 8th ed.; rpt. New York: Garland, 1986), 86. This work was originally published as *An Unfortunate Mother's Advice to Her Absent Daughters* in 1761.

16. Jane West, *Letters to a Young Lady in Which the Duties and Character of Women Are Considered* (Troy: O. Penniman, 1806), 376.

17. Caroline Wiggett Workman, "Reminiscences of Life at the Vyne," HRO 31M57/1070. Material in the next two pages is drawn from this unpaginated manuscript.

18. Historical demographers Schofield and Wrigley had originally put the eighteenth-century figure at 5.9 percent, but Schofield subsequently told MacFarlane that he thought the number was nearer to 9 percent. See MacFarlane, 25, and n. 17 on that page.

19. Stone, *The Family, Sex and Marriage*, 44, 47, 380–86. See also Ian Watt's discussion of spinsters in *The Rise of the Novel* (Berkeley: Univ. of California Press, 1957), 142–47.

20. H. J. Habakkuk, "Marriage Settlements in the Eighteenth Century," *Transactions of the Royal Historical Society*, 4th ser., 32 (1950): 15-30. See also Susan Staves, *Married Women's Separate Property in England, 1660-1833* (Cambridge: Harvard Univ. Press, 1990), 217-18.

21. Stone, *The Family, Sex and Marriage*, 44, 48.

22. Ibid., 44.

23. Hester Chapone, *Letters on the Improvement of the Mind* (1773; rpt. Boston: James B. Dow, 1834), 87.

24. West, 379.

25. John Gregory, *A Father's Legacy to His Daughters* (1774; rpt. London: John Sharpe, 1828), 93. Edward Copeland has shown that novelists of the period also stressed the importance of a competence. See his "What's a Competence? Jane Austen, her Sister Novelists, and the 5%'s," *Modern Language Studies* 9, no. 3 (1979).

26. Gisborne, 275-76.

27. E. A. Wrigley and R. S. Schofield, *The Population History of England 1541-1871* (Cambridge: Harvard Univ. Press, 1981), 255-56.

28. Mary Bramston's letters to Henrietta Hicks Beach reveal the couple's very limited knowledge of one another prior to the marriage proposal. See especially, HRO 20M64/9.

29. Caroline Wiggett Workman, "Reminiscences," HRO 31M57/1070.

30. Richard Vann, "Toward a New Lifestyle: Women in Preindustrial Capitalism," in *Becoming Visible: Women in European History*, ed. Renate Bridenthal and Claudia Koonz (Boston: Houghton Mifflin, 1977), 192-216.

31. Lawrence Stone and Jeanne Fawtier Stone, *An Open Elite? England, 1540-1800* (Oxford: Oxford Univ. Press, 1986), 123-24. The Stones' figures, however, are only for widows who married heirs.

32. *Reminiscences of Caroline Austen*, ed. Deirdre Le Faye (Overton: Jane Austen Society, 1986), 45.

33. See, for example, Fanny Austen's view of Lady Sondes's remarriage in Chapter 2. For a useful analysis of attitudes toward women's remarriages in a slightly earlier period, see Barbara J. Todd, "The Remarrying Widow: a Stereotype Reconsidered," in *Women in English Society, 1500-1800*, ed. Mary Prior (New York: Methuen, 1985), 54-92.

34. Such clauses may have become more common between 1549 and 1800. See Staves, 216.

35. Ad. Prob 6/178, 396, Public Record Office, London.

36. Evidence of the friendship between John Harwood and the Rev. William Heathcote appears in letters from Anne Lefroy to her son Christopher Edward, especially 12 April 1802, LF.

37. *Reminiscences of Caroline Austen*, 27-28.

38. Ibid., 28.

39. Stone, *The Family, Sex and Marriage*, 63, 65.

40. Wrigley and Schofield, 254. Catherine Hall and Leonore Davidoff have

also found the average number of births to be just over seven for the social group they have recently studied—the middle class from 1780 to 1850 in the town of Birmingham and the counties of Essex and Suffolk. See their *Family Fortunes: Men and Women of the English Middle Class, 1780-1850* (Chicago: Univ. of Chicago Press, 1987), 281.

41. The information that follows has been reconstructed from the family papers and other biographical sources cited in this and the next two chapters.

42. Noticing an unusually long interval between the births of Edward and Henry Austen, Deirdre Le Faye has surmised that Cassandra Austen miscarried in 1768. See William Austen-Leigh and Richard Arthur Austen-Leigh, *Jane Austen: A Family Record,* revised and enlarged by Deirdre Le Faye (London: The British Library, 1989), 17, 258 n. 35.

43. For a history of the painting of this portrait, see Sir Hughe Knatchbull-Hugessen, *Kentish Family* (London: Methuen, 1960), 157-60.

44. Angus McLaren, *Reproductive Rituals: The Perception of Fertility in England from the Sixteenth Century to the Nineteenth Century* (New York: Methuen, 1984), 4. My discussion of family planning is indebted to McLaren's study.

45. Thomas Crawford, "Boswell's Temple and the Jane Austen World," *Scottish Literary Journal* 10, no. 2 (1983): 58.

46. David Hopkinson, "'The Later Life of Sir Francis Austen," Jane Austen Society, *Report for the Year 1983* (Alton: Jane Austen Society, 1984), 9.

47. See MacFarlane, 66, for other, earlier recommendations of this strategy.

48. Sir Richard Hardinge to Thomas Papillon, 5 Feb. 1817, CKS U1015 C115/5.

49. "To Fanny Knight," 20 Feb. 1817, Letter 140, *JAL,* 480.

50. McLaren, 66-72; Stone, *The Family, Sex and Marriage,* 64.

51. The average interval between births was between 24 and 36 months. Stone, *The Family, Sex and Marriage,* 63; McLaren, 66-70.

52. Trumbach agrees; see *The Rise of the Egalitarian Family,* 170-76. Stone disagrees; see *The Family, Sex and Marriage,* 415-24.

53. Sir Richard Hardinge to Thomas Papillon, 5 Feb. 1817, CKS U1015 C115/5.

54. Rev. James Wiggett to William Chute, 3 Aug. 1792, HRO 31M57/953.

55. See MacFarlane's discussion of the Malthusian marriage, particularly 20-48.

56. McLaren, 65.

57. J. H. George Lefroy to Christopher Edward Lefroy, 13 Aug. 1805, LF.

58. Ibid., 12 Sept. 1805, LF. On 2 Feb. 1807, the older brother urged the younger in more direct terms to postpone marriage until he had a sufficient income: "I hope you will not marry till You have the means of keeping a Wife & whenever Your union with Miss W. does take place may the Almighty bless you both."

59. West, 24.

60. Maria Edgeworth and Richard Lovell Edgeworth, *Practical Education* (1798, rpt. New York: Self & Brown & Stansbury, 1801), 1:267.
61. Hannah More, *Strictures on the Modern System of Female Education*, ed. Gina Luria (1799; rpt. New York: Garland, 1974), 1:52.
62. Anne Lefroy to Christopher Edward Lefroy, 1 July 1801, LF.
63. Ibid., 29 Sept. 1801, LF.
64. F. Awdry, *A Country Gentleman of the Nineteenth Century: Being a Short Memoir of the Right Honourable Sir William Heathcote, Bart., of Hursley. 1801–1881* (Winchester: Warren & Son, 1906), 21.
65. *Reminiscences of Caroline Austen*, 13.
66. Charles John Austen, Journals and Diaries, 8 Feb. 1817 NMM AUS/109.
67. Fanny Austen to Dorothy Chapman, 23 April 1806, CKS U951 C105/4.
68. "Mrs. Knight to Edward Austen," 24 Nov. 1797, *AP*, 230.
69. Caroline Wiggett Workman, "Reminiscences of Life at the Vyne," HRO 31M57/1070.
70. See, for example, Fanny Austen's letters to Dorothy Chapman, CKS U951 C102, C103, and C105.
71. "To Cassandra Austen," 1 Sept. 1796, Letter 4, *JAL*, 10; Fanny Austen to Dorothy Chapman, 1 Sept. 1805, CKS U951 C104/5.
72. "To Cassandra Austen," 15 June 1808, Letter 51, *JAL*, 190.
73. Fanny Austen to Dorothy Chapman, 24 Sept. 1808, CKS U951 C108/9.
74. See "To Cassandra Austen," Letters 57, 58, 59, *JAL*, 219–30.
75. "To Cassandra Austen," 24 Oct. 1808, Letter 59, *JAL*, 225.
76. F. M. L. Thompson, *English Landed Society in the Nineteenth Century* (London: Routledge & Kegan Paul, 1963), 25–26.
77. "Lady Bridges to Mrs. Fielding," 2 March 1791, *Letters of Jane Austen*, ed. Edward, Lord Brabourne (London: Richard Bentley & Son, 1884), 2:357.
78. Gregory, 42.
79. For the uses of the term in the social context of patronage relationships, see Harold Perkin, *The Origin of Modern English Society, 1780–1880* (London: Routledge & Kegan Paul, 1969), 46–51.
80. "T. S. Hancock to Philadelphia Hancock," 23 Nov. 1769, *AP*, 41.
81. Gisborne concurs. In his *Enquiry* he observes: "Letters which pass between men, commonly relate in a greater or a less degree to actual business" (110–11).
82. Rev. James Wiggett to William Chute, 25 June 1800, HRO 31M57/954.
83. "Mrs. Knight to Mr. Knatchbull," 1808 or 1809, *Letters of Jane Austen*, 2:360–61.
84. Ibid., 2:362.
85. Fanny Knight's Diaries, CKS U951 F24/13.
86. Caroline Gore Diaries, 23 Dec. 1788, JAH.
87. Ibid., 29 March 1789.
88. "To Cassandra Austen," 26 June 1808, Letter 53, *JAL*, 201.
89. Annabella Knatchbull to Mary Knatchbull, 20 March 1814, CKS U951 C49/2.

90. Dorothea Banks to Mary Knatchbull, 30 March 1816, CKS U951 C59/3.

91. Fanny Palmer Austen to Esther Esten, 8 March 1814, PML MA4500.

92. Caroline Austen, *My Aunt Jane Austen: A Memoir* (London: Spottiswoode, Ballantyne & Co., 1952), 10.

93. "To Cassandra Austen," 27 Aug. 1805, Letter 46, *JAL*, 166.

94. Fanny Austen to Dorothy Chapman, 1 March 1803, CKS U951 C102/1.

95. Ibid., 9 April 1805, CKS U951 C104/3.

96. Ibid., 31 Aug. 1803, CKS U951 C102/2.

97. Ibid., 28 July 1805, CKS U951 C104/4.

98. Fanny Knight to Dorothy Chapman, 18 July 1815, CKS U951 C109/5.

99. "To Cassandra Austen," 23 Sept. 1813, Letter 84, *JAL*, 333.

100. Fanny Austen to Dorothy Chapman, 15 March 1812, CKS U951 C108/14.

101. B. M. Willmott Dobbie, "An Attempt to Estimate the True Rate of Maternal Mortality, Sixteenth to Eighteenth Centuries," *Medical History* 26, no. 1 (1982): 82–83.

102. Stone and Stone, *An Open Elite?*, 94–95.

103. J. H. George Lefroy to Christopher Edward, 8 June 1807, LF.

104. "To Cassandra Austen," 17 Nov. 1798, Letter 11, *JAL*, 30.

105. Rev. James Wiggett to William Chute, 23 Jan. 1801, HRO 31M57/955.

106. "To Fanny Knight," 13 March 1817, Letter 141, *JAL*, 483.

107. Poovey, 30–35; Judith Lowder Newton, *Women, Power, and Subversion: Social Strategies in British Fiction, 1778–1860* (Athens: Univ. of Georgia Press, 1981), 1–5, 15.

108. Newton, 4.

109. Gisborne, 11.

110. Ibid., 251.

111. West, 331.

112. Ibid., 381.

113. Gisborne, 11.

114. West, 34.

115. Charles Powlett to Anne Temple, 25 Jan. 1791, PL.

116. Henry Austen, "Biographical Notice of the Author," in *Northanger Abbey: and Persuasion*, vol. 1 (London: John Murray, 1818); rpt. in *The Novels of Jane Austen*, ed. R. W. Chapman, 3rd ed. (Oxford: Clarendon Press, 1933), 5:3. For a discussion of the history of biographical representations of Jane Austen's "uneventful" life, see my "The Disappearance of the Woman Writer: Jane Austen and Her Biographers," *Prose Studies* 7, no. 2 (1984): 129–47.

117. Trumbach, 119–20.

118. Caroline Gore Diaries, 12 April 1789, JAH.

119. "To Cassandra Austen," 26 June 1805, Letter 53, *JAL*, 200–201.

120. Chapone, *Letters on the Improvement of the Mind*, 94.

121. Gregory, 45–46.

122. Ibid., 26.

123. Ibid., 24, 26.

124. West, 50.
125. Ibid., 376.

CHAPTER 2
Compliant Women

1. "To Cassandra Austen," 14 Oct. 1813, Letter 87, *JAL*, 353. The less astute, twenty-year-old Fanny Knight, who also met him for the first time, was more impressed, describing him in her diary as "a darling! . . . has a lovely voice and is quite delightful!" See Deirdre Le Faye, "Fanny Knight's Diaries: Jane Austen through Her Niece's Eyes," in *Persuasions: Occasional Papers*, no. 2 (1986), Jane Austen Society of North America, 18. Many years later Fanny's son Edward, Lord Brabourne, also provided a brief sketch of Lushington; his account of the "pleasant and agreeable man of the world" is good-humored but ambivalent. See his *Letters of Jane Austen* (London: Richard Bentley & Son, 1884), 1:130–32.
2. For a portrait of their marital relations as well as their relations with Anne's father, see CKS U624 C67 and U624 C51.
3. Anne Lushington to George Harris, 4 May 1800, CKS U624 C51/4.
4. Ibid., 21 Sept. 1803, CKS U624 C51/5.
5. Sir Edward Knatchbull's Diary, 7 April 1816, CKS U951 F20.
6. Ibid., 4 April 1817, CKS U951 F20.
7. Ibid., 23 April 1818, CKS U951 F20.
8. Ibid., 9 April 1820, CKS U951 F20.
9. Fanny Knight to Sir Edward Knatchbull, 21 Sept. 1820, CKS U951 C12/10.
10. Ibid., n. d., CKS U951 C12/4.
11. Ibid., 8 Sept. 1820, CKS U951 C12/1.
12. Ibid., 14 Sept. 1820, CKS U951 C12/7.
13. Ibid.
14. Maria Edgeworth and Richard Lovell Edgeworth, *Practical Education* (1798; rpt. New York: Self, & Brown & Stansbury, 1801), 1:148.
15. Anne Powlett to Padgy Peters, 20 June 1799, PL.
16. Ibid., 8 July 1801, PL.
17. "To Cassandra Austen," 24 Jan. 1809, Letter 65, *JAL*, 255–56.
18. Fanny Austen to Dorothy Chapman, 11 Jan. 1809, CKS U951 C107/1.
19. "To Cassandra Austen," 25 Nov. 1798, Letter 12, *JAL*, 32.
20. Mary Bramston to Henrietta Hicks Beach, Jan. 1790, HRO 20M64/5.
21. Ibid., 15 Jan. 1790, HRO 20M64/6.
22. "To Cassandra Austen," 14 Jan. 1801, Letter 31, *JAL*, 110.
23. Anne Powlett to Charles Powlett, 7 Nov. 1805, PL.
24. "To Cassandra Austen," 15 June 1808, Letter 51, *JAL*, 186; and 20 June 1808, Letter 52, *JAL*, 197.
25. Fanny Austen to Dorothy Chapman, 27 May 1806, CKS U951 C105/5

26. Ibid., Feb. 1809, CKS U951 C107/2.

27. Ibid., 2 Nov. 1809, CKS U951 C107/11.

28. "Eliza de Feuillide to Philadelphia Walter," 1 Aug. 1791, *AP*, 142.

29. Elizabeth Chute to William Chute, 1805, A-L.

30. "Cassandra Elizabeth Austen to Mrs. Whitaker," 20 March 1812, *AP*, 250.

31. "To Cassandra Austen," 11 Feb. 1801, Letter 34, *JAL*, 121.

32. "Mary Bramston to Henrietta Hicks Beach," 6 July 1793, HRO 31M57/952.

33. "To Cassandra Austen," 21 Jan. 1799, Letter 18, *JAL*, 54.

34. Anne Powlett to Padgy Peters, 3 Nov. 1799, PL.

35. Ann Oakley, *Woman's Work: The Housewife, Past and Present* (New York: Vintage, 1974), 43–56.

36. Anna Austen Lefroy, "Memoranda," LF, 8. For more information on the Littleworth family, see Deirdre Le Faye, "The Austens and The Littleworths," in Jane Austen Society, *Report for the Year 1987* (Overton: Jane Austen Society, 1988), 14–21.

37. "Rev. James Austen to James Edward Austen," 28 April 1818, *AP*, 258.

38. "James Edward Austen to Rev. James Austen," 1? May 1818, *AP*, 259–60.

39. Caroline did, in fact, leave school in 1818, although not at Midsummer as her parents had intended but in December of that year. She may have been removed from school because her parents were still intent on economizing, but, more likely, Caroline was taken out of school at the end of the year because James Austen's health was rapidly declining.

40. If *penalties* seems an exaggeration, it is worth keeping in mind historian Richard Vann's words: "During by far the greatest part of human history, women have been relatively deprived of life. . . . for millennia females had a lower life expectancy than males. There are several possible explanations for this. They may simply have had less to eat than men." See "Towards a New Lifestyle: Women in Preindustrial Capitalism," in *Becoming Visible: Women in European History*, ed. Renate Bridenthal and Claudia Koonz (Boston: Houghton Mifflin, 1977), 195.

41. *Reminiscences of Caroline Austen*, ed. Deirdre Le Faye (Overton: Jane Austen Society, 1986), 2–3.

42. M. A. Austen-Leigh, *James Edward Austen Leigh, a Memoir* (1911), 48–49, cited in *Reminiscences of Caroline Austen*, 3.

43. Caroline Wiggett Workman, "Reminiscences of Life at the Vyne," HRO 31M57/1070.

44. *Reminiscences of Caroline Austen*, 35.

45. Ibid., 36.

46. Ibid., 37, 36.

47. *The Memorial* (London: Gosnell, Little Queen St., 1812). This published paginated work can be found in the Knatchbull manuscript collection, CKS U951 Z49/19.

48. Ibid., 10.

49. Ibid., 23.

50. Ibid., 26.
51. Ibid., 45.
52. Ibid., 11.
53. "To Cassandra Austen," 6 Nov. 1813, Letter 91, *JAL*, 372. See also Fanny Knight to Edward Knatchbull, 8 Sept. 1820, CKS U951 C12/1, and their son Edward, Lord Brabourne's opinion of Lady (Mary Anne) Honywood in his *Letters of Jane Austen*, 2:25–26.
54. For a discussion of women's ownership of "paraphernalia," see Susan Staves, *Married Women's Separate Property in England, 1660–1833* (Cambridge: Harvard Univ. Press, 1990), 148.
55. Annabella Honywood to Edward Knatchbull, 25 Nov. 1812, CKS U951 C49/1.
56. Mary Poovey, *The Proper Lady and the Woman Writer: Ideology as Style in the Works of Mary Wollstonecraft, Mary Shelley, and Jane Austen* (Chicago: Univ. of Chicago Press, 1984), 10.
57. Ibid., 15.
58. Sarah Smith to Elizabeth Chute, 18 Feb. 1794, A-L.
59. Ibid., 6 Feb. 1794, A-L.
60. Although these letters from Sarah Smith to Elizabeth Chute do not provide enough evidence to say for certain, it is possible that Chute's preferences for modesty in dress and self-denial may indicate a subtle form of resistance to patriarchal social relations akin to that Nancy Cott has identified in "Passionlessness: An Interpretation of Victorian Sexual Ideology, 1790–1850," *Signs* 4, no. 2 (1978): 219–36.
61. Sarah Smith to Elizabeth Chute, 18 Feb. 1794, A-L.
62. Hester Chapone, *Letters on the Improvement of the Mind* (1773; rpt. Boston: James B. Dow, 1834), 18–19.
63. Charles John Austen, Journals and Diaries, 6 May 1815, NMM AUS/102.
64. Edward Knatchbull's Diary, 7 April 1816, CKS U951f F20.
65. "Cassandra Elizabeth Austen to Mrs. Whitaker," 18 Aug. 1811, *AP*, 248.
66. Quoted in Geoffrey Grigson, "New Letters from Jane Austen's Home," *Times Literary Supplement*, 19 Aug. 1955, 484, col. 2–4.
67. "To ——," end of May? 1817, Letter 147, *JAL*, 498.
68. Anne Lushington to George Harris, 19 Aug. 1799, CKS U624 C51/3.
69. "To Cassandra Austen," 26 Oct. 1813, Letter 89, *JAL*, 361–62.
70. Mary Bramston to Henrietta Hicks Beach, Jan. 1790, HRO 20M64/5.
71. Ibid., 6 July 1793, HRO 31M57/952.

CHAPTER 3
The Women's Culture

1. Sir Edward Knatchbull to Fanny Knight, 13 Sept. 1820, CKS U951 C75/17; ibid., 18 Sept. 1820, CKS U951 C75/24; Fanny Knight to Dorothy Chapman, 18 Sept. 1820, CKS U951 C109/12.

2. Sir Edward Knatchbull to Fanny Knight, 18 Sept. 1820, CKS U951 C75/24.

3. Ibid.

4. For the development of Fanny's affection for her fiancé, see her letters to Sir Edward Knatchbull, CKS U951 C12/1–12.

5. Anna Austen Lefroy, *Jane Austen's Sanditon: A Continuation by Her Niece together with "Reminiscences of Aunt Jane,"* ed. Mary Gaither Marshall (Chicago: Chiron Press, 1983), 158; Austen scholar Deirdre Le Faye estimates in her study of Fanny's diaries that she and Cassandra exchanged letters approximately every three weeks; see Le Faye, "Fanny Knight's Diaries: Jane Austen through Her Niece's Eyes," in *Persuasions: Occasional Papers*, no. 2 (1986), Jane Austen Society of North America, 6.

6. Sir Edward Knatchbull to Fanny Knight, 13 Sept. 1820, CKS U951 C75/17.

7. John Gregory, *A Father's Legacy to His Daughters* (1774; rpt. London: John Sharpe, 1828), 57–58.

8. Hester Chapone, *Letters on the Improvement of the Mind* (1773; rpt. Boston: James B. Dow, 1834), 81.

9. Hannah More, *Strictures on the Modern System of Female Education*, ed. Gina Luria (1799; rpt. New York: Garland, 1974), 1:134–37.

10. Jane West, *Letters to a Young Lady in which the Duties and Character of Women Are Considered* (Troy: O. Penniman, 1806), 370.

11. Lady Sarah Pennington, *A Mother's Advice to Her Absent Daughters*, ed. Randolph Trumbach (1817, 8th ed.; rpt. New York: Garland, 1986), 55. This work was originally published as *An Unfortunate Mother's Advice to Her Absent Daughters* in 1761.

12. See, for example, West, 369; Gregory, 52; and Chapone, 66–69; Sarah Smith to Elizabeth Chute, 6 Feb. 1794 and 18 Feb. 1794, A-L.

13. The terms "dominant" and "alternative" belong to the theory of culture offered by Raymond Williams in "Base and Superstructure in Marxist Cultural Theory," in his *Problems in Materialism and Culture* (London: Verso, 1980), 31–49.

14. For discussions of the concepts of women's culture and cultural duality, see the Introduction.

15. Gerda Lerner's statement is in Ellen Dubois et al., "Politics and Culture in Women's History: A Symposium," *Feminist Studies* 6, no. 1 (1980): 52.

16. Gregory, 55–56.

17. "Mrs. George Austen to Mary Lloyd," 30 Nov. 1796, *AP*, 228.

18. Mary Bramston to Henrietta Hicks Beach, 8 Oct. 1793, HRO 20M64/13.

19. Elizabeth Gosling to Elizabeth Chute, 17 Oct. 1793, A-L.

20. See, for example, Gregory, 56–57, and Pennington, 35.

21. Chapone, 77.

22. Fanny Knatchbull to Dorothy Chapman, 9 Oct. 1838, CKS U951 C109/20.

23. Fanny Austen to Dorothy Chapman, 29 May 1808, CKS U951 C108/5.

24. Judgments about sexual expression in female friendships of this period

are, of course, very difficult to make, for a highly charged affective language, which may be understood as a form of eroticism in itself, is not, by itself, evidence of homosexual practice. But female bonds among English and American middle- and upper-class women in the late eighteenth and nineteenth centuries have been extensively documented, and it is useful at least to compare Hampshire and Kent gentlewomen's language of affection with the more passionate language of other women in other social circles. For a range of examples and treatments of the issue, see Nancy Cott, *The Bonds of Womanhood: "Woman's Sphere" in New England, 1780–1835* (New Haven: Yale Univ. Press, 1977); Carroll Smith-Rosenberg, "The Female World of Love and Ritual: Relations between Women in Nineteenth-Century America," *Signs* 1, no. 1 (1975): 1–29; Lillian Faderman, *Surpassing the Love of Men: Romantic Friendship and Love Between Women from the Renaissance to the Present* (New York: William Morrow, 1981); Elizabeth Mavor, *The Ladies of Llangollen: A Study in Romantic Friendship* (Harmondsworth, Middlesex: Penguin Books, 1971).

25. "Eliza de Feuillide to Philadelphia Walter," 27 March 1782, *AP*, 99.
26. Mary Bramston to Henrietta Hicks Beach, 15 Jan. 1790, HRO 20M64/6.
27. Fanny Austen to Dorothy Chapman, 20 Dec. 1806, CKS U951 C105/11.
28. Anne Powlett to Padgy Peters, 1 May 1814, PL.
29. Gregory, 52.
30. Pennington, 56.
31. "To Cassandra Austen," 7 Jan. 1807, Letter 48, *JAL*, 173.
32. Mary Bramston to Henrietta Hicks Beach, 8 Oct. 1793, HRO 20M64/13.
33. Charles Powlett to Anne Temple, 25 Jan. 1791, PL.
34. Anne Powlett to Charles Powlett, 20 Jan. 1801, PL.
35. Mary Bramston to Henrietta Hicks Beach, n.d., HRO 20M64/20.
36. Anne Powlett to Padgy Peters, 12 Aug. 1798, PL.
37. Chapone, 82.
38. *Letters of Jane Austen*, ed. Edward, Lord Brabourne (London: Richard Bentley & Son, 1884), 2:118.
39. Eliza de Feuillide to Philadelphia Walter, 11 Feb. 1789, A-L.
40. "Mrs. George Austen to Mary Lloyd," 30 Nov. 1796, *AP*, 228.
41. Fanny Knight's Diaries, CKS U951 F24/13.
42. "To Cassandra Austen," 3 Nov. 1813, Letter 90, *JAL*, 364.
43. "To Fanny Knight," 30 Nov. 1814, Letter 106, *JAL*, 418–19.
44. Mary Bramston to Henrietta Hicks Beach, 6 July 1793, HRO 31M57/952.
45. Ibid., 14 March 1793, HRO 20M64/10.
46. "Eliza de Feuillide to Philadelphia Walter," 26 Oct. 1792, *AP*, 150.
47. Chapone, 67.
48. Mary Bramston to Henrietta Hicks Beach, 13 Feb. 1793, HRO 20M64/9.
49. Ibid., 1793, HRO 20M64/12.
50. Ibid., 1800, HRO 20M64/21; and 15 Jan. 1790, HRO 20M64/6.
51. Anna Austen Lefroy, *"Reminiscences,"* 164.
52. Caroline Gore Diaries, 13 June 1791, JAH.

53. "Eliza Hancock to Philadelphia Walter," 16 May 1780, *AP*, 92.
54. "To Cassandra Austen," 27 Oct. 1798, Letter 10, *JAL*, 26.
55. Chapone, 109; Elizabeth Chute to Elizabeth Gosling, 29 Sept. 1800, A-L.
56. "To Cassandra Austen," 1 Dec. 1798, Letter 13, *JAL*, 35–36.
57. "Eliza Austen to Philadelphia Walter," 16 Feb. 1798, *AP*, 170.
58. Elizabeth Chute to Elizabeth Gosling, 29 Sept. 1800, A-L.
59. Mary Bramston to Henrietta Hicks Beach, n.d., HRO 20M64/16.
60. Fanny Knight to Dorothy Chapman, 13 Dec. 1819, CKS U951 C109/11.
61. Anne Powlett to Padgy Peters, 13 Oct. 1803, PL.
62. "Eliza de Feuillide to Philadelphia Walter," 27 March 1782, *AP*, 100–101.
63. Ibid., 22 Aug. 1788, *AP*, 133.
64. "To Cassandra Austen," 24 Dec. 1798, Letter 15, *JAL*, 42.
65. In other moods and sometimes to other correspondents, Austen also reversed the point of her irony, exaggerating the importance of what she did to signal its triviality. In 1798, to her brother Frank, then stationed in the Baltic, she wrily portrayed her trip to Godmersham as an event of international significance: "I wonder whether You & the King of Sweden knew that I *was* to come to G^m with my B^r. Yes, I suppose you have rec^d due notice of it by some means or other. I have not been here these 4 years, so I am sure the event deserves to be talked of before & behind as well as in the middle" (*JAL*, 336–37). For a more extended discussion of the humor and stylistic devices stimulated by Austen's experience of cultural duality, see my "Representing Two Cultures: Jane Austen's Letters," in *The Private Self: Theory and Practice of Women's Autobiographical Writings*, ed. Shari Benstock (Chapel Hill: Univ. of North Carolina Press, 1988), 211–29.
66. "To Cassandra Austen," 15 June 1808, Letter 51, *JAL*, 191.
67. Ibid., 20 June 1808, Letter 52, *JAL*, 192–93.
68. Ibid., 2 March 1814, Letter 92, *JAL*, 377.
69. Mary Bramston to Henrietta Hicks Beach, 24 Aug. 1788, HRO 20M64/4.
70. Ibid., 13 Feb. 1793, HRO 20M64/9.
71. Ibid., 1793, HRO 20M64/12.
72. Eliza de Feuillide to Philadelphia Walter, 22 Aug. 1788, A-L.
73. Ibid., 7 Jan. 1791, A-L.
74. Ibid., 23 Nov. 1787, A-L.
75. "Eliza de Feuillide to Philadelphia Walter," 17 Jan. 1786, *AP* 116.
76. Elizabeth Chute to Elizabeth Gosling, 29 Sept. 1800, A-L.
77. Mary Bramston to Henrietta Hicks Beach, 14 March 1793, HRO 20M64/10.
78. Fanny Palmer Austen to Esther Esten, 1 June 1810, PML MA4500.
79. "To Cassandra Austen," 25 Nov. 1798, Letter 12, *JAL*, 33.
80. Elizabeth Chute to Elizabeth Gosling, 29 Sept. 1800, A-L.
81. Jane Cresset Pelham to Elizabeth Papillon, 17 Jan. 1793, CKS U1015 C117/3.
82. "To Cassandra Austen," 14 Oct. 1813, Letter 87, *JAL*, 349.
83. Elizabeth Chute to Elizabeth Gosling, 29 Sept. 1800, A-L.

84. Anne Powlett to Padgy Peters, 1804, quoted in Charles John Powlett's "Abstract" of family papers, 1903, PL.
85. "To Cassandra Austen," 26 June 1808, Letter 53, *JAL*, 203.
86. "Eliza de Feuillide to Philadelphia Walter," 30 Dec. 1796, *AP*, 157.
87. Fanny Knatchbull to Dorothy Chapman, 9 Oct. 1838, U951 C109/20.
88. West, 50, 31.
89. Anne Powlett to Padgy Peters, 12 Feb. 1801, PL.
90. Fanny Palmer Austen to Harriet Palmer, 1814, PML MA4500.
91. "To Cassandra Austen," 11 Oct. 1813, Letter 86, *JAL*, 346.
92. Augusta Smith to Elizabeth Chute, 4 March 1794, A-L.
93. Mary Bramston to Henrietta Hicks Beach, n.d., HRO 20M64/20.
94. Barbara Taylor, *Eve and the New Jerusalem: Socialism and Feminism in the Nineteenth Century* (New York: Pantheon Books, 1983), 5.
95. Eliza de Feuillide to Philadelphia Walter, 3 July 1797, A-L.

CHAPTER 4
Circles of Support

1. Jane Aiken Hodge, *Only a Novel: The Double Life of Jane Austen* (New York: Coward, McCann, & Geoghegan, 1972); David Cecil, *A Portrait of Jane Austen* (New York: Hill and Wang, 1978); John Halperin, *The Life of Jane Austen* (Baltimore: Johns Hopkins Univ. Press, 1984).
2. Cecil, *A Portrait*, 141.
3. What I refer to as Austen's extant letters are in some cases only copies. The originals of approximately thirty letters have not been found. In addition, a few of the letters are brief fragments. See *Jane Austen's Manuscript Letters in Facsimile*, ed. Jo Modert (Carbondale: Southern Illinois Univ. Press, 1990).
4. Henry Austen, "Biographical Notice of the Author," in *Northanger Abbey: and Persuasion*, vol. 1 (London: John Murray, 1818); rpt. in *The Novels of Jane Austen*, ed. R. W. Chapman, 3rd ed. (Oxford: Clarendon Press, 1933), 5:3.
5. J. E. Austen-Leigh, *Memoir of Jane Austen*, 2nd ed., ed. R. W. Chapman, (1871; rpt. Oxford: Clarendon Press, 1926), 12.
6. See, for example, B. C. Southam, *Jane Austen's Literary Manuscripts: A Study of the Novelist's Development through the Surviving Papers* (Oxford: Clarendon Press, 1964), 4–5, 8; A. Walton Litz, *Jane Austen: A Study of Her Artistic Development* (New York: Oxford Univ. Press, 1965), 14–15, 17; and Jane Aiken Hodge, *Only a Novel*, 34.
7. Southam, *Jane Austen's Literary Manuscripts*, 4–5. Southam names James, Henry, and Charles, but I have found no evidence of Charles's penchant for literary writing.
8. A collection of James Austen's poetry and a few prose pieces is located at Jane Austen's house at Chawton. For a discussion of his writings, see

George Holbert Tucker, *A Goodly Heritage: A History of Jane Austen's Family* (Manchester: Carcanet New Press, 1983), 99–114.

9. Austen-Leigh, *Memoir*, 9.

10. David Cecil, *A Portrait*, 35.

11. Austen's knowable community was very literate; the general adult population of England was not. See Roger S. Schofield, "Dimensions of Illiteracy in England 1750–1850," in *Literacy and Social Development in the West: A Reader*, ed. Harvey J. Graff (Cambridge: Cambridge Univ. Press, 1981), 201–13. According to Schofield, "long before the mid eighteenth century the subculture of the social elite presupposed literacy, and literacy was also essential to the economic functions of men in the professions and official positions" (210). By contrast, in the late eighteenth and early nineteenth centuries male illiteracy in the general population hovered at about 40 percent and female illiteracy was between 50 and 60 percent. This larger context should remind us of Austen's good fortune in being born to parents who were part of a genteel community.

12. Elizabeth Chute to Elizabeth Gosling, 16 August 1800, A-L.

13. "To Cassandra Austen," 9 Feb. 1813, Letter 78, *JAL*, 304.

14. Lady Frances Heathcote, HRO 63M84/233/56.

15. J. E. George Lefroy to Christopher Edward Lefroy, Nov. 1801, LF.

16. Wither Bramston to Mrs. Beach, 3 March 1782, HRO 20M64/1.

17. William Heathcote, HRO 63M84/234/7.

18. Augusta Bramston to Mrs. Hicks, 20 Jan. 1790, HRO 20M64/8.

19. Anne Lefroy to Christopher Edward Lefroy, 1 Aug. 1803, LF. The poem was "The Address of Robert Bruce to his Soldiers on the Eve of the Battle of Bannockburn" ("Scots, Wha Hae"). The Scottish Burns's nationalistic poem, written in 1793, was partly inspired by the French Revolution. When Lefroy transformed it into a pro-English, anti-French poem, she showed no awareness of the irony of her undertaking.

20. "Old Hampshire Hunt Songs," Jan. 1880, 31. This article, in the possession of the Hampshire Record Office and cited with permission, bears no accession number. See also *The Diaries of Dummer*, ed. A.M.W. Stirling (London: Unicorn Press, 1934), 78.

21. Park Honan provides the most elaborated version of this view in *Jane Austen: Her Life* (New York: St. Martin's Press, 1987) and in his subsequent article, "The Austen Brothers and Sisters," *Persuasions*, no. 10 (1988): 59–64.

22. Mary Lascelles, *Jane Austen and Her Art* (1939; rpt. London: Oxford Univ. Press, 1963), 146, 32.

23. Mary Poovey, *The Proper Lady and the Woman Writer: Ideology as Style in the Works of Mary Wollstonecraft, Mary Shelley, and Jane Austen* (Chicago: Univ. of Chicago Press, 1984), 202. See also Alison Sulloway, *Jane Austen and the Province of Womanhood* (Philadelphia: Univ. of Pennsylvania Press, 1989), 86, 87, 92. Sulloway stresses the lifelong role of the family, particularly Austen's father and her brother Henry. She also singles out

Austen's mother and sister as decidedly unsupportive and unhelpful.

24. "George Austen to Mr. Cadell," 1 Nov. 1797, in W. and R. A. Austen-Leigh, *Jane Austen: Her Life and Letters*, 2nd ed. (London, 1913; rpt. New York: Russell and Russell, 1965), 97–98.

25. Quoted in Tucker, *A Goodly Heritage*, 113.

26. Cecil, *A Portrait*, 142.

27. Halperin, *The Life of Jane Austen*, 189.

28. See, for example, J. M. S. Tompkins, *The Popular Novel in England: 1770–1800* (1932; rpt. Lincoln: Univ. of Nebraska Press, 1961), 116–22; and Elaine Showalter, *A Literature of Their Own: British Women Novelists from Brontë to Lessing* (Princeton: Princeton Univ. Press, 1977).

29. Anne Lefroy to Christopher Edward Lefroy, 3 Nov. 1802, LF.

30. Ibid., 9 Nov. 1802, LF.

31. Anna Austen Lefroy, *Jane Austen's Sanditon: A Continuation by her Niece Together with "Reminiscences of Aunt Jane,"* ed. Mary Gaither Marshall (Chicago: Chiron Press, 1983), 106. Anna Lefroy remembers the manuscript as "P & P" [*Pride and Prejudice*] in retrospect; in the late 1790s it was called "First Impressions."

32. W. and R. A. Austen-Leigh probably adapted the story from the account given by Anna's daughter, Fanny C. Lefroy, in her "Family History," A-L.

33. W. and R. A. Austen-Leigh, *Her Life and Letters*, 73.

34. "To Cassandra Austen," 8 Jan. 1799, Letter 17, *JAL*, 52.

35. Ibid., 11 June 1799, Letter 21, *JAL*, 67.

36. "To Crosbie & Co.," 5 April 1809, Letter 67, *JAL*, 263.

37. *Emma* actually appeared in December 1815, but its title page is dated 1816. Similarly, *Persuasion* and *Northanger Abbey* were published in December 1817, but their title pages are dated 1818.

38. W. and R. A. Austen-Leigh, *Life and Letters*, 236.

39. For a comprehensive review of the information that has survived about Austen's older brother George, see George Holbert Tucker, *A Goodly Heritage*, 115–17.

40. This information appears in a letter of reminiscence written by one of the Middleton children more than fifty years later, probably in the 1870s. Two of her letters were published in "Recollections of Chawton," *Times Literary Supplement*, 3 May 1985, 495, col. 2–3.

41. "To Cassandra Austen," 29 Jan. 1813, Letter 76, *JAL*, 297. Despite her efforts, word of her authorship trickled out among some of her neighbors and acquaintances. Austen's collections, "Opinions of *Mansfield Park*" and "Opinions of *Emma*," in *The Works of Jane Austen*, 6: 431–39, provide the names of some of those who knew her secret by 1814.

42. Quoted in Deirdre Le Faye, "Fanny Knight's Diaries: Jane Austen Through her Niece's Eyes," in *Persuasions: Occasional Papers*, no. 2 (1986), Jane Austen Society of North America, 1986, 15.

43. "To Fanny Knight," 13 March 1817, Letter 141, *JAL*, 484.

44. Anna Austen Lefroy, *"Reminiscences,"* 160.

45. Caroline Austen, *My Aunt Jane Austen: A Memoir* (Alton: Jane Austen Society, 1952), 9.

46. J. E. Austen-Leigh, *Memoir*, 102–3.

47. Constance Hill, *Jane Austen: Her Home & Her Friends* (1901; rpt. Folcroft: Folcroft Library Editions, 1977), 202.

48. Elizabeth Jenkins, "Some Notes on Background," in Jane Austen Society, *Report for the Year 1980* (Alton: Jane Austen Society, 1981), 26.

49. "To Fanny Knight," 23 March 1817, Letter 142, *JAL*, 486–87. For other evidence that Austen's confidantes discussed her writing with her, see William Austen-Leigh and Richard Arthur Austen-Leigh, *Jane Austen: A Family Record*, revised and enlarged by Deirdre Le Faye (London: The British Library, 1989), 214, 219.

50. "To Francis Austen," 3 July 1813, Letter 81, *JAL*, 317.

51. "To Fanny Knight," 30 Nov. 1814, Letter 106, *JAL*, 419–20.

52. "To Francis Austen," 3 July 1813, Letter 81, *JAL*, 317.

53. Jane Austen described his reading experience to her sister in Letters 92, 93, and 94 of *JAL*.

54. "To Fanny Knight," 23 March 1817, Letter 142, *JAL*, 487.

55. See, for example, Henry Austen, "Biographical Notice," 6–7.

56. Sandra Gilbert and Susan Gubar, *The Madwoman in the Attic: The Woman Writer and the Nineteenth-Century Literary Imagination* (New Haven: Yale Univ. Press, 1979), 108.

57. "To J. Edward Austen," 16 Dec. 1816, Letter 134, *JAL*, 469.

58. "To James Stanier Clarke," 11 Dec. 1815, Letter 120, *JAL*, 443.

59. "To Cassandra Austen," 24 May 1813, Letter 80, *JAL*, 311.

60. Ibid., 4 Feb. 1813, Letter 77, *JAL*, 299–300.

61. Ibid., 29 Jan. 1813, Letter 76, *JAL*, 297–98.

62. "To Anna Austen," 10 Aug. 1814, Letter 98, *JAL*, 394.

63. "To Cassandra Austen," 17 Oct. 1815, Letter 111, *JAL*, 425; and ibid., 24 Nov. 1815, Letter 116, *JAL*, 433, 435.

64. Ibid., 15 Sept. 1813, Letter 82, *JAL*, 320.

65. Ibid., 2 March 1814, Letter 92, *JAL*, 378.

66. "To Fanny Knight," 18 Nov. 1814, Letter 103, *JAL*, 411.

67. See, for example, Honan, *Jane Austen: Her Life*, 156, 175, and 205.

68. See, for example, ibid., 403.

69. Ibid., 351; see also 251. But elsewhere in the biography Honan stresses the impact of Austen's brothers on her writing and downplays the influence of Martha or other female friends; see, for example, 62.

70. See, for example, ibid., 27 and 119.

71. J. E. Austen-Leigh, *Memoir*, 102.

72. W. and R. A. Austen-Leigh, *Life and Letters*, 236.

73. Elizabeth Jenkins, *Jane Austen* (London: Victor Gollancz, 1938), 181.

74. J. E. Austen-Leigh, *Memoir*, 103.

75. Cecil, *A Portrait*, 141.

76. Halperin, *The Life of Jane Austen* 190.
77. Hodge, *Only a Novel*, 116.

CHAPTER 5
Assuming Spinsterhood

1. Only the interpretations of Susan Lanser and Jane Aiken Hodge have linked Austen's decision to remain single to her writing. See Hodge, *Only a Novel: The Double Life of Jane Austen* (New York: Coward, McCann & Geoghegan, 1972), 83; and Lanser, "No Connections Subsequent: Jane Austen's World of Sisterhood" in *The Sister Bond: A Feminist View of a Timeless Connection* (New York: Pergamon Press, 1985), 59.
2. See, for example, Park Honan, "Jane Austen and Marriage," *Contemporary Review* (Nov. 1984), 257, and Honan's biography, *Jane Austen: Her Life* (New York: St. Martin's, 1987), 193–96; see also Elizabeth Jenkins, *Jane Austen* (London: Victor Gollancz, 1938), 147.
3. J. E. Austen-Leigh, *Memoir of Jane Austen*, 2nd ed., ed. R. W. Chapman, (1871; rpt. Oxford: Clarendon Press, 1926), 28.
4. See R. W. Chapman, *Jane Austen: Facts and Problems* (Oxford: Clarendon Press, 1948), 61–62; and Joan Austen-Leigh, "New Light Thrown on JA's Refusal of Harris Bigg-Wither," *Persuasions*, no. 8 (1986): 34–35.
5. Chapman, *Facts and Problems*, 62.
6. Jenkins, *Jane Austen*, 131.
7. Ibid., 146.
8. John Halperin, *The Life of Jane Austen* (Baltimore: Johns Hopkins Univ. Press, 1984), 135.
9. Reginald Bigg-Wither, *Materials for a History of the Wither Family* (Winchester: Warren & Son, 1907), 58.
10. Quoted in Joan Austen-Leigh, "New Light," 35.
11. Honan, "Jane Austen and Marriage," 256–57. Honan softens Bigg-Wither's portrait in *Jane Austen: Her Life* but only slightly. See, for example, 193: "He might improve. He was still young."
12. J. H. George Lefroy to Christopher Edward Lefroy, 16 April 1802; Anne Lefroy to Christopher Edward Lefroy, 12 April 1802, 12 Sept. 1802, 12 Oct. 1804, 9 Nov. 1804, LF.
13. These versions are provided in Chapman, *Facts and Problems*, 64–68.
14. Chapman, *Facts and Problems*, 67.
15. Ibid., 64.
16. Ibid., 66.
17. David Cecil, *A Portrait of Jane Austen* (New York: Hill and Wang, 1978), 98.
18. John Halperin, "Jane Austen's Lovers," *Studies in English Literature 1500–1900* 25, no. 4 (1985): 735. The essay extends and in places slightly exag-

gerates similar points made in his full-length biography. I have sometimes wondered whether Halperin intended this article as an ironic joke, but I can find no internal or external evidence to support that reading.

19. Halperin, "Jane Austen's Lovers," 727.
20. Ibid., 733.
21. Ibid., 735.
22. "To Cassandra," 2 Dec. 1815, Letter 118, *JAL*, 441, 440.
23. Halperin, "Jane Austen's Lovers," 735.
24. "To Cassandra Austen," 26 Nov. 1815, Letter 117, *JAL*, 438.
25. Anne Powlett to Padgy Peters, 3 Nov. 1799, PL.
26. Quoted in Joan Austen-Leigh, "New Light," 35.
27. See, for example, Cecil, *A Portrait*.
28. J. M. S. Tompkins, *The Popular Novel in England, 1770–1800* (Lincoln: Univ. of Nebraska Press, 1961), 122; *A Dictionary of British and American Women Writers, 1660–1800*, ed. Janet Todd (Totowa, N.J.: Rowman & Littlefield, 1987), 6.
29. Todd, ed., *A Dictionary*, 7.
30. Sarah Smith to Elizabeth Chute, 2? Jan. 1794, A-L.
31. See Chapter 2.
32. Although his *Jane Austen: Her Life* does not make this argument, in a subsequent article Park Honan says, "If she had married Harris or almost any other man, she would have been less free to talk or even to write just as she wished. (How many wives today have complete expressive freedom?)." See "The Austen Brothers and Sisters," *Persuasions*, no. 10 (1988): 63.
33. "To Cassandra Austen," 24 Dec. 1798, Letter 15, *JAL*, 43.
34. Ibid., 8 Jan. 1799, Letter 17, *JAL*, 51–52.
35. "Mrs. George Austen to Mary Lloyd," 30 Nov. 1796, *AP*, 228.
36. "To Cassandra Austen," 27 Oct. 1798, Letter 10, *JAL*, 24.
37. Elizabeth Gosling to Elizabeth Chute, 17 Oct. 1793, A-L.
38. "To Cassandra Austen," 18 Dec. 1798, Letter 14, *JAL*, 40.
39. Ibid., 1 Nov. 1800, Letter 24, *JAL*, 79–80.
40. Ibid., 8 Jan. 1799, Letter 17, *JAL*, 50.
41. Ibid.
42. Only Lanser and Hodge have linked Austen's decision not to marry to her relationship with other women, though they focus on only one—Cassandra. See "No Connections Subsequent," 59; and *Only a Novel*, 83.
43. "To Cassandra Austen," 27 Aug. 1805, Letter 46, *JAL*, 164.
44. Ibid., 24 Jan. 1809, Letter 65, *JAL*, 255–56.
45. Ibid., 7 Jan. 1807, Letter 48, *JAL*, 171.
46. Ibid., 1 Oct. 1808, Letter 55, *JAL*, 211.
47. Ibid., 4 Feb. 1813, Letter 77, *JAL*, 300.
48. "To Martha Lloyd," 16 Feb. 1813, Letter 78.1, *JAL*, 503.
49. "To Cassandra Austen," 26 Nov. 1815, Letter 117, *JAL*, 437.
50. Ibid., 8 Sept. 1816, Letter 133, *JAL*, 466.

51. Ibid., 6 Nov. 1813, Letter 91, *JAL*, 370.

52. Ibid., 14 Oct. 1813, Letter 87, *JAL*, 349.

53. "To Fanny Knight," 30 Nov. 1814, Letter 106, *JAL*, 419.

54. Caroline Austen, *My Aunt Jane Austen: A Memoir* (Alton: Jane Austen Society, 1952), 5.

55. Anna Austen Lefroy, *Jane Austen's Sanditon: A Continuation by Her Niece Together with "Reminiscences of Aunt Jane,"* ed. Mary Gaither Marshall (Chicago: Chiron Press, 1983), 158.

56. Anna Austen Lefroy, *"Reminiscences of Aunt Jane,"* 159. The "Family History" composed by Anna's daughter, Fanny Lefroy, offers this version, presumably of Anna's account: "They seemed to lead a life to themselves, within the general family life, which was shared only by each other. I will not say their true but their full feelings and opinions were known only to themselves."

57. "To Cassandra Austen," 13 Oct. 1808, Letter 57, *JAL*, 220.

58. Ibid., 30 Aug. 1805, Letter 47, *JAL*, 168.

59. Ibid., 31 May 1811, Letter 73, *JAL*, 284.

60. Ibid., 20 June 1808, Letter 52, *JAL*, 194.

61. Ibid., 17 Jan. 1809, Letter 64, *JAL*, 251.

62. "To Alethea Bigg," 24 Jan. 1817, Letter 139, *JAL*, 476.

63. "To Cassandra Austen," 26 June 1808, Letter 53, *JAL*, 201.

64. Ibid., 7 Oct. 1808, Letter 56, *JAL*, 217.

65. Ibid., 2 Dec. 1815, Letter 118, *JAL*, 441.

66. Anna Austen Lefroy, *"Reminiscences of Aunt Jane,"* 160.

67. "To Cassandra Austen," 9 Dec. 1808, Letter 61, *JAL*, 236.

68. Ibid., 20 June 1808, Letter 52, *JAL*, 195.

69. Ibid., 26 Oct. 1813, Letter 89, *JAL*, 361.

70. "To Fanny Knight," 30 Nov. 1814, Letter 106, *JAL*, 416.

71. "To Anna Austen," 28 Sept. 1814, Letter 101, *JAL*, 404.

72. "To Fanny Knight," 20 Feb. 1817, Letter 140, *JAL*, 478–79.

73. Ibid., 480. For diverse discussions of Austen's attitudes toward childbearing and children, see, for example, Christopher Ricks, "Jane Austen and the Business of Mothering," *Report for the Year 1982* (Alton: Jane Austen Society, 1983), 27–44; and Nina Auerbach, "Artists and Mothers: A False Alliance," *Women and Literature* 6, no. 1 (1978): 3–9.

74. "To Fanny Knight," 23 March 1817, Letter 142, *JAL*, 488.

75. Edward Copeland, "What's a Competence? Jane Austen, her Sister Novelists, and the 5%'s," *Modern Language Studies* 9, no. 3 (1979): 164.

76. Patrick Piggott, "Jane Austen's Southampton Piano," *Report for the Year 1980* (Alton: Jane Austen Society, 1981), 7.

77. "To Fanny Knight," 13 March 1817, Letter 141, *JAL*, 483.

78. "To Cassandra Austen," 30 June 1808, Letter 54, *JAL*, 209.

79. "To Cassandra Austen," 9 Feb. 1813, Letter 78, *JAL*, 302.

80. "To Martha Lloyd," 16 Feb. 1813, Letter 78.1, *JAL*, 505.

81. *Gentleman's Magazine*, Vol. 82 (Nov. 1812), 495.

82. "Mrs. Knight to Miss Knight," 26 Oct. 1809, *Letters of Jane Austen*, ed. Edward, Lord Brabourne (London: Richard Bentley & Son, 1884), 2:365.
83. "To Cassandra Austen," 20 June 1808, Letter 52, *JAL*, 194.
84. Ibid., 26 June 1808, Letter 53, *JAL*, 200.
85. Ibid.
86. Ibid., 199.
87. Ibid., 30 June 1808, Letter 54, *JAL*, 207.
88. "To Charles Austen," 6 April 1817, Letter 144, *JAL*, 491–92.
89. Lanser, "No Connections Subsequent," 59.
90. "To Francis Austen," 3 July 1813, Letter 81, *JAL*, 317.
91. "To Cassandra Austen," 15 Sept. 1813, Letter 82, *JAL*, 324.

CHAPTER 6

The Juvenilia: Convenient Ambiguities

1. I rely for the dating of the juvenilia on B. C. Southam's *Jane Austen's Literary Manuscripts: A Study of the Novelist's Development through the Surviving Papers* (Oxford: Clarendon Press, 1964), 14–19.
2. The writings in these manuscripts do not constitute all of Austen's earliest productions. A few pages have been torn from the notebooks, and a few of the dedications Austen appended to the juvenilia seem to refer to works that have not survived. Moreover, Austen probably wrote at least part of "Sir Charles Grandison," a play until recently attributed to Austen's niece Anna, in the early 1790s. See B. C. Southam, *Jane Austen's Literary Manuscripts*, 19; and *Jane Austen's "Sir Charles Grandison,"* ed. Brian Southam (Oxford: Clarendon Press, 1980), 1–34.
3. Southam, *Jane Austen's Literary Manuscripts*, 17, 18.
4. A. Walton Litz, *Jane Austen: A Study of her Artistic Development* (New York: Oxford Univ. Press, 1965), 13; Southam, *Jane Austen's Literary Manuscripts*, 13.
5. Sandra Gilbert and Susan Gubar, *The Madwoman in the Attic: The Woman Writer and the Nineteenth-Century Literary Imagination* (New Haven: Yale Univ. Press, 1979), 116.
6. Litz, 17; Southam, *Jane Austen's Literary Manuscripts*, 6, 14, 24, 29–30.
7. Gilbert and Gubar, 120, 112.
8. Scholars disagree about how parodic some of the pieces are and have counted the juvenilia overall in different ways. I have counted separately the parodic items in groupings such as "Scraps" and "A Collection of Letters."
9. For discussions of domestic ideology in Richardson's novels, see, for example, Nancy Armstrong, *Desire and Domestic Fiction: A Political History of the Novel* (New York: Oxford Univ. Press, 1987) and Margaret Anne Doody, *A Natural Passion: A Study of the Novels of Samuel Richardson,*

(Oxford: Clarendon Press, 1974). Richardson was not the first eighteenth-century novelist to dramatize the precepts of conduct books for women. See Doody; John J. Richetti, *Popular Fiction Before Richardson: Narrative Patterns 1700–1739* (Oxford: Clarendon Press, 1969); and Jane Spencer, *The Rise of the Woman Novelist: From Aphra Behn to Jane Austen* (Oxford: Basil Blackwell, 1986).

10. Few of these writers have been subject to the revisionary treatments of feminist criticism (or any treatment at all). Of those mentioned, Frances Burney has received the most attention. See, for example, three important recent works: Julia Epstein, *The Iron Pen: Frances Burney and the Politics of Women's Writing* (Madison: Univ. of Wisconsin Press, 1989); Kristina Straub, *Divided Fictions: Fanny Burney and Feminine Strategy* (Lexington: Univ. Press of Kentucky, 1987); and Margaret Anne Doody, *Frances Burney: The Life in the Works* (New Brunswick: Rutgers Univ. Press, 1988).

11. J. M. S. Tompkins, *The Popular Novel in England, 1770–1800* (1932; rpt. Univ. of Nebraska Press, 1961), 74–75.

12. In "Jack & Alice," for example, although Alice is "charming" and "amiable," she also happens to drink, gamble, and have a bad temper.

13. George Levine, *The Realistic Imagination: English Fiction from Frankenstein to Lady Chatterley* (Chicago: Univ. of Chicago Press, 1981), 72. But see also Margaret Rose, *Parody//Meta-Fiction: An Analysis of Parody as a Critical Mirror to the Writing and Reception of Fiction* (London: Croom Helm, 1979). Rose suggests that although parody may lead the way to a more realistic style, it also criticizes "the myth of realistic representation in mimetic art; and . . . the assumption that art may truthfully mirror other worlds" (67).

14. Levine, 21.

15. See, for example, the "little adventure" of the bonnet in "Frederic & Elfrida" (6:5–6).

16. Susanna Keir, *The History of Miss Greville* (Edinburgh: E. Balfour and W. Creech, 1787), 1:22–23.

17. Frances Sheridan, *Memoirs of Miss Sidney Bidulph*, 4th ed. (London: J. Dodsley, 1772), 1:28. This work was originally published in 1761.

18. In *Jane Austen: A Study of her Artistic Development*, A. Walton Litz argues that "although the narrative breaks over occasionally into pure burlesque," the work "is Jane Austen's first attempt to create a variety of believable characters, and to place them in a wholly realistic social milieu" (26–27). Although I do see passages of realistic portraiture in "Lesley Castle," I find much more parody in the work than Litz does.

19. For discussions of sensibility in the eighteenth-century novel, see Marilyn Butler, *Jane Austen and the War of Ideas* (Oxford: Oxford Univ. Press, 1975); Jean Hagstrum, *Sex and Sensibility: Ideal and Erotic Love from Milton to Mozart* (Chicago: Univ. of Chicago Press, 1980); Janet Todd, *Sensibility: An Introduction* (London: Methuen Press, 1986); and George Rousseau, "Nerves, Spirits, and Fibres: Towards Defining the Origins of Sensibility,"

in *Studies in the Eighteenth Century*, ed. R. F. Brissendon and J. C. Eade (Canberra: Australian National Univ. Press, 1977), 3:137–57.

20. The odd mix of domestic ideology and melodrama in Richardson's novels has been widely noted. Nancy Armstrong's *Desire and Domestic Fiction* is particularly interesting on Richardson's incorporation of a seduction tale within *Pamela*. See 109.

21. For another interpretation of this character and her experience, see Claudia Johnson's "'The Kingdom at Sixes and Sevens': Politics and the Juvenilia" in *Jane Austen's Beginnings: The Juvenilia and Lady Susan*, ed. J. David Grey (Ann Arbor: UMI Research Press, 1989), 51–52.

22. Keir, 1:238.

23. Sheridan, 1:52.

24. Ian Watt, *The Rise of the Novel: Studies in Defoe, Richardson and Fielding* (Berkeley: Univ. of California Press, 1957), 297, 300–301.

25. Terry Eagleton, *The Rape of Clarissa: Writing, Sexuality and Class Struggle in Samuel Richardson* (Minneapolis: Univ. of Minnesota Press, 1982), 30.

26. Eagleton, 33.

27. See Levine's discussion of "realism's effort to make the ordinary significant" (13).

28. Levine, 8.

29. The spelling of the name in the title is "Catharine," but the spelling in the text is more often "Catherine" (when the briefer "Kitty" is not used). When referring to the heroine, I have used "Kitty" to avoid confusion.

30. See 6:206.

31. Quite diverse critics have subscribed to the notion that the bower is a symbol of adolescent and romantic illusions. See Litz, 36, and Gilbert and Gubar, 122. The bower is, at the beginning and end of the fragment, the site of a sentimentalism, first about female friendship and then about Edward Stanley, and such sentimentalism, certainly where Stanley is concerned, rests on illusions. But I maintain that in most of the text the bower takes on a quite different set of associations. Although I disagree in many instances with her treatment of female friendship in Austen's works, I join Deborah Knuth in seeing the bower as a symbol of significant, unsentimental female bonds. See her "'You, Who I Know will enter into all my feelings': Friendship in Jane Austen's Juvenilia and *Lady Susan*," in *Jane Austen's Beginnings*, 103, 105.

32. Joseph Allen Boone, *Tradition Counter Tradition: Love and the Form of Fiction* (Chicago: Univ. of Chicago Press, 1987), 8.

33. Rachel Blau DuPlessis, *Writing Beyond the Ending: Narrative Strategies of Twentieth-Century Women Writers* (Bloomington: Indiana Univ. Press, 1985), 5, 3.

34. Boone, 8. See also DuPlessis, 5.

CHAPTER 7
The "Middle" Fictions: Visible Conflicts

1. Throughout this chapter I follow the dating of Austen's early works proposed by B. C. Southam in *Jane Austen's Literary Manuscripts: A Study of the Novelist's Development through the Surviving Papers* (Oxford: Clarendon Press, 1964).

2. Frank Bradbrook, "Jane Austen and Choderlos De Laclos," *Notes & Queries* 199 (1954): 75; and Jay Arnold Levine, "*Lady Susan*: Jane Austen's Character of the Merry Widow," *SEL* 1, no. 4 (1961): 23–34.

3. See, for example, Southam, 63–78.

4. Most critics have also treated the character Lady Susan as the center of the piece, either ignoring the other characters or seeing them as opposites of and foils for the cunning and aggressive widow. See, for example, Southam, 45–62; Mary Poovey, *The Proper Lady and the Woman Writer: Ideology as Style in the Works of Mary Wollstonecraft, Mary Shelley, and Jane Austen* (Chicago: Univ. of Chicago Press, 1984), 173–79; A. Walton Litz, *Jane Austen: A Study of Her Artistic Development* (New York: Oxford Univ. Press, 1965), 39–45; and Marvin Mudrick, *Jane Austen: Irony as Defense and Discovery* (1952; rpt. Berkeley: Univ. of California Press, 1968), 127–39. But in singling out Lady Susan or in placing her in opposition to other characters, most critics have overlooked her structural similarities to at least some of those characters. Lady Susan participates in the social world in precisely the same manner as the text's other women—not only her sophisticated town friend, Alicia Johnson, but the domestic and provincial Catherine Vernon and Vernon's mother. Only Lloyd Brown has also noted such similarities in his discussion of Catherine Vernon and Lady Susan. See his *Bits of Ivory: Narrative Techniques in Jane Austen's Fiction* (Baton Rouge: Louisiana State Univ. Press, 1973), 145–55.

5. Natalie Zemon Davis, "Women on Top," in her *Society and Culture in Early Modern France: Eight Essays* (Stanford: Stanford Univ. Press, 1975), 124–51.

6. Janet Altman, *Epistolarity: Approaches to a Form* (Columbus: Ohio State Univ. Press, 1982), 118.

7. For a comparison of *Lady Susan* with other, earlier epistolary novels, see Patricia Spacks, "Female Resources: Epistles, Plots, and Power," *Persuasions*, no. 9 (1987): 88–98.

8. "To Cassandra Austen," 14 Jan. 1796, Letter 2, *JAL*, 5.

9. Ibid., 15 Sept. 1796, Letter 6, *JAL*, 14.

10. Ibid., 17 Jan. 1809, Letter 64, *JAL*, 253.

11. Ibid., 14 Jan. 1796, Letter 2, *JAL*, 6.

12. Poovey, 178. It should be noted that critics have charged some novels in *third-person* narration with a similar "moral anarchy." They have found Lady Delacour (before her reformation) in Maria Edgeworth's *Belinda*

more appealing than the heroine, and, of course, many have felt more regard and sympathy for Austen's Mary Crawford than her very moral Fanny Price.

13. Altman, 122–27.

14. Southam, 54–62. See also Margaret Lenta, "Form and Content: A Study of the Epistolary Novel," *University of Cape Town Studies in English*, no. 10 (1980): 14–29.

15. Litz, 44, 52, 45.

16. Without the first and second 1790s drafts of "Elinor and Marianne," we can never know whether a powerful women's discourse was the source of Austen's discontent with the very first version. It is worth noting, however, that she wrote this work just after *Lady Susan* and rewrote it relatively soon—within two years of completing the first draft.

17. J. E. Austen-Leigh, *A Memoir of Jane Austen*, 3rd ed. (London: Richard Bentley, 1872), 364.

18. Nina Auerbach has suggested that whereas in *Pride and Prejudice* food appears only when men are present, in *The Watsons* women are shown preferring to eat alone together. Men are in their way at the dinner hour. According to Auerbach, when Lord Osborne and Tom Musgrave visit, the "unwelcoming imminence of food hints that a woman's primary hunger is the need to feed herself rather than a man." See *Communities of Women: An Idea in Fiction* (Cambridge: Harvard Univ. Press, 1978), 47.

19. James Heldman, "Where is Jane Austen in *The Watsons?*" *Persuasions*, no. 8 (1986): 90.

20. Ibid., 91.

21. Margaret Drabble, Introduction, *Lady Susan/The Watsons/Sanditon*, by Jane Austen (London: Penguin Books, 1974), 16.

22. Joseph Wiesenfarth, "*The Watsons* as Pretext," *Persuasions*, no. 8 (1986): 110.

23. Austen-Leigh, 296.

24. Southam, 68.

25. Juliet McMaster, "'God Gave Us Our Relations': The Watson Family," *Persuasions*, no. 8 (1986): 71–72.

26. For a good analysis of those revisions, see Southam, 86–99.

27. Wiesenfarth, 104–11.

28. "To Cassandra Austen," 30 June 1808, Letter 54, *JAL*, 209.

CHAPTER 8

Pride and Prejudice: Cultural Duality
and Feminist Literary Criticism

1. Quoted in Malcolm Elwin, *Lord Byron's Wife* (London: MacDonald, 1962), 159.

2. The adjective "American" has increasingly served as a label for a specific feminist critical tradition rather than the national identity of those contributing to this tradition. For sympathetic and unsympathetic overviews of "American" or "Anglo-American" feminist criticism, see Kathy E. Ferguson, "Interpretation and Genealogy in Feminism," *Signs* 16, no. 21 (1991): 322–39; Janet Todd, *Feminist Literary History* (New York: Routledge, 1988), 17–50; Toril Moi, *Sexual/Textual Politics: Feminist Literary Theory* (London: Methuen, 1985), 21–88; and Rita Felski, *Beyond Feminist Aesthetics: Feminist Literature and Social Change* (Cambridge: Harvard Univ. Press, 1989), 19–30.

3. Conventions of sensibility, so frequently lampooned in her earliest works, make scant appearance in the "Plan." Also, in contrast to the parodic early pieces, the "Plan" places much more emphasis on the theme of persecution, a legacy of the Jacobin fiction of the 1790s still prevalent in novels such as Mary Brunton's *Self-Control* (published in 1810 and read by Austen, probably in 1811 or 1812).

4. "Unsigned Review, *Critical Review*," in *Jane Austen: The Critical Heritage*, ed. B. C. Southam (London: Routledge & Kegan Paul, 1968), 46. Mary Russell Mitford was one Austen contemporary who did not like Elizabeth Bennet; she found the heroine not improper but vulgar. See *The Life of Mary Russell Mitford*, ed. A. G. L'Estrange (London: Richard Bentley, 1870), 1:300.

5. For a discussion of post-World War II Austen criticism, see *Jane Austen: A Collection of Critical Essays*, ed. Ian Watt (Englewood Cliffs: Prentice Hall, 1963), 12–14. For examples of this treatment of the heroine, see Tony Tanner, *Jane Austen* (Cambridge: Harvard Univ. Press, 1986), 105, 122; and A. Walton Litz, *Jane Austen: A Study of Her Artistic Development* (New York: Oxford Univ. Press, 1965), 99.

6. Claudia Johnson, *Jane Austen: Women, Politics, and the Novel* (Chicago: Univ. of Chicago Press, 1988), 75; see also Judith Lowder Newton, *Women, Power, and Subversion: Social Strategies in British Fiction, 1778–1860* (Athens: Univ. of Georgia Press, 1981), 76; and Mary Poovey, *The Proper Lady and the Woman Writer: Ideology as Style in the Works of Mary Wollstonecraft, Mary Shelley, and Jane Austen* (Chicago: Univ. of Chicago Press, 1984), 194.

7. See Terry Eagleton, *Literary Theory: An Introduction* (Minneapolis: Univ. of Minnesota Press, 1983).

8. Johnson, 76; Newton, 74, 76.

9. Ferguson, 328.

10. Sandra Gilbert and Susan Gubar, *The Madwoman in the Attic: The Woman Writer and the Nineteenth-Century Literary Imagination* (New Haven: Yale Univ. Press, 1979), 74, 73.

11. This position is sometimes reinforced (though not in the case of Gilbert and Gubar's expression of it) by neo-Marxist or Foucauldian critical premises. Feminist criticism has been very eclectic, and a work such as

Poovey's *The Proper Lady and the Woman Writer*, for example, bears the influence of both American feminist and neo-Marxist criticism.

12. Johnson, 76–77.

13. Newton, 76, 77.

14. Even a "mortified" Elizabeth who repudiates her own conduct after reading Mr. Darcy's letter cannot suppress her spirits for long. At several points in the last third of the novel, she is, again, verbally direct and aggressive—with Mr. Wickham, with Lady Catherine de Bourgh, and, in a more playful way, with Mr. Darcy.

15. See, for example, Newton, 73; Marvin Mudrick, *Jane Austen: Irony as Defense and Discovery* (Berkeley: Univ. of California Press, 1952), 94–95, 117; and Darrel Mansell, *The Novels of Jane Austen: An Interpretation* (London: Macmillan, 1973), 80. Mansell does suggest similarities between Elizabeth's witty remarks and comments in Austen's letters, but he doesn't perceive the letters as the medium by which we know the novelist.

16. "To Fanny Knight," 23 March 1817, Letter 142, *JAL*, 488.

17. "To Cassandra Austen," 20 Feb. 1807, Letter 50, *JAL*, 186.

18. "To Anna Lefroy," 22 Nov. 1814, Letter 104, *JAL*, 413.

19. "To Cassandra Austen," 7 Jan. 1807, Letter 48, *JAL*, 173.

20. Ibid., in *JAL*: 30 Jan. 1809, Letter 66, 260; 30 June 1808, Letter 54, 206; 26 June 1808, Letter 53, 200; 24 Aug. 1805, Letter 45, 160; 14 Oct. 1813, Letter 87, 350.

21. Feminist critics have in recent years commented extensively on these bonds. Viewing relationships among female characters as a measure of an author's concern for women's self-sufficiency and their solidarity as well, some have been critical of the representation of female ties in *Pride and Prejudice* and in Austen's other novels. See Nina Auerbach, *Communities of Women: An Idea in Fiction* (Cambridge: Harvard Univ. Press, 1978), 35–55; and Janet Todd, *Women's Friendship in Literature* (New York: Columbia Univ. Press), 298. More recently, other feminist critics have found such readings of the novel too severe. Defending *Pride and Prejudice* against charges that it favors marriage at the expense of female solidarity, Claudia Johnson has argued that the novel allows Jane and Elizabeth Bennet to have *both* love and friendship (91–92). See also Susan Lanser, "No Connections Subsequent: Jane Austen's World of Sisterhood," in *The Sister Bond: A Feminist View of a Timeless Connection* (New York: Pergamon Press, 1985), 53–67.

22. Johnson and Lanser focus only on Jane and Elizabeth Bennet's bond. Deborah J. Knuth's more comprehensive discussion of affectionate female friends in the novel provides the notable exception. See her "Sisterhood and Friendship in *Pride and Prejudice*," *Persuasions*, no. 11 (1989): 99–109.

23. One other exception is presented: Elizabeth and Jane's improving influence over Kitty, mentioned in the novel's last chapter. But their didactic connection with this younger sister makes too brief and belated an appearance in *Pride and Prejudice* to have any impact.

24. Compare 6:347–48.
25. "Unsigned notice, *British Critic*," in *Jane Austen: The Critical Heritage*, 41.
26. "Unsigned review, *Critical Review*," in *Jane Austen: The Critical Heritage*, 46. Similarities between the language of these two reviews and the parodic language in "Plan of a Novel" suggest that in that work Austen also may have been mocking, if not these reviews of her book, then reviewers' clichéd language in general.
27. Stuart M. Tave, *Some Words of Jane Austen* (Chicago: Univ. of Chicago Press, 1973), 157.
28. Joseph Wiesenfarth, *The Errand of Form: An Assay of Jane Austen's Art* (New York: Fordham Univ. Press, 1967), 83.
29. Lionel Trilling, *The Opposing Self: Nine Essays in Criticism* (New York: Viking Press, 1955), 222.
30. Tanner, 141.
31. For an attack on feminist treatments of marriage in Austen's novels, see Julia Prewitt Brown's "The Feminist Depreciation of Austen: A Polemical Reading," *Novel* 23, no. 3 (1990): 303–13. Brown wants to rescue Austen's endings from feminist analyses of the social inequality of marriage—to return, in effect, to a prefeminist, "de-gendered" view of the meaning of Austen's marital resolutions.
32. Poovey, 237.
33. Carolyn Heilbrun, "Women Writers: Coming of Age at 50," *The New York Times Book Review*, 4 Sept. 1988, 25, col. 1. See also Gilbert and Gubar, 154–55, 169.
34. Lanser, 66. Lanser argues that Austen subtly inscribed in her novels her preference for the bonds of sisters over heterosexual unions. See also Rachel Brownstein's "Jane Austen: Irony and Authority," *Women's Studies* 15, nos. 1–3 (1988): 67, which makes, for one passage in the narrative, a similar claim. Brownstein argues that the bond between Elizabeth and Georgiana Darcy, described briefly at the end of the novel, constitutes a "subtle subversion of the conventional romantic plot." As Brownstein explains, "One woman will make a man the object of her pleasantries while another one listens and learns" (69). As Brownstein acknowledges, however, the two women are not talking *to one another* about Mr. Darcy. There is no suggestion in this passage that they are generating an alternative and dissenting discourse of their own. Learning from her sister-in-law the possibility of adopting an unconventional and unladylike female voice, Georgiana is, in effect, in training to be a heroine.
35. Karen Newman, "Can This Marriage Be Saved: Jane Austen Makes Sense of an Ending," *English Literary History* 50, no. 4 (1983): 705, 704. This essay is not an example of *American* feminist literary criticism. Although its neo-Marxist premises have less overlap with that feminist tradition than Mary Poovey's more eclectic study, many of Newman's conclusions are nevertheless similar to those produced within American feminist criticism.
36. Joseph Allen Boone, *Tradition Counter Tradition: Love and the Form of*

Fiction (Chicago: Univ. of Chicago Press, 1987), 18. See also George Levine, *The Realistic Imagination: English Fiction from Frankenstein to Lady Chatterley* (Chicago: Univ. of Chicago Press, 1981), 21.

37. See Todd, 401, and Auerbach, 49.

38. See, for example, Fredric Jameson, *The Political Unconscious: Narrative as a Socially Symbolic Act* (Ithaca: Cornell Univ. Press, 1981), 76–83.

39. Ferguson, 322, 324, 326.

40. "To Fanny Knight," 23 March 1817, Letter 142, *JAL*, 486–87.

41. Her taste in heroines differed from some but not all of her female friends and kin. For a sense of their views, see "Opinions of *Mansfield Park*" and "Opinions of *Emma*" in *The Works of Jane Austen*, 6:431–39.

42. J. E. Austen-Leigh, *Memoir of Jane Austen*, 2nd ed., ed. R. W. Chapman, 2nd ed. (1871; rpt. Oxford: Clarendon Press, 1926), 157.

43. "To Fanny Knight," 23 March 1817, Letter 142, *JAL*, 487.

INDEX

Altman, Janet, 161, 167
Armstrong, Bet, 51
Auerbach, Nina, 193, 233n.18
Austen, Anna. *See* Lefroy, Anna Austen
Austen, Caroline, 24, 52, 53, 102–3, 111, 112, 122, 217n.39; *Reminiscences of Caroline Austen*, 25
Austen, Cassandra (mother), 7–8, 21, 26, 60, 66, 70, 101, 126–27, 213n.42, 223–24n.23
Austen, Cassandra (sister), 7, 8, 32–33, 37, 48, 49, 50, 59–60, 62–63, 68, 70, 72, 90, 111, 113, 117, 122, 123, 126–28, 129, 170, 181, 219n.5, 223–24n.23; Jane Austen's letters to, 50, 56, 71, 75, 80, 82, 90, 117, 120–21, 124, 127, 166, 180, 191; as reader of Jane Austen's manuscripts, 3, 99, 102, 104, 106, 107, 157
Austen, Charles (brother), 39, 50, 59, 79, 82, 133
Austen, Edward (brother), 7, 26, 32, 33, 39, 47, 56, 71, 80, 101, 122, 127, 128
Austen, Eliza de Feuillide. *See* Feuillide, Eliza de
Austen, Elizabeth, 26, 31, 32–33, 120, 122, 125
Austen, Fanny Palmer, 37, 79, 82
Austen, Frank (brother), 17, 23, 27, 39, 68, 75, 97, 104, 127, 129, 133, 221n.65
Austen, George (father), 21, 26, 91, 101, 223–24n.23
Austen, George (brother), 101, 133, 224n.39
Austen, Henry (brother), 7, 41, 50, 73, 90, 91, 92, 97, 100, 104, 105, 106–7, 115, 116, 120, 124, 127, 129, 223–24n.23
Austen, James (brother), 8, 17, 18, 20, 21, 39, 50, 52, 68, 92, 97, 99, 119, 122, 127, 217n.39, 222–23n.8
Austen, James Edward. *See* Austen-Leigh, James Edward

Austen, Jane, 43, 68, 70, 72; cultural duality as experienced by, 4, 6, 11–12, 90–91, 124–25, 136, 147, 221n.65; as dependent of brothers, 80–81, 82, 101, 126–27; development of as writer, 4, 6, 9–10, 12–13, 19–20, 85, 90–93, 96–108, 153–54, 158, 182–83; early writings of, 96–97; family as influence on, 90–93, 96–98, 101, 223–24n.23, 225n.69; on family size, 27, 28; female friendships of, 3–4, 9, 12, 63, 107–8, 122–24, 200; and identification with concerns of men, 48–49; letters of, 8, 32, 36, 48–49, 50, 56, 63, 67, 71, 73, 75, 79, 80, 82, 90, 96, 147, 222n.3; attitude toward marriage of, 119–20; neighbors of, 1–2, 20–21, 24–25, 26, 92–95, 102; and proposal of Harris Bigg-Wither, 109–17, 227n.32; role of in family, 32–33, 38; secrecy of, 98–99, 101–4; self-effacement of, 47, 49, 60–61, 73, 75, 105, 221n.65; similarities of to Elizabeth Bennet, 191, 235n.15; attitude of toward single life, 118–19, 121, 122, 125–30; social obligations of, 120–25; women's culture as supportive of, 91, 99–100, 102–8, 111, 118–19, 122, 130, 150, 157, 165. *See also* Juvenilia; *Lady Susan; Pride and Prejudice; The Watsons;* and other specific works
Austen, Martha Lloyd, 23, 31, 62, 66, 77, 99, 101, 103, 107, 117, 119, 120, 133, 157, 225n.69
Austen, Mary Gibson, 17, 101
Austen, Mary Lloyd, 8, 31, 33, 39, 52, 66, 70, 99, 111, 117, 119, 122, 123, 127, 133
Austen-Leigh, James Edward, 52, 105, 107, 133, 170, 178, 181, 204; *A Memoir of Jane Austen*, 11, 92, 103, 111–12, 113
Austen-Leigh, W. and R. A., 107; *Jane Austen: Her Life and Letters*, 99, 101, 210n.16

Designed by Laury A. Egan.

Composed by Blue Heron, Inc.,
in Baskerville text and display.

Printed on 50-lb., Glatfelter Eggshell Cream
and bound in Holliston Roxite
by The Maple Press Company.